Doc Shores

An authorized reprint of *Memoirs of a Lawman*

Edited by

Wilson Rockwell

Lake City, Colorado

An authorized reprint published by
Western Reflections Publishing Company
P.O. Box 1149
951 N. Highway 149
Lake City, CO 81235

www.westernreflectionspublishing.com

Cover art and design by Angela Hollingsworth
APH creative design, Lake City, CO

Printed in the United States of America

ISBN 978-1-937851-05-7

Publisher's Foreword

When historical author Wilson Rockwell received a letter from the great niece of renowned Old West lawman Cyrus W. (Doc) Shores in January of 1957, he humbly and heartily accepted the task of putting Shores' writings in readable form, thus making the fascinating, firsthand memories of early western life available to everyone. In the preface of *Memoirs of a Lawman*, published in 1962, Rockwell compares his access to Shores' "untapped" manuscripts to "stumbling on to a hitherto unknown personal autobiography of Butch Cassidy or Wyatt Earp."

The experiences penned by Shores during his eventful lifetime range from mule trains and cattle drives to holdups and shootouts. His acquaintances at times outshine those experiences, with the likes of Wild Bill Hickok, Tom Horn, Jim Clark, the Marlow Brothers, and Alferd Packer topping the list. Researched, condensed, edited, and rewritten, yet staying "religiously within the spirit and detail" of Doc Shores' original notes, *Memoirs of a Lawman* includes early frontier reminiscences from such environs as Montana, Oklahoma, Texas, and the Colorado Territory, with Part II of the book focusing on Shores' lawman days in the late 1800s and his eight years as sheriff of Gunnison County, Colorado.

As a tribute to Rockwell – Western Slope historian, former Colorado State Senator, extraordinary author and editor – Western Reflections Publishing is offering this authorized reprint, *Doc Shores: Memoirs of a Lawman*, for future generations to treasure and share.

Wilson Rockwell, a native Coloradoan who died in 2007, was one of the most prolific and respected writers of western Colorado history. Because all of his western Colorado titles fell out of print for years, Western Reflections is continuing its efforts to reprint Rockwell's works. *Doc Shores: Memoirs of a Lawman* will be joining *Sunset Slope*, *Uncompahgre Country*, *Utes: a Forgotten People*, and *New Frontier* as works that lovers of Colorado history will be excited to read.

"Doc" Cyrus Wells Shores when he was sheriff of Gunnison County. *Photo courtesy of Mrs. Lucille B. Hartman.*

MEMOIRS OF A LAWMAN

Edited by

WILSON ROCKWELL

SAGE BOOKS
DENVER 1962

Library of Congress Catalog Card Number: 62-19354

Sage Books are published by

Alan Swallow, 2679 South York Street, Denver 10, Colorado

Dedication

To my son, Danny, whose interest in true stories about the Old West inspired my contribution to this work.

Preface

In January, 1957, I received a letter from Mrs. Lucille B. Hartman of Denver which read:

"There has come into my possession the personal memoirs of Cyrus Wells Shores, better known as 'Doc' Shores. He was my great uncle and I was brought up on his stories.

"While discussing the matter with two of my uncles, Lee Savage and Harry Savage, your name was mentioned as an authority on the history of the Western Slope. They both felt that only a writer of your experience could utilize this material to its fullest possibility. The rewriting and publishing of these stories would make a very substantial contribution to the knowledge of early western life.

"Cyrus Wells Shores was born in Michigan in 1844. As a boy he was more interested in the woods than in his books. As a young man he went to Montana via a steamer and paid passage by hunting game along the route. After prospecting and hunting in Montana he worked in Wyoming hauling ties for the railroad. Later he drove cattle up from Texas. After many experiences with Indians, blizzards, and rustlers in Kansas he took his wife and settled in Gunnison. He was sheriff of Gunnison County from 1884 until 1892 when he moved to Grand Junction and was employed by the Rio Grande Express . . ."

I, of course, was interested in seeing these memoirs of one of Colorado's most celebrated early-day peace officers, and I so advised

Mrs. Hartman. She sent me around eighty manuscripts, some of great length, which Doc had written about his varied experiences on the frontier. It was genuine source material which had never been tapped—like stumbling on to a hitherto unknown personal autobiography of Butch Cassidy or Wyatt Earp. While the accounts were poorly written, the facts were there, and in checking through contemporary newspaper reports, I found them to be remarkably accurate.

I have digested and re-written these memoirs, still using the first person since I stayed religiously within the spirit and detail of the original version. I did occasionally supply missing facts from other source material. To illustrate, in writing about the train holdup near Grand Junction, Shores fails to mention how the bandits held up the train. The *Rocky Mountain News* dated Nov. 4, 1887, gives a full account of the robbery, and, to round out the story, I took the liberty of supplying this important detail, giving the newspaper due credit in the footnotes.

Doc's excellent memory was occasionally at fault. To cite an example, in his recounting of the Cotopaxi train robbery near the Royal Gorge, he called one of the robbers he arrested "Burt McCarty." All other accounts of this case, including the one by the reliable historian Jay Monaghan in his book *Last of the Bad Men,* refer to this outlaw as "Burt Curtis." I have corrected such obvious errors in my revision.

Another important task in re-composing Shores' extensive memoirs was the condensation and selection of material. I discarded the lesser stories and combined many which were related. Footnotes at the end of each chapter specify where I obtained my information.

In dealing with Shores' thirty-year career as an investigator and peace officer in part II of this book, I have limited his activities to the eight years he was sheriff of Gunnison County. They are a good cross section of his diversified adventures in the criminal field, and mark the highlight of his colorful life. In so doing I have omitted a good many interesting cases which he encountered as a special investigator for the railroads and as chief of police of Salt Lake City. These accounts may also be found in their unedited form at the Western History Department of the Denver Public Library.

Doc Shores wrote his memoirs in the latter part of the 1920's when he was more than eighty years old. After their completion he went to New York City to offer them to a publisher. He staunchly refused to have the manuscripts edited, and the publisher would not accept them without revision. Indignant, Shores returned home and filed his memoirs away.

After his death in 1934, they came into the possession of his older son, Frank, who did nothing with them. When Frank died unexpectedly in December, 1948, a note was found with the manuscripts bequeathing them to Lucille Burch Hartman and Louis Burch, grand-neice and grand-nephew of Doc Shores, who as children provided Doc with an enthusiastic and ever-ready audience. Upon completing this book, I persuaded Lucille and Louis to turn the documents over to the Western History Department of the Denver Public Library for reference and safekeeping.

Table of Contents

Table of Illustrations

Prologue

When "Doc" Shores and his wife, Agnes, arrived in Gunnison the forepart of May, 1880,[1] the town was going through the most dramatic period of its history. Although the versatile Sylvester Richardson attempted to establish a colony there in the spring of 1874, the real founding of Gunnison did not begin until five years later in 1879 when carbonate deposits were discovered at the head of Quartz Creek, where the town of Pitkin sprang up overnight. Other mining camps also began mushrooming forth in the area, including Tin Cup, Hillerton, White Pine, Gothic, and Irwin. Gunnison became the hub and supply center for these rapidly growing silver mining camps. An entirely new town organization was formed, and it was believed that Gunnison would soon become the metropolis of the Rockies.

Thousands were arriving daily. On May 17, 1880, a correspondent writing to the *Pueblo Chieftain* from Parlin's Ranch—twelve miles from the booming town—reported that on the previous day he counted 250 teams bound for Gunnison.

"One would think," he wrote, "that there must be an end to this procession, but the end is not yet, for far away on the Saguache road, there is (another) long line of white covers."[2]

During the rush days of 1880 two hundred houses were built in Gunnison over only a three-month period from May 15th to August 15th. The town was wide open, and every kind of business sprang up and flourished, including grocery stores, saloons, livery barns,

Gunnison as it looked during boom days of 1881. *Photo courtesy of Denver Public Library Western Collection.*

hotels, pool halls, sporting houses, clothing stores, hardware stores, general stores, a newspaper office, and a school.

During these boom days the stage line of J. L. Sanderson was established in Gunnison, and two big railroad companies began a feverish race to the new El Dorado. The Denver & Rio Grande won the race, reaching Gunnison on August 8, 1881, while the Denver and South Park arrived a year later on September 2, 1882.

The mining boom lasted until 1886. Before the bubble burst, the Denver & Rio Grande invested heavily in the gold, silver, and copper mines of the region, and eastern capitalists spent hundreds of thousands of dollars in Gunnison Valley enterprises. The nationally known LaVeta Hotel, costing $200,000, was built during this period.

In the winter of 1879-80 part of the Gunnison Town Company withdrew and laid out about 200 acres as the townsite of West Gunnison. Sylvester Richardson, who had brought a colony to Gunnison in 1874, was the leading promoter of West Gunnison while Alonzo Hartman, who in 1872 took over management of the Ute Indian Agency Cowcamp at Gunnison[3] during the reservation days, was the chief promoter of East Gunnison.

Doc Shores and his wife arrived upon the scene at the time all these activities were taking place. Shortly after his arrival Doc built a cabin of hewed logs between the expanding, rival towns of East Gunnison and West Gunnison on what was known as Boulevard Street.

For a time he freighted supplies to the surrounding mining camps, but in the latter part of October, 1880, an event occurred which was destined to change the entire course of his life. He was thirty-six years old at the time—tall, dark, ramrod straight, with a weather-beaten face and piercing, steely, blue eyes.

Early on that momentous day before daylight two horsemen, mounted on clay bank colored mustangs, jogged out of the White Pine mining camp[4]—forty miles east of Gunnison. About a half-mile from White Pine they turned their mounts off the wagon road and dismounted. Tying their horses behind some oak brush out of sight from anyone approaching along the road, they squatted down at the foot of a large cedar tree. They were dressed in dark woolen coats and trousers with their pant-legs tucked in long, high-heeled boots, typical of that day. They both wore white, grimy sombreros, and one of them had long, bushy hair protruding from under his hat brim. He pulled a nearly-empty pint bottle of whiskey from his coat pocket and handed it to his companion.

"Here, take a drink of this. It'll help quiet your nerves."

"We've just about killed this bottle," the other man said, tilting it to his lips. "We'll have to tank up again in Gunnison." After draining the bottle, he tossed it into the brush.

A buckboard wagon rattled into view from White Pine. The two cowboys immediately ground out their cigarettes and reached for their six-shooters.

In the approaching wagon was a prisoner, handcuffed and shackled, who was being escorted to Gunnison to stand trial for making and passing counterfeit money. An officer sat on each side of him. The trio had spent the night in White Pine and were off to an early start for Gunnison, where the prisoner was to be turned over to the Gunnison County sheriff.

When the wagon had nearly reached the spot where the two cowboys were hiding, they ran out in front of the surprised group and held them up. The holdup men then ordered the officers to remove the irons from the prisoner and set him free. After giving the alleged counterfeiter time to hide out somewhere in the surrounding hills, the highwaymen ran over to their horses and started for Gunnison at a fast gallop. Apparently they had no motive for releasing the prisoner other than to show their contempt for the law.

When the hard-riding cowboys came riding into East Gunnison late that afternoon, they tied their lathered horses to a hitching rail in front of a saloon and strode inside for a few quick bracers before continuing on their way.

Emerging a half-hour later, they jumped on their mounts and started down Boulevard Street toward West Gunnison as fast as their refreshed horses could travel. As they pounded through town yelling like drunken Indians, they took pot shots at anyone on the streets who happened to be in sight.

One of the bullets hit a pedestrian who was walking up Boulevard

Street carrying a dinner bucket. The bucket clattered out of his hand as he fell to the ground badly hurt.

Doc Shores was rocking his fretting, two-weeks old son in a homemade cradle when he heard the horsemen thundering up the street. The baby was running a slight fever, and Doc's wife had gone to summon a physician.

Wondering what all the commotion was about, Doc ran over to his cabin window just in time to see the pedestrian fall. The outlaws laughed and spurred their horses' bloody sides with renewed vigor. The street they were riding on ran directly past Doc's cabin; so instinctively he grabbed his Winchester rifle, which was hanging on the wall, and ran out the door. When he appeared, the outlaws whirled their mounts and stampeded up a side street.

In the excitement of the moment Doc completely forgot about his sick baby. Quickly catching and saddling a small, iron-gray horse, which he had bought that morning and happened to have staked out in back of his house, Doc was soon in pursuit. The two desperados had checked their speed somewhat to reload their guns, and when Doc caught sight of them again, they were within rifle range. Doc braced himself in the stirrups as solidly as he could and raised his Winchester to shoot at them from his running horse.

"Put down your rifle," someone shouted at Doc from behind. "Don't let them see it."[5]

Lowering his gun Doc glanced around to see Childers, the city marshal, riding up. Behind him came Deputy Sheriff J. F. Spencer, followed by a posse of about fifteen other horsemen.

"What are you going to do," Doc yelled back at Childers, "let those fellows get away?"[6]

Before the city marshal could answer, the deputy sheriff cried out, "No, damn them. Go ahead and kill the bastards."

During this brief exchange of words, the fugitives again pulled out of gun range. When they reached the toll bridge which led across the Gunnison River, they held up the gate keeper and made him let down the chain and allow them to pass over without payment of the customary toll.

Although Doc was well ahead of the posse, who did not seem anxious to pass him, he had a slow and unshod horse. It was not the kind of animal that one would have picked for such a chase. Most of the men following him had bigger and faster mounts, but they were being held back. Apparently their riders did not want to get within firing range of the outlaws who kept turning and shooting back at the pursuers.

After crossing the toll bridge, the road curved around a dense growth of brush back to the river. In an effort to head off the fugitives, Doc took a shortcut through the undergrowth, which clawed at his face and clothing. He came within sight of the road again on the other side of the bend as the two fugitives came pounding around it.

Jumping off his horse, Doc took aim at the lead outlaw when he came into view. Before he could pull the trigger, two big four-horse teams on their way to Gunnison unexpectedly pulled in between Shores and his target.

With an oath at this interference of fate, Doc vaulted back into his saddle and once more gave chase. When he galloped up onto the road, the bandits were again out of rifle range. They were riding stronger and faster horses than Doc and easily held their lead.

The winding road was so full of turns and dust that much of the time Doc could not even see the fugitives. Rounding one of the corners, however, he caught sight of their white sombreros bobbing along above the dust as they ascended a hill. They were closer than before, apparently having slowed their horses to reload again.

Once more Doc pulled up his rifle to get a shot at them, but before he could shoot, two six-horse stages—one directly behind the other—came rattling over the crest of the hill. Both coaches were loaded with people; so Doc again held his fire.

As the stages shot past the two fugitives, one of the outlaws yelled to the teamsters, "Tell those greenhorns riding back of us to get a move on."[7]

After the stagecoaches had rushed by in a cloud of dust, Doc stood up in his stirrups and began shooting at the outlaws through the haze before they once more pulled away out of sight around a bend. Hearing the reports, several members of the posse, trailing a half-mile behind and unable to see clearly, took some random shots at Doc, apparently believing him to be one of the fleeing outlaws.

Doc whirled around and cursed the bungling, slow-moving posse. Fortunately they were not good marksmen, and the bullets whistled by wide of their mark.

It was nearly dark by this time, and Doc did not see the fleeing horsemen again. When there were no longer any clouds of dust ahead of him to mark their flight, Doc reined in his horse and dismounted to look for tracks. He lit matches and examined the road carefully. As he had suspected, there was no sign of any fresh horse tracks. The fugitives had evidently, under cover of darkness, turned off the road somewhere into the concealing brush.

When the fifteen or twenty members of the posse finally came thundering up, Doc informed them that he had lost the outlaws' trail.

"They're probably hidin' out someplace in the brush," the deputy sheriff said, "but sooner or later they'll probably hit the road again and ride on into Sapinero, Montrose, or Lake City. About all we can do now is go back to Gunnison and telegraph the authorities there to keep an eye out for them. My guess is they'll take the trail south to Lake City."[8]

It was a long ten-mile ride back to Gunnison, and Doc's tenderfooted, slow pony could not keep up with the others. As the posse had let him take the lead in pursuit of the two gunmen, they left him far behind in the dust on the return trip home.

On the way back Doc suddenly remembered the fretting baby he had deserted to take part in the manhunt. He worried about the child all the way home and was greatly relieved to find that everything was all right. Fortunately, Doc's wife, Agnes, and the town doctor had arrived to look after the sick baby within a few minutes after Doc's sudden departure.

When the marshal of Lake City received the wire, he organized a posse and was on hand to greet the unsuspecting fugitives when they came riding into town the next day. The surprised desperados were taken prisoner without a struggle. They gave their names as Jack Smith and Tom Lewis.

The captives were brought back to Gunnison and locked up in the county jail. At the ensuing trial in the district court they were convicted of assault with intent to kill and given terms in the state penitentiary at Canon City. Doc was one of the witnesses who testified against them.

After serving his sentence Jack Smith, one of the outlaws, visited Gunnison. Doc Shores was sheriff at the time, and Smith dropped around at his office. Doc shook hands with the visitor, who apparently bore him no malice.

"Well, I'm glad you're out," Doc said. "I hope you'll behave yourself from now on."

"I've learned my lesson," Smith answered. "I'll be good."[9]

Before leaving Smith said, "By the way, who was that fellow who rode the little iron gray pony and kept shooting at us?"

"That was me," Doc said with a smile.

"Well, I've often wondered. So far as Tom and me were concerned, you were the only one in the whole damned posse who had guts enough to give us a good race. After that chase I can understand why the people of Gunnison County elected you sheriff."

A man's background largely determines how he will act in a crisis. The roots of Doc Shores single-handed pursuit of the two gunmen and his later outstanding success as sheriff, deputy U. S. marshal, special investigator for the Denver & Rio Grande Railroad, and Chief of Police of Salt Lake City lie buried in his early training on the frontier.

FOOTNOTES

[1]C. W. Shores, "Autobiography of C. W. Shores," original manuscript, Denver, Colo., Feb. 17, 1928, p. 50. In possession of Western History Dept. of Denver Public Library.

[2]C. E. Hagie (former professor of history at Western State College), "Gunnison in the Early Days," *The Colorado Magazine,* Vol. VIII, No. 4, July 1931, p. 121.

[3]This cow camp was located one mile below the present town.

[4]Now a ghost town.

[5]C. W. Shores, "Two Desperados named Jack Smith and Tom Lewis," original manuscript, Denver, Colo., Mar. 1927, p. 2. In possession of Western History Dept. of Denver Public Library.

[6]*Ibid.*

[7]*Ibid.*

[8]Lake City was a prospering mining camp about 45 miles southwest of Gunnison.

[9]In spite of his promise, time proved that Jack Smith had not learned his lesson. In White Pine, shortly after serving his sentence, he met a little man by the name of Barrett who at one time had been a peace officer in Canon City and in Gunnison. Smith seemed to have it in for lawmen generally, and he found some excuse to beat up Barrett with a gun. He then fled to Aspen where Sheriff Doc Shores had him arrested and brought back to Gunnison to stand trial for assault and battery.

However, Barrett failed to appear at the trial to testify against Smith; so Doc turned him loose. He later went to Cripple Creek where he got mixed up in the Bull Hill War as one of the leaders of the men who were defying the authorities. During these troublesome times at Cripple Creek there were many riots and killings, and several mines were blown up.

One day Jack Smith rode up to the city jail at Cripple Creek and began shooting the lock off the door to free one of his associates who had recently been arrested. Hearing the reports, the city marshal rushed over and shot Smith, bringing his career of violence to an abrupt end.

Part I

FRONTIER REMINISCENCES

Chapter I

I was born on November 11, 1844, in a small village called Hickville about thirty miles from Detroit, Michigan. I was named Cyrus Wells after the doctor who brought me into the world. When I was five years old, the doctor gave me an orphan lamb. My two older brothers were envious of this gift and got their revenge by teasing me. They told me that since I was named after a doctor I would probably become one and spend my time riding around on an old horse with a bag of pills visiting the sick. They then started calling me "Doc." I objected to this title since my ambition then was to become a hunter and trapper. However, the nickname stuck for the rest of my life.[1]

When I was about seven years old, I visited a great-uncle who showed me how to set the first steel trap that I had ever seen. This was the beginning of my career in trapping and hunting.[2] When I walked to the little country school house where I received my limited formal education, I often took an old flintlock musket along with me. If I happened to run across the tracks of some wild animal, I usually played hookey and would spend the day following the trail like a bloodhound. When I finally returned home at night, I was generally carrying the skin of the animal I had been tracking.

My father invariably gave me a good, old-fashioned whipping for such escapades, and upon my arrival in the school the next day, my teacher would repeat the punishment in front of the class. Using a ruler, the teacher once hit my hand with such force that it knocked my thumb out of joint. However, I took these necessary unpleasantries in stride and didn't allow them to interfere with my favorite pastime. While I did not learn much in school during these formative years, I earned the equivalent of several degrees in the art of hunting and trapping.

There was a big bully in school who made a habit of picking on boys smaller than himself. One day he kicked me hard in the seat of the pants. I started for the school house, crying, to report it to my older brother. As I passed the wood pile, which provided fuel for the school's pot-bellied stove, I had an inspiration. Picking up a big, heavy stick, I held it behind me while I returned to the playground where the bully was playing baseball. As I walked up behind him, he raised his arms to catch a high fly. Using both hands I hit him on the head with the club, and he fell to the ground unconscious. I then ran back to the school house and informed my brother of the disagreement.

A little while later the bully walked up to the door, sobbing, and yelled, "Come on out here, Doc. I want to see you."

I was afraid to go out; but my brother pushed me through the open doorway where the irate bully was standing, and said to him, "Go ahead and touch him, and I'll beat the hell out of you."[3]

From that time on he left me strictly alone, but I occasionally caught him looking at me out of the corner of his eye with an expression of puzzled frustration.

Late in the fall of 1866 when I was twenty-two, I started out for Montana Territory to seek my fortune. I took with me a .44-caliber breech loading rifle, known as a "Thunderbolt," and a big hunting knife made by a blacksmith. I carried my blankets and extra wearing apparel in a sack. My father gave me $200 in greenbacks, which I sewed up in an inside pocket of my shirt.[4]

Upon arriving at Council Bluffs, Iowa, on the Missouri River, I got a job with a mule train, which was being managed by Colonel J. M. Chivington. It was two years before this that Chivington had staged his notorious Indian massacre at Sand Creek in eastern Colorado. He and his soldiers had shot down 500 defenseless Indians, including women and children, who were camped there.

As a result, he had been court martialed and discharged from the army.

The following spring (1867) when Chivington's mule outfit was getting ready to pull out for Montana, the sheriff attached it for nonpayment of bills. This threw me and the other mule skinners working for Chivington out of a job.

Fortunately, a river steamer, called the Huntsville, unexpectedly came up the Missouri and stopped at Council Bluffs to refuel. It had started out from St. Louis and was on its way to Fort Benton, Montana—a distance of 3,100 miles by river. Since the boat was going to my intended destination, I picked up a ride on it, agreeing to work at various jobs to pay for my passage.

Yankton, South Dakota, was the last outpost of civilization that we stopped at before entering Indian country. During the remainder of the long trip we passed only an occasional isolated fort, including Fort Randall and Fort Perrie Sully in present South Dakota, and Fort Union in Montana Territory. The Hunstville stopped at these fortifications to deliver government supplies and sometimes a few soldiers.

On the deck of the steamboat was a small four-pound canon, which could be moved about on wooden wheels. Before entering Indian territory this canon was loaded with powder and grapeshot. Also, the elevated pilot house was planked up on the sides with only the front exposed in order to protect the ship's pilot from Indian arrows shot from the shore. The pilot used this lookout perch, high above the deck, to direct the course of the steamer. From this vantage point he would signal to the engineer far below in the engine room who did the actual steering.

Whenever the boat landed to obtain wood, which was used for fuel, the deck hands or roustabouts cut up dry cottonwood trees with a saw and carried the logs aboard to be split later on deck.

During these landings I, who proved to be the best hunter of the 150 men on board, brought in supplies of fresh meat. Buffalo and antelope were plentiful, and it was not difficult to keep the passengers and deck hands well provided for.

One day while out looking for game, I noticed a bundle tied with rawhide to the forks of a tree. Thinking that it might contain some

River steamer going up Missouri River in 1867 between St. Louis and Ft. Benton. *Photo courtesy of Denver Public Library Western Collection.*

jerked meat placed there by the Indians for safekeeping, I climbed the tree and cut the thongs. The buffalo hide fell to the ground, and I descended to examine its contents.

Inside the dried-up crinkly hide was a much finer fringed buffalo calf robe, covered with beads. Opening the robe I was startled to find the grisly remains of a papoose. I wrapped up the body as it was before, but the boat whistle began blowing; so I didn't have time to replace it in the tree.[5]

At another time while the deck hands were ashore gathering wood, a big band of Indians appeared on horseback. They wore nothing but breech-clouts and moccasins, and their bodies and faces were painted. They acted so hostile that the old canon on board ship was wheeled around and pointed above them. When it was fired, it made such a blast and emitted so much smoke that for a few minutes the Indians were demoralized. They held up their hands toward the steamer as a token of peace, which gave the woodcutters and me an opportunity to scurry on board. As soon as the boat began moving out into the river, the band recovered from its initial shock and began shooting arrows at us.

A number of times on the long journey such attacks were made on the boat as it steamed up the river, arrows piercing the protecting planks of the pilot house and other exposed portions of the vessel. However, none of the passengers were hit, and sometimes we would return the fire as the Indians were seen running and dodging behind the trees along the shore.[6]

It was spring, and the rampaging Missouri was full of sand and dirt. For passengers traveling first-class the river water was hauled up in buckets and poured into barrels, where the sediment was allowed to settle. We roustabouts, who cooked our own food, did not enjoy this luxury. Our drinking water was taken directly from the riley stream and was full of dregs. It gave a distinct flavor to our coffee, which we soon got used to.

Many events occurred to break the routine drudgery of the trip. Once a small group of stranded white men were sighted along the shore as they yelled and waved frantically at us to attract our attention. The captain of the steamer lowered a yawl which was rowed over to the castaways. They proved to be mountain traders from Fort Benton, Montana. They informed us that they had started down the river en route to Yankton, South Dakota, on a raft of cottonwood logs. They brought with them 300 large gray wolf skins, wrapped in bales. These bales were worth three dollars each. After several days on the river, the raft became watersoaked and began to sink. The traders landed their floundering craft and hid their wolf hides in the brush. Being in hostile Indian country, they were badly frightened and asked the captain of our steamer for a ride to the next fort, where they could catch a boat going down the river to Yankton.[7]

During another stop to procure wood we ran across the scalped, mutilated bodies of a less fortunate group of traders. Nearby were the charred remains of a stockade and blockhouse which had been built for defense against Indian attacks. On the bank was a partially burned stack of corded wood, which the ill-fated party had cut to sell to passing river steamers. The Indians had apparently cut loose the traders' boats and stolen all of their grub, axes, tools and supplies.[8]

A day or so after discovering this gruesome sight, we noticed a man on shore waving at us. The yawl was again sent to the rescue and the man brought aboard. He was a wild-looking creature, covered with lice and somewhat demented from his ordeal. He explained that he had been lost from a steamship, but he was too irrational to give a coherent account of just what had occurred. Although it was bitterly cold, he took off his clothes and tried vainly to wash off in the river the crawling vermin. He then put on the wet clothing, shivering like one with palsy. We gave him a wide berth and put him off at the next fort.[9]

Navigation of the turbulent river presented its share of adventure. Whenever rapids were encountered which the boat couldn't steam through, a long cable attached to the ship was carried ashore and all the able-bodied men on board, including the captain, pulled the heavy steamer to navigable water.[10]

Snags and trees in the swollen stream were continually striking the boat or getting caught in the wheel. Sometimes when traveling close to shore, hidden snags leaning downstream with the current would jab big holes in the side of the steamer. Tarpaulins were

Bull train leaving Fort Benton, Montana, with freight for mining camps. *Photo courtesy of Denver Public Library Western Collection.*

used to plug up these holes in order to keep the boat from sinking until more permanent repairs could be made.

Once when pulling out from the bank after a landing, the coiled cable, which had not been disconnected, suddenly drew tight, catching one of the deck hands around the leg and jerking him overboard. He was unconscious when rescued, and his leg was badly mangled. But such tragic incidents were all a part of the long river journey up the Missouri in the 1860's.

Upon finally reaching Fort Benton, Montana Territory, after an eventful sixty-day trip, I got a job as a bullwhacker at sixty dollars a month. This salary was paid in gold dust, which was the main currency in Montana at this time, since greenbacks were only worth eighty cents on a dollar.[11]

Gold had recently been discovered in Montana Territory, and mining camps had sprung up all over the region.[12] Mule and ox trains camped at Fort Benton all of the time to meet incoming steamboats from St. Louis in order to load and carry freight to the various mining camps. This freight included flour, bacon, coffee, clothing, blankets, drugs, tobacco, whiskey, wine, hardware, picks, shovels, and pans.

The ox or bull train that I got a job with consisted of twenty-four big Murphy freight wagons[13] with five or six yokes of oxen to each wagon. Six thousand pounds was considered a normal load to a wagon when pulled by ten or twelve bulls, although it was large enough to hold ten thousand pounds.

Each bullwhacker had a bull whip about fourteen feet long, and an experienced driver could make it crack like the report of a gun. Since warlike Indians abounded in the territory,[14] a bullwhacker also came equipped with a six-shooter and a butcher knife, which he carried at his belt. The butcher knife not only served as a weapon but also as an eating utensil since forks, spoons, and knives were not plentiful in the chuck wagon.

Unlike a mule skinner, a bullwhacker did not ride as he drove but walked up and down beside his yokes of oxen, cracking his whip and swearing like only a bullwhacker could. Even when coming to a river, he would walk right on through it, oftentimes wading in water up to his armpits. He seldom took time on such occasions to

Bullwhacker with improvised bull whip. *Photo courtesy of Denver Public Library Western Collection.*

empty the water which collected in his boots or shoes, and, as a result, his watersoaked feet often became sore or swollen.[15] A mule skinner was considered a higher occupation than that of a bull-whacker, and instead of walking beside his teams, he rode a saddle mule.[16]

The life of a bullwhacker was a rough one. He often went for weeks at a time without washing his hands or face since most of the available water had alkali in it, which burned his skin and eyes.[17] Consequently, after a short time on the freighting trail his face became so layered with dirt and alkali dust that a white bullwhacker could not be distinguished from a black one, except by his features or his hair.

After a long day's drive in hot weather, it was not uncommon for the thirsty oxen to stampede when nearing water, capsizing many of the wagons and smashing up the freight. When crossing rivers, wagons often got bogged down in quicksand, and in straining to pull them out, the oxen occasionally would rip off the front gearing, dropping the wagon beds and their contents down into the water and mud.

As a bullwhacker, I experienced all of these trials and tribulations. One of my chores was to go in search of water each evening when the bulltrain stopped for the night. I carried the water back in big kettles, which I often had to fill by dipping water out of stagnant pools with a tin cup. Upon returning to camp, I ground the coffee, filled the coffee pots, and put them on the camp fire. One evening while I was pouring water into a coffee pot, a dead, partly decomposed frog fell out of the kettle into the pot. Not wanting anyone to notice this catastrophe, I let the frog remain since if I had been seen fishing it out, I would have had to make another long trip to the water-hole to refill the kettle with fresh water. So, I proceeded to grind the coffee, put it in the pot containing the dead frog, and placed the contents on the fire to boil just as if nothing had happended. Although it did not appeal to my aesthetic sense, I was so tired and hungry after bullwhacking all day that I drank as much of the polluted coffee as my unsuspecting companions.[18]

Such experiences cured me of any finickiness that I might have had. It was more common than not to break open a piece of freshly cooked bread and find hairs sticking through it. But, like my fellow bullwhackers, my appetite was so keen after a long day's drive that I seldom took the time to pull out the unappetizing objects but would eat the bread—hairs and all.

Each of the twenty-four wagons in my outfit had a large number painted on its side. At night when making camp the wagons were driven in two semicircles, the even numbers forming on one side and the odd numbers on the other until the train was in a perfect circle. The oxen were then unyoked and turned out to graze for the night, while we tired bullwhackers rolled ourselves up in our blankets for a few hours of well-earned sleep on the hard ground. We usually slept out in the open, but in case of rain we lay under the wagons, which afforded us a little protection.

On one such occasion when my sleeping companion and I crawled out of our rain-soaked blankets, he said, "Shores, sometime we may see better days."[19]

At daybreak the night herder drove the bulls into the improvised wagon circle or corral, crying "Roll out! Roll out! Roll out!"

With groans and oaths we would reluctantly comply. Dressing ourselves hurriedly in the cold morning air, we rolled up our blankets and threw them into the wagons on top of the freight. Then we yoked up our oxen and started out, number one wagon taking the lead, followed by number two wagon on the opposite side of the circle, and so on in alternating fashion until all twenty-four wagons were moving single file in their proper order.[20]

About ten o'clock the wagons were again driven into two half circles as before, with even numbers on one side and odd numbers on the other. The bulls were then turned out to water and graze while breakfast was prepared and eaten. After breakfast we usually spent a couple of hours in doing odd jobs, such as repairing yokes, bull whips, and bow keys. It was not until after eating lunch that we drove the oxen back into the wagon corral, where they were harnessed and the journey resumed. This ordinarily took place about three or four o'clock in the afternoon, and night camp was not made until nine or ten that evening, depending on when we reached a favorable site equipped with grass and water.

When I think back on my days as a bullwhacker, I can honestly

Wagon train circled for night camp. *Photo courtesy of Denver Public Library Western Collection.*

say that it was an experience I wouldn't take anything for, but I wouldn't go through it again for a million dollars.

It reminds me of the story about a bullwhacker's young daughter who once asked, "Mother, what is a bullwhacker? Does it eat grass?"

"No, honey," the mother replied. "It's part human."

FOOTNOTES

[1]C. W. Shores, "Autobiography of C. W. Shores," original manuscript, Denver, Colo., Feb. 17, 1928, p. 2. In possession of Western History Dept. of Denver Public Library.

[2]*Ibid.,* p. 6.

[3]*Ibid.,* p. 5.

[4]*Ibid.,* p. 11.

[5]*Ibid.,* p. 14.

[6]*Ibid.,* p. 15.

[7]*Ibid.,* p. 16.

[8]*Ibid.,* pp. 13-14.

[9]*Ibid.,* p. 17.

[10]*Ibid.,* p. 16.

[11]*Ibid.,* pp. 18-19.

[12]Discoveries of gold between 1857-1863 produced the rush. Bandits held up unlucky miners who had found gold, and the miners struck back by organizing Vigilantes in Dec., 1863. The Vigilantes soon hung, shot, or frightened most of the "road agents" from the area. In 1863 Idaho Territory was organized and included practically all of present Montana. On May 26, 1864, Montana Territory was formed from Eastern Idaho.

[13]So-called because they were made down along the Missouri River, at Leavenworth or St. Joe, by a man named Murphy. They had wooden axles.

[14]Indian uprisings against the settlers began in the late 1860's. The Sioux were the most belligerent, and on June 25, 1876 (ten years after Doc Shores landed at Fort Benton), they killed General Custer and his men at the famous Battle of the Little Big Horn. (*The Encyclopedia Americana,* Vol. 19, "Montana," pp. 390-394.)

[15]Shores, *op. cit.,* p. 25.

[16]*Ibid.,* pp. 26-27.

[17]*Ibid.,* p. 25.

[18]*Ibid.,* p. 23.

[19]*Ibid.,* p. 25.

[20]*Ibid.,* p. 20.

Chapter II

After working all the summer and fall of 1867 as a bullwhacker, I got a job that winter hunting and trapping for an old rancher in what is now Madison County, Montana. The chief game in that area consisted of deer, antelope, and mountain sheep. I packed the meat in on a little black Spanish mule, and my employer sold what we didn't eat at twenty-five cents a pound in gold dust.[1]

The mountain sheep proved to be the most dangerous game to bag. When shot at, they would stampede into the inaccessible crags of rocky gulches or percipitous canyons. In attempting to follow my nimble victims, I had to scale cliffs and cross ledges as narrow as tightropes. At such times I had to carefully place one foot directly in front of the other to keep from falling into the tremendous voids which stretched out below me.

When these razor-backed ledges came to a dead end, as they often did, I, unable to turn around, would drop my rifle on the rocks below and work myself back out, step by step, while hugging the sheer walls of the cliff. More than once I came close to slipping and plunging to my death. Upon regaining more substantial footing I then would feel my way down the slope to recover my gun.[2]

A number of times I brought in jack rabbits with my other game. Whenever I did so, my elderly employer would cook the jacks for our use, thereby saving the more savory meat to sell. Since the old jacks were pretty strong, the rancher cooked them in a lot of gravy to diminish somewhat the wild taste. He kept warming up this unpalatable rabbit stew day after day until it was all gone. While heating the soupy concoction he stirred it with a spoon, sampling it frequently. He had no teeth and the long whiskers covering his chin and upper lip so concealed the sunken line of his mouth that when he tasted the stew, it looked as if he were pushing the spoon in and out of his dirty beard. This unappetizing sight made me so sick of rabbit stew that I quit bringing the jacks in, much to the consternation of the well-meaning rancher, who apparently considered them quite a delicacy.[3]

By spring[4] I had saved enough gold dust to buy four mules and a freight wagon. I quit my job killing game and started out for Laramie, Wyoming Territory, which was situated near where the Union Pacific Railroad was being built across the plains. Not far from Green River, Wyoming, I overtook an acquaintance of mine by the name of Ebenezer Jones, who was driving a wagon through the region peddling vegetables, which he had raised on his little farm along Willow Creek near where I had spent the winter hunting and trapping. Jones was a big, genial, naive-looking farmer about fifty-five years old. Because of his grandfatherly air, he was called "Uncle Eb" by his neighbors. However, despite his kindly, harmless appearance he was an expert card player and gambler.

Since we were going in the same direction, Uncle Eb and I traveled together for several days. One evening we made our camp near a tent where a couple of fellows had a little stock of canned goods, tobacco, cigars, and whiskey, which they sold to passers-by on their way to the new railroad that was being constructed out of Laramie. When Uncle Eb and I entered, the two proprietors were sitting around a table playing poker and drinking with several of their patrons. They were very friendly to Uncle Eb and me as we bought some drinks and cigars. After we had made our purchases, one of the proprietors offered us a drink and invited us to join in the game.

I declined, but Uncle Eb accepted both, saying, "Well, I hardly ever gamble myself, but I might take a dollar's worth of chips just to be sociable."

By nightfall Uncle Eb was still playing and apparently half drunk.

I left to cook supper, and upon returning found my companion getting a little more reckless but still nearly holding his own.

"Soup's on, Uncle Eb," I said.

"Yes, you'd better take the old man back to camp with you," one of the owners of the establishment said. "He's had his fun, and he'd better stop now before he loses all of his money."

"I don't wanta go yet," Uncle Eb protested, taking another drink. "I'm just beginning to feel lucky."

I, knowing Uncle Eb's aptitude with cards, played along with him. After a token attempt to get him to go back to our camp with me, I turned to the smiling proprietors and said, "I can't do anything with him when he gets in one of these moods. He works hard all year and earns a lot of money. Then, he goes on a spree, gets to gamblin', and usually ends up by losing everything he has on earth."[5]

Uncle Eb played poker with them all night, and by morning he had won all their money, tent, and entire stock of goods. The unfortunate victims had discovered too late that they were dealing with a professional.[6]

In August, 1868, I reached Laramie, which was then the terminus of the Union Pacific Railroad. The railroad was being constructed westward, and Laramie was one of the toughest towns in the entire West. Gambling of all kinds flourished, including Three Card Monte, Union Pacific Lottery, dice games, and all kinds of poker.[7] There were three big dance halls full of sporting women, and gun fights were daily occurrences. The more conservative citizens were even afraid to venture out on the streets after dark[8]

I set up my camp just across the Laramie River from the wide-open town. The following afternoon, seeking respite from the heat, twenty-seven dance hall girls, accompanied by two men, went swimming in the nude in full view of my camp. Some of the bathers were old and fat while others were young and comely. However, I was not used to such immodesty and turned my back in embarrassment on the activity.[9]

Late that fall a vigilante committee was organized to clean up the town. My partner and I, who were camped about twenty miles away hauling ties for the railroad, were asked to serve on the committee. We refused to participate in the proposed lynchings but agreed to stand guard at the bridge over the Laramie River, while others performed the more violent work in town.

During the raid a man came hurrying from town up to the bridge. I stopped him, and he looked at me pleadingly and said, "Please let me get the hell out of here. The vigilante committee is hanging lots better men than me."[10]

I let him pass, and he crossed the river and went into Alec Lawson's saloon—the only one on that side of the river. After restoring his courage and undermining his judgment with a few stiff drinks, he staggered back across the bridge and returned to Laramie, where he was also strung up to the branch of a handy tree.

Three or four other hoodlums got lynched that day, including the proprietor of the unsavory Diana Dance Hall, where one man had been found behind the bar beaten to death and another corpse discovered in a big box under the dance hall. This proprietor was hung to a telegraph pole. More fortunate rowdies—including the corrupt city marshal—were told by the vigilantes to get out of town or suffer a like fate.[11] This forced exodus of the worst element in early-day Laramie made it a safe place to live.

At the time of the raid I was working for a firm which had contracted to haul ties for the westward-moving Union Pacific Railroad. My camp consisted of an improvised slab shack on one of the forks of the Little Laramie River about twenty miles west of town. I had traded my mules for four yoke of oxen, which pulled a large freight wagon capable of carrying three thousand feet of green lumber or seventy-five railroad ties. My partner was a former Prussian soldier by the name of Gus Grames, who had three yoke of oxen and a wagon. We hauled ties and lumber out of the timber to our camp, where we kept them for a time before hauling them down to the Little Laramie River. From here they were run down the river to a section house, called Wyoming City, where they were loaded on railroad cars to be shipped to the end of the line.[12]

One day I took time out from my work to go hunting in order to break a steady diet of old yellow sowbelly (salted pork). Four or five miles from camp I shot an antelope. After removing the entrails and bracing the carcass open to let in the cold air, I covered it with my overcoat to keep away the wolves until I could return with a pack horse.

The next morning when I came back with a borrowed pack horse, an Indian had put on my overcoat and was struggling to load the frozen antelope on his pony. He was having a hard time since he had no knife or tomahawk to quarter the animal.

I quickly reclaimed my possessions and proceeded to cut up the fresh meat and place it in the panniers on the packsaddle. The Indian kept begging for some of the meat, but after his attempt to steal it, I refused to give him any. That evening my partner and I had our first square meal in many weeks.[13]

Hauling ties during that winter of 1868-69 was a lonely job. Many of my fellow bullwhackers and muleskinners made occasional visits to Laramie to break the monotony. They usually had a pretty wild time, and some never returned.

For example, one time when a group of my companions were going into town I asked a bullwhacker by the name of Murphy to inquire at the post office about any mail for me. Murphy was an educated man from New York City and had a certain air of refinement about him which was seldom seen on the frontier. Well, I didn't get my mail, for that night Murphy got in some kind of a jam and was shot and killed.[14]

Alec Howie, another bullwhacking buddy of mine, had a similar experience. He visited Laramie and nearly got in a shooting scrape at Pat Doran's place, which was part saloon and part hotel. Like Murphy, Howie was a college graduate, which was not a common characteristic among bullwhackers. However, I met men of all professions in this lowly kind of work, including lawyers, teachers, bookkeepers, and even preachers. The job sort of went against the grain of a preacher, though, because the man wasn't made who could whack oxen all day without swearing.[15]

After returning from Laramie, Alec Howie brooded about the trouble that he had at Pat Doran's saloon. He told me that the next time he went back he was going to settle the score. I advised him to stay away from Laramie and forget about the disagreement, whatever it was. But Alec did not follow my advice. Several weeks later he went to Laramie for another celebration, and while there he shot and killed a man. He was locked up and tried for murder. His brother, Neil Howie, who was a prominent vigilante in Montana, came down to Laramie to attend the trial. But, in spite of his support, Alec received a life sentence and was sent to the penitentiary at Yankton, South Dakota.[16] So, Alec obtained his revenge but in so doing ruined his life.

One day while we were working, my partner Gus Grames, the former Prussian soldier, complained of a violent toothache. By evening his jaw was badly swollen, and he was in a great deal of pain. I tried to pull out the infected tooth with an old pair of bullet molds, but they kept slipping off. Finally, in desperation, I got a spike, and holding it against the tooth, I knocked it out with a hammer.[17]

The contracting firm we were working for was called Sprague, Davis & Company with headquarters at Fort Saunders, about two miles from Laramie. When spring arrived we received word to come over to Laramie and receive pay for our winter's work. We lay around our respective camps near town for several weeks waiting for the contracting company to settle with us.

Finally one tie hauler went up to the office of Sprague, Davis & Company and demanded his pay.

"We can't pay you," Mr. Davis said, "until we get our books straightened out."

"That's what you fellows have been tellin' us for the past month," the irate bullwhacker said. "I don't believe you intend to pay us at all."

"That's pretty rough talk," Davis retorted. "Get out of my office before I throw you out."

As Davis advanced threateningly, the bullwhacker pulled out a six-shooter and shot the contractor through the heart.[18]

This occurrence brought matters to a head. A big crowd of us muleskinners and bullwhackers gathered in Laramie and started out for Fort Saunders to make Sprague, the surviving contractor, dig up our money or hang.

When we arrived at the fort, one of our leaders explained to the commander of the post that we were just going up to the office of Sprague, Davis & Company to demand our rightful pay checks. The commander said that he and his soldiers would not interfere so long as there was no violence. This sobered us down considerably, but we continued on up to the firm's headquarters.

As soon as Sprague saw the threatening crowd, he came rushing out. He was badly scared, and when he heard our demands, he agreed to give us each a little cash, which the company had on hand, and pay us the balance in checks. I received about $25 in cash and a check made out for $1400, as I remember. However, by the time I got to the Laramie bank to cash my check, Sprague had made out a stop payment order and had left the country. So, all my winter's work and privations had gone for nothing. I yoked up my oxen and started out in search of another job.

FOOTNOTES

[1]C. W. Shores, "Autobiography of C. W. Shores," original manuscript, Denver, Colo., Feb. 17, 1928, p. 27. In possession of Western History Dept. of Denver Public Library.

[2]*Ibid.*, p. 28.

[3]*Ibid.*

[4]1868.

[5]C. W. Shores, "The Story of a Gambler," original manuscript, Denver, Colo., Dec. 27, 1927, p. 4. In possession of Western History Dept. of Denver Public Library.

[6]*Ibid.*, pp. 1-5.

[7]C. W. Shores, "Helping to Build the Union Pacific Railroad across the Plains in 1868," original manuscript, Denver, Colo., Mar. 16, 1927, p. 2. In possession of Western History Dept. of Denver Public Library.

[8]Shores, "Autobiography of C. W. Shores," *op. cit.*, p. 33.

[9]Shores, "Helping to Build the Union Pacific Railroad across the Plains in 1868," *op. cit.*, p. 2.

[10]*Ibid.*, p. 7.

[11]This Laramie marshal was later hung in Denver.

[12]Shores, "Helping to Build the Union Pacific . . . ," *op. cit.*, p. 1.

[13]*Ibid.*, pp. 3-4.

[14]*Ibid.*, p. 5.

[15]Shores, "Autobiography of C. W. Shores," *op. cit.*, p. 25.

[16]Shores, "Helping to Build the Union Pacific Railroad across the Plains in 1868," *op. cit.*, p. 5.

[17]*Ibid.*, p. 10.

[18]*Ibid.*, p. 8.

Chapter III

After quitting my job hauling ties for the Union Pacific Railroad, I spent the following year (1870) carrying freight to and from many frontier outposts, including Cheyenne, Laramie, and Denver.

One night while camped out on a flat near Cheyenne ready to start for Denver in the morning, I encountered one of the hardest windstorms of my career.

When the wind struck, I was sleeping under the bows of my wagon between boxes of freight. I awakened to see the heavy canvas cover of my wagon blow off into the moonlit night. The gale ripped off the door of my mess box, and soon my cooking utensils were bouncing along on the ground like rabbits. The full moon made the turbulent night as light as day, and the canvas covers of the other wagons around me were flying and flapping like cavorting ghosts on a spree. Empty wagons were blown over, loaded wagons like mine rocked precariously, and tents were flattened out. Bullwhackers and muleskinners sleeping on the ground scurried around, piling their yokes and harnesses on the edges of their blankets to keep them from also blowing away.[1]

While observing all of this wild and confused commotion, I pulled one of the flapping canvas sheets from the side of my wagon and wrapped it around me and my few blankets to keep from freezing to death.

I weathered out the night, and the next morning after the wind had subsided I walked around the area looking for my cooking utensils, which I had last seen bounding along in the wind. The only thing I could find was a big coffee pot, which I carried back to camp. I was starting to make some coffee when another bullwhacker came along and said that the coffee pot belonged to him. So, before I could prepare breakfast, I had to go into Cheyenne and purchase a new mess outfit.

Arriving in Denver with my load of freight, I sold it and spent the winter with two other freighters in a crude adobe cabin at the mouth of Chico Creek where it empties into the Arkansas River east of Pueblo. Between us we had 160 head of oxen which wintered on the dried-up grass over an area of from five to ten miles.

During the latter part of March, 1870, these oxen were yoked up to our train of wagons, and the three of us with our employees started southward toward the Huerfano River, a branch of the Arkansas. Here we loaded our wagons with corn, raised by some Indians and Mexicans, and headed north for Kit Carson. At that time Kit Carson was the terminus of the Kansas Pacific Railroad, later called the Union Pacific.[2]

Just north of the Arkansas River near Bent's Fort, which was the only outpost bewteen the Huerfano and Kit Carson, an unexpected blizzard broke out late one night while we were asleep in our tent. Toward morning the roaring wind had reached such a velocity that it blew down our tent and ripped off the wagon covers. We gathered up our blankets and started back for the river to seek shelter in the brush and build a fire. On the way we luckily ran across an old building which had apparently been used at one time as a blacksmith shop. We remained in the refuge for three days and nights until the blizzard had ended.

During the storm our 160 head of oxen drifted to the Arkansas and scattered up and down the river. A few were so badly frozen that they were never worth anything again. Many men caught in this blizzard were not so fortunate as we and froze to death. We probably would have met a like fate if we hadn't stumbled on to the old blacksmith shop.[3]

Upon finally reaching the terminus of the Kansas Pacific Railroad at the newly formed town of Kit Carson, my partners and I sold our corn to the government to be used as feed for cavalry horses. Several companies of cavalry were on their way to be stationed there to give protection against hostile Indians, who were expected to go on the warpath at any time.

After disposing of our corn, my two partners and I loaded our wagons with more government freight to haul to Fort Union, New Mexico. At Rush Creek, ten miles south of Kit Carson, it took twenty-seven yoke of oxen to pull one loaded wagon across since the stream was full of quicksand.

After pasturing through the long winter months our oxen were not in their best condition, but the new spring grass was getting started and they fed on it greedily when given the opportunity.

Between Rush Creek and Kiowa Springs there was a forty-five mile stretch where no water could be obtained. Along this route the terrain was so sandy that our oxen could pull only half the wagons through at a time. I waited with the parked wagons until the oxen and other bullwhackers could make the first trip through and return. I was out of drinking water and only had a small amount of alkali water to cook with. Toward the end of the day I was so thisty that my tongue became swollen and dry. A few Mexican freight trains from the south passed by on their way to Kit Carson, but the oxen and their drivers were also suffering from lack of water. The bullwhackers called over to me asking in hoarse voices how far it was to the next water hole.

In one of the freight wagons was a keg of whiskey; so when my thirst became almost unbearable, I poured out a little whiskey from this keg into a tin cup. When I swallowed a little of it, I nearly choked to death. After recovering my breath I tried eating some jam which I found in another wagon, but it also strangled me.[4]

During the following night I suddenly noticed little lights appearing and vanishing in the darkness. When a passing Mexican bullwhacker drove up and asked for some water, I called his attention to the strange phenomenon.

"Mon Dios," he cried, "they look like Indian signals. They must be gettin' ready to attack us."

We both grabbed our rifles and waited expectantly, watching the mysterious lights with fearful fascination.

As they came nearer, we finally realized with relief that they were not Indian signals but the headlamps of a stagecoach moving up and down the hilly road on its way to Kit Carson.

About midnight one of my men rode in on a horse which we had brought along for emergencies. He said that the others were coming along behind him with the oxen. He had come on ahead to let me drink from a gallon keg of water which he was carrying for the group. However, when he dismounted to untie it from his saddle, we found that the cork had come out and all the water was gone. By this time my throat and mouth were so dry that I could only talk in a hoarse whisper. During my life as a bullwhacker I had become so inured to disappointments and hardships that I accepted my bad luck with the usual stoicism of one accustomed to the mishaps of frontier life.

Upon arrival of the other bullwhackers, we yoked the oxen to the remaining wagons and set forth on the difficult forty-five mile trip to Kiowa Springs, where the other wagons and a guard were awaiting us. I drove one of the wagons, but since I was unable to talk or yell, I was severely handicapped. To keep my tired steers going I had to keep pounding them with my bull whip all the way to the springs. When we reached there late the next morning, I rushed over to the nearest spring and lay there drinking out of it until I was sick.[5]

We remained at Kiowa Springs for the remainder of the day and night. At daybreak the next morning we started out on another forty-mile dry drive to the Arkansas River, which we intended to ford near old Fort Lyons. At about two o'clock that afternoon the oxen began to hold their heads high in the yokes as they got the smell of water from the still distant river.

To prevent a stampede while they were hitched to the freight wagons, we immediately unyoked them. Each time that the bow was pulled out of a yoke, releasing a steer, he started out on a run for the Arkansas. Soon there was a whole string of them moving along at a fast trot with their tongues hanging out and frothing at the mouths.

Knowing the oxen would not stray from the river, we lay down under our wagons for a nap. I was awakened by something crawling across my hand. I jumped up to discover that the intruder was a small rattlesnake. Instinctively, I threw myself backward, striking my hand against the axle of the wagon I had been sleeping under.

"Look out for the rattler," I yelled, crawling out into the open.

This warning abruptly ended our brief siesta. Everyone was instantly on his feet looking around for the rattlesnake which had disappeared.

"You must've had a nightmare, Doc," one of the men commented. "There ain't no rattler around here."[6]

Everyone seemed to have reached the same conclusion until I happened to look under a big empty barrel. There was the rattlesnake, coiled and ready to strike.

After this unpleasant experience I developed a phobia about snakes, which lasted for many months. The slightest noise or movement near me during the night would send me into a frenzied search through my blankets for an imaginary rattler.

South of the Arkansas River roamed the warlike Comanche and Kiowa Indians, who were more unfriendly to the whites than were the Cheyenne and Arapaho tribes, who lived north of the river. We fortunately did not come into contact with any Indians on our trip south to Fort Union, New Mexico, but on the return trip we were not so lucky.

On our way back to Kit Carson quite a number of Mexican freighters, driving up from Old Mexico, gathered behind our camp on the south side of the Arkansas River. While the Cheyennes and Arapahoes often tolerated the whites coming through their territory north of the river, they were very hostile toward Mexicans. Since our train had an escort of six or seven soldiers because we were carrying government freight, the Mexican bullwhackers followed us closely across the river into the land of their mortal enemies. They came empty intending to load their wagons at the railhead and return to Chihuahua, Mexico.[7]

In spite of the Indian threat, the Mexicans were not equipped with good firearms or other weapons. Some had knives; others carried old-time horse pistols, and a few were provided with old-fashioned muzzle loading rifles.[8] They were deathly afraid of the Indians and kept close to us for protection.

On the first night after crossing the Arkansas River, our bull train made camp in its customary circle, and the oxen were turned out to graze under the supervision of a night herder.[9] The Mexican trains behind us followed suit. After eating and completing the night's chores, we crawled into our welcome blankets beside the wagons, while our soldier escort retired in a small tent, except for the sentry shift.

Not long after everyone had quieted down in the various camps, a Mexican youth, who had strayed away from the group while chasing a stray pony, came running into our camp yelling, "Indios! Indios! Indios!" The pursuing Indians could be heard yelling and shooting right behind him.

We all jumped out of our blankets and ran for our guns. An old sergeant, who was in charge of the soldiers, rushed out of the tent and started barking orders. He had difficulty getting his small command out of its quarters. His men were so panic-stricken that some of them in their confusion finally ventured forth with their pants on backward.[10]

They began shooting at the oncoming Indians with needle guns, but their aim was so high that the Indians were in little danger. Seeing the white wagon covers the Cheyenne raiding party turned off to one side and galloped away into the darkness.

The fleeing Mexican youth continued to run and scream until all of the camps in the area became a scene of wild disorder.

Although the soldiers' aim was bad, they kept reloading and firing into the night, which token show of force kept the Indians from returning. This was fortunate since our military escort apparently would not have been very effective in case the Indians had made a serious attack.

Indian attacks on bull and mule trains going to and from Kit Carson were not uncommon at this time. When our freighting wagons pulled into Kit Carson, a big, tall Irishman by the name of Irwin was camped just outside of town with a bull outfit. One morning while he and his bullwhackers were out on foot rounding up their oxen, a band of Indians came galloping toward them. The leader struck at Irwin with his lance as he sped by. Irwin, who, in spite of his size, was an agile man, grasped the lance and jerked it out of the Indian's hand. At the same time he grabbed the running horse by the tail. As he was dragged along, stepping about twenty feet at a stride, he kept slashing the Indian over the head and shoulders with his long black bull whip.

This whip, known as a "black snake" and carried by most wagon bosses in charge of bull trains, was a lethal weapon about ten feet long, equipped on its extreme end with a heavy lash. The Indian had nothing on but a thin calico shirt over his shoulders and a blanket around his hips. He yelled each time that Irwin hit him. The big Irishman finally lost his grip on the horse's tail, and the Indian galloped away, yipping like a frightened dog.[11]

FOOTNOTES

[1]C. W. Shores, "Autobiography of C. W. Shores," original manuscript, Denver, Colo., Feb. 17, 1928, pp. 39-40. In possession of Western History Dept. of Denver Public Library.

[2]C. W. Shores, "Caught with a Bull Outfit in an Awful Blizzard," original manuscript, Denver, Colo., Dec. 31, 1927, p. 1. In possession of Western History Dept. of Denver Public Library.

[3]*Ibid.*, p. 2.

[4]*Ibid.*, p. 3.

[5]*Ibid.*, p. 4.

[6]*Ibid.*, p. 5.

[7]C. W. Shores, "Navajo Indian Story," original manuscript, Denver, Colo., April 23, 1929, p. 1. In possession of Western History Dept. of Denver Public Library.

[8]Shores, "Autobiography of . . . ," *op cit.*, p. 42.

[9]Shores, "Caught With a Bull Outfit in an Awful Blizzard," *op. cit.*, p. 6.

[10]Shores, "Autobiography of . . . ," *op. cit.*, p. 42.

[11]Shores, "Caught with a Bull Outfit in an Awful Blizzard," *op. cit.*, pp. 7-8.

Chapter IV

After arriving at Kit Carson, Colorado Territory, with our government freight, the contractors who were employing me and my two partners sent us to Fort Hays, Kansas, to haul government supplies from this point to Fort Dodge, Kansas, and Camp Supply, Indian Territory, in present Oklahoma.

While traveling from Kit Carson toward our new headquarters at Fort Hays, we came upon a big herd of buffalo, which were commonplace all through the plains country. We saw many other herds during our two hundred mile trip and, consequently, kept well supplied with fresh meat.

Fort Hays was situated about half a mile from Hays City with a stream called Big Creek running between. Soldiers stationed at the fort came over to the little town for entertainment and often got into trouble.

On the outskirts of town was a graveyard known as Boot Hill, where men who died violently were buried. When we arrived during the summer of 1870, I was told that Boot Hill already had a population of twenty-seven.

While in Hays City I occasionally saw the famous gunman, Wild Bill Hickock, who was marshal there at that time. His appearance alone made him an unforgettable character. His curly, blonde silken hair hung to his shoulders, a style popular with plainsmen and buffalo hunters in the early days. He usually wore a fancy Prince

Albert coat, checkered trousers, embroidered silk waistcoat, polished boots, and a black sombrero. He was living with a half-breed Indian girl, and he occasionally drank and gambled—but never excessively. When cavalry troops were moved to Fort Hays in 1870, Wild Bill's job of keeping the peace was made much more difficult.[1]

That fall while my two partners and I were camped for the night about forty miles south of Hays City en route to Camp Supply with a load of freight, an army ambulance from Fort Hays stopped nearby. One of the soldiers accompanying the ambulance walked over for a short visit. He informed us that several nights previously Marshal Hickock had got into a rough and tumble fight in Ned Waters' saloon with a group of drunken soldiers from the seventh cavalry. Two of the cavalrymen had thrown Wild Bill to the floor and were holding him on his back when the marshal somehow managed to pull out his gun. He shot one of the men on top of him. Then, struggling to his feet, he shot over his shoulder and killed the other soldier who was hanging on to his back.

Our guest went on to say that right after the fight Hickock caught a freight train to Junction City, Kansas—about 125 miles distant. He apparently feared reprisals from the fellow soldiers of the two men whom he had killed, for he never returned to Hays city.[2] A few months later he was appointed marshal of Abilene, Kansas, after his distinguished predecessor—efficient, soft-spoken Tom Smith—was killed.[3]

In order to keep freight from being molested along the 160-mile wagon road from Fort Hays to Camp Supply, the government required that all Indians keep twelve miles away from both sides of the route. But, in spite of this ruling, Indians often slipped into our camp at night to trade moccasins, buckskin, and tanned buffalo hides for whiskey, ox bows, powder, lead, and percussion caps.

Muzzle loading rifles were issued to the Indians along with a limited amount of ammunition to use in hunting. Trading lead, powder, or whiskey to the Indians was illegal, but the law was difficult to enforce since the Indians would never testify in court against the men with whom they traded.[4]

On my last trip to Camp Supply the night herder went to sleep, and all the oxen got away, mixing with the buffalo. They were hard to trail because the tracks of the unshod oxen looked the same as those of the buffalo.

I took a man with me, and riding two of the three horses, which we took along for such emergencies, we found thirty-six head which we herded back into camp. With these oxen we pulled a few wagons at a time to Bluff Creek where water could be obtained. We remained here for several weeks until I had rounded up the remaining strays, bringing in a few each day.[5]

Our bad luck continued. It rained continually, causing the rivers and creeks to be swollen and boggy. As a result of the frequent downpours and losing our oxen, it took us six weeks to make the 160-mile journey from Fort Hays to Camp Supply.

It was a heart-breaking trip, and we were a sorry-looking lot of men when we finally arrived at our destination. Our clothes were threadbare, and we had replaced our sodden, worn out shoes with pieces of buffalo hide wrapped around our feet and tied with whangs.

The outfit and cargo looked as travel-worn as we did. Many of the patched-up wagons had been pulled apart in the mud and quicksand, and the freight, consisting of forage, corn, oats, and bran for cavalry horses, was badly damaged by the inclement weather. The oats and corn had grown out through the water-soaked gunny sacks, and the bran was hard and caked.

The quartermaster, as was the custom, appointed a board of surveyors to inspect the freight and pass judgment on it. Three young captains were chosen to perform this job, and upon seeing in what bad shape our freight was, they rejected our cargo in no uncertain terms.

"Where in hell have you been?" one of them asked in disgust. "Take your damned outfit and get off the reservation."

This forceful rejection was a shade too much for one of my partners, who had already endured about as much as he could stand in getting these needed supplies to their destination. He lost his temper and called the inspectors and quartermaster every name in the book.

My other partner and I managed to control our sentiments a little better and were more diplomatic about the situation.

"I know this stuff we're carrying looks like the devil," I said to the elderly quartermaster, "but we've had every bad break in the game hauling it down here."

I then proceeded to explain in a tactful way all the hardships and trials we had been through. After a little persuasion the quartermaster, who himself had once been a bullwhacker, finally appointed a new board of inspectors, composed of older officers more familiar with the hazards of hauling freight by oxen across the plains. After due consideration this board proved more tolerant and agreed to accept our damaged load.[6]

Among the soldiers stationed at Camp Supply were several companies of Negro cavalrymen. Some of the Indians had never before seen Negroes, who were quite a curiosity to them. Once, as a humorous gesture, I saw an Indian wet a finger in his mouth and then rub it on a colored soldier's face, pretending to rub off some of the black. The Negro cavalryman seemed to enjoy the joke as much as the Indians.[7]

After making the return trip back to Fort Hays in November, 1870, I sold my oxen and wagons, and caught a train for Detroit to visit my folks, whom I had not seen in four years.

A month later, accompanied by a friend from back home who wanted to see the West, I returned as far as Fort Scott, Kansas. Here my companion and I bought a yoke of oxen and a covered chuck wagon, equipped with cooking utensils, blankets, and a small tent. Then, we set out for Texas with the intention of buying a bunch of cattle and driving them back up the famous Chisholm Trail to sell at the railhead in Abilene, Kansas.[8]

This was the era of the big cattle drives from Texas, and being young and of an adventurous disposition, I for some time had longed to try my hand at this colorful and lucrative business.

In 1870, a man could buy a good four-year-old steer in Texas for five dollars. If the steer was held and wintered in Kansas before being sold, he would bring as much as fifty dollars.[9] These good prices so stimulated trade that fully 600,000 cattle were herded up the trail from Texas in 1871 bound for the northern railroads. This was the biggest year of the Texas Trail drives and, interestingly enough, was the year that I made the trip. A year later in 1872

Dodge City was fast replacing Abilene as the capital of the cattle trade.

The reason for the overabundance of cattle in Texas was that during the Civil War the Union Army, by controlling the Mississippi and the Gulf of Mexico, prevented the Texans from supplying the Confederate Army or any other market with beef. As a result, their herds increased rapidly. On the other hand, the supply of beef in the North for the Union Army did not keep pace with the demand, resulting in a scarcity of cattle north of the Mason and Dixon line.[10]

Consequently, Texas had the cattle, and the North had the demand and money. The Union Stock Yards in Chicago was opened on Christmas Day, 1865, and railroads began nosing their way westward across the plains into Missouri and Kansas. The only problem that remained was to get the cattle from Texas over the intervening thousands of miles to the railroads in Missouri and Kansas, and the immediate answer to that lay in bringing them up on the hoof. The first cattle drive from Texas to the railroad began in 1866, and they continued for the next twenty years. Between 1867 and 1890 almost ten million cattle were driven out of Texas to be sold in the northern markets.

After 1880, however, trail driving declined rapidly due to the increasing number of farms and fences, and because the railroads began extending their lines southward into Texas.

The most famous and for a time the most widely used of these cattle trails to the north was the Chisholm Trail, which ran from San Antonio, Texas, across the Red River at Red River Station and north through Indian Territory, later known as Oklahoma, to Abilene, Kansas—the capital of sin and violence as well as the cattle trade. This trail was named after Jesse Chisholm, a half-breed Indian trader who established a wagon route for freighters to military posts across present Oklahoma before the Civil War.

Leaving Fort Scott, my companion and I drove southward in our covered wagon through Kansas into Oklahoma, then known as Indian Territory. This was the home of the Five Civilized Tribes—the Cherokees, Creeks, Choctaws, Chickasaws, and Seminoles. These tribes were removed by the government from their original holdings in the eastern part of the United States during 1830 to 1840 to territory in what comprised practically all of present Oklahoma.[11] The Osage and Quapaw Tribes, who originally claimed dominion over Oklahoma, also had reservations in this region.

Until the Civil War members of the Five Civilized Tribes established little farms, formed tribal governments, and became quite prosperous in their new surroundings. When the Civil War broke out, the various tribes tried to remain neutral, but they were eventually drawn into the struggle. Most of the Choctaw and Chickasaw Indians joined the Confederate forces while most of the Cherokee, Creek, and Seminole Indians aligned themselves with the Union Army.[12]

As a result, much fighting occurred in their territory with devastating effects. Their fields were laid waste, their livestock killed or run off, and their houses burned to the ground. Feuds between the Indians were created which took many years to heal.

Because factions from all the tribes had served with the South, each of the Five Civilized Tribes was required in 1866 to enter into a peace treaty with the United States in which they all had to surrender the western half of present Oklahoma at from fifteen to thirty cents an acre, as a penalty for their lack of loyalty to the northern cause. This land, which was ceded to the government, subsequently became known as Oklahoma Territory. The eastern half continued as Indian Territory and the home of the Five Civilized Tribes.[13]

Such was the status of the Indian Territory in the winter of 1870-71 when my partner and I drove down through that area from Kansas on our way to Texas.

Along the way we stayed for a few days in an old deserted cabin near a little log store and post office in the Choctaw nation. The post office was called McAlester, and an educated Choctaw Indian was both proprietor of the store and postmaster.[14]

Early each morning a small Indian boy about seven or eight years old would walk by our camp, carrying an ax on his shoulder and followed by three mongrel dogs. In the evenings he would return home, often carrying a skunk on his back which he had killed during the day. The Choctaws and Chickasaws considered skunk or pole cat meat quite a delicacy.

I inquired about this boy from the postmaster, who informed me that his father and mother were dead and that he was living nearby with an uncle, who was an educated Choctaw Indian.

The little orphan could speak some English, and if I happened to be around when he passed, I would engage him in conversation.[15] Since all Indians, young and old alike, enjoyed tobacco from the time they were born, I occasionally gave the boy a quid. As a result, he became quite devoted to me. He occasionally helped me hunt for my yoke oxen, following their tracks as unerringly as a bloodhound.

Each day he asked me, "When you go?"

"In a day or two," I would reply, "but I'll let you know before I do."[16]

One day my partner discovered and killed a possum crawling under the old cabin where we were staying. He dressed it out and saved the carcass for our little Indian friend, believing that it would be better eating than the skunks he was bringing in.

Much to our consternation, he turned down our delectable gift saying, "Indian never eat possum."

The next day the postmaster explained to us the reason for the boy's refusal. He said that members of the Choctaw and Chickasaw tribes believed that when a Negro dies he is reincarnated into a possum.[17] So the boy's antipathy to eating the animal was understandable.

The Five Civilized Tribes had formerly lived in Georgia, Florida, and the Carolinas, and when they were transferred to the Indian Territory in present Oklahoma, they were accompanied by many Negroes who had adopted the Indian language and customs. These Negroes and their descendants were scattered throughout the territory and were usually more thrifty and better workers than the Indians.[18]

One moonlight night I was awakened by the sound of horses' hoofs. I looked out of the cabin door to see a man on horseback hurrying by, leading a large gray stallion. The next evening two other riders rode up and asked my partner and me if we had seen a man go past with a gray stud. I told them that such a man had passed by the night before.

Since it was about supper time, I asked the newcomers to dismount and have a bite to eat with us. They did not say much during the meal, but apparently the man they were after had stolen the horse from one of them.

Several days later the two riders stopped by again on the return trip. They were leading the stolen stallion and the horse thief's mount, which they said they had taken in payment for their trouble.

The horse thief's body was found a few days later with a bullet hole in his head. This was a common method of dealing with rustlers in those days.[19]

When my partner and I decided to break camp and continue on our journey, I informed my little Indian friend that I was leaving the next day. He was on hand early the following morning to help us find our oxen and yoke them up to the chuck wagon. He had made up his mind to go along with us, and I had a difficult time persuading him to remain. Finally, after bribing him with a number of trinkets, the boy promised not to follow.

It was with great reluctance that I bid my small admirer a last goodby.

FOOTNOTES

[1]C. W. Shores, "Story of the Kind of Men who Caused Graves along the Old Texas Cattle Trail from Texas to British Columbia," original manuscript, Denver, Colo., April 18, 1929, pp. 3-4. In possession of Western History Dept. of Denver Public Library.

Also see Thomas Penfield, *Western Sheriffs and Marshals,* Grosset & Dunlap, N.Y., 1955, pp. 19-20.

[2]*Ibid.* The stories about this affair differ and the record is cloudy. The above version is Doc Shores' account of the story as he heard it from the ambulance driver from Fort Hays shortly after the fight happened.

[3]Penfield, *op. cit.,* p. 20.

[4]C. W. Shores, "Navajo Indian Story," original manuscript, Denver, Colo., April 23, 1929, p. 2. In possession of Western History Dept. of Denver Public Library.

[5]C. W. Shores, "Autobiography of C. W. Shores," original manu-

script, Denver, Colo., Feb. 17, 1928, pp. 43-44. In possession of Western History Dept. of Denver Public Library.

[6]*Ibid.*

[7]Shores, "Navajo Indian Story," *op. cit.,* p. 2.

[8]C. W. Shores, "Going in the Cattle Business," original manuscript, Denver, Colo., p. 1. In possession of Western History Dept. of Denver Public Library.

[9]William MacLeod Raine and Will C. Barnes, *Cattle,* Doubleday, Doran and Company, Garden City, N. Y., 1930, pp. 59 and 111. Also see James D. Horan and Paul Swann, *Pictorial History of the West,* Crown Publishers, Inc., N. Y., 1954, pp. 91-93.

[10]Ralph W. Steen, *The Texas Story,* The Steck Co., Austin, Texas, 1948, pp. 295-299.

[11]"Oklahoma," *The Encyclopedia Americana,* Vol. 20, p. 640a.

[12]*Ibid.,* p. 640b.

[13]In 1867 as a result of the Treaty of Medicine Lodge Creek made in Kansas, the Cheyenne, Arapaho, Apache, Wichita, Kiowa, and Comanche tribes were assigned reservations in present western Oklahoma. Smaller and more peaceful tribes were also brought into this area, most of whom were removed from Kansas where they had lived briefly since their removal from eastern states. In the midst of these reservations was an unoccupied region which much later on April 22, 1889, was opened to white settlement, resulting in the famous land rush.

[14]A short distance from this store and post office was an outcropping of coal, which was often used by neighboring blacksmiths. The present big coal mining town of McAlester, Oklahoma, sprang up years later at this spot.

[15]C. W. Shores, "Eating Pole Cat," original manuscript, Denver, Colo., Jan. 20, 1928, p. 1. In possession of Western History Dept. of Denver Public Library.

[16]Shores, "Going in the Cattle Business," *op. cit.,* p. 2.

[17]Shores, "Eating Pole Cat," *op. cit.*

[18]Shores, "Going in the Cattle Business," *op. cit.,* p. 6.

[19]*Ibid.,* pp. 2-3.

Chapter V

After leaving the post office of McAlester in the Choctaw nation of present Oklahoma, my partner and I drove our covered wagon southward through Indian Territory along one of the cattle trails, which in the spring would be lined with Texas Longhorns plodding north to the railheads in Kansas.

I had two Indian mustangs tied to the back of the rattling wagon. One of these was a small sorrel gelding which I had bought from a Choctaw Indian while camped at McAlester. I prized it much more than the other horse, which I had procured before reaching McAlester. It was a bag of bones with a razor-sharp back—the type of backbone which would soon cut a man in two if he rode without a saddle.

The trail we were following led across streams, over open prairies, and through timbered country, covered with large bodock trees. One evening we camped on a stream near a corral and several log cabins. It proved to be the habitation of a young Chickasaw Indian woman, commonly referred to as Widow Pusley. Because of her striking beauty, she was widely known throughout the area. Her light hair and skin evidenced some cross breeding in her ancestry. However, she could speak no English, and her manner of life was strictly Indian. Her husband, who had been a prosperous rancher, was killed during the Civil War. She was living with her sixteen-year-old daughter, who was much darker than her mother.[1]

Two days later we drove our yoke of oxen into the Indian village of Stonewall Jackson, located in the Chickasaw nation of present Oklahoma. We made camp here on the outskirts of town and staked my two horses out to graze.

The next morning as I was leading the horses down to water, something frightened the sorrel, and he shied back, jerking his halter rope out of my hand. Before I could catch him, he started off at a gallop back up the trail toward his old home range near McAlester—fifty miles away. I jumped on the razor-backed horse and gave chase.[2]

The sorrel was much faster than the bag of bones I was riding, and although I rode at full speed, I could not get around the loose horse to head him back toward camp. Using a heavy eight-foot rope, which had been used to stake out the horse I was riding, I tried to ride up close enough to the sorrel to lasso him. The only times that this was possible were when he hesitated at some stream before plunging in to cross over. However, all of my throws were short; so I stopped and peeled some hickory bark off a tree and fastened it to the end of my rope to make it longer.

Before I got a chance to use my improvised, extended lariat, we had splattered across so many streams that the bark became too soggy and heavy to throw with any accuracy.

The rivers and creeks were up with the approach of spring, and I had to swim my mount across many of them, holding on to his mane or tail until he reached the other side. Consequently, I got soaked clear up to my neck.

There were a number of small bands of mustangs scattered throughout the region, and whenever the sorrel came in sight of one, he tried to join the herd. However, I managed to keep between my stray horse and the mustangs, and kept him headed up the trail toward McAlester.

As I moved farther and farther into the wilds of the Indian country, I began keeping a sharp lookout for bushwhackers. I was carrying all of my savings, amounting to $2000 in currency, sewed up in my red undershirt, and I had no firearm with me.

Because of the feuds created by the Civil War among the Indians, bushwhacking was a common occurrence. Even when out plowing,

Indian farmers in this country customarily carried rifles tied to their plow handles to protect themselves from chance marauders.

About evening the sorrel I was following trotted up the trail to Widow Pusley's ranch, which was about thirty-one miles from Stonewall. Luckily, the pole gate to her corral happened to be open, and I managed to head the wayward pony into it. Otherwise, I probably would be still chasing that broomtail.

I was a bedraggled looking sight when I dismounted in front of the Indian woman's door. I had ridden bareback on a razor-backed horse all day at a dead run. My clothes were soaked through from swimming many rivers, and I was dog-tired, sore, and cold.

Widow Pusley saw my plight at a glance, and although she could not speak a word of English, by means of gestures she showed me where I could get grain for my tired horses while she prepared a meal for me.

I had had nothing to eat since breakfast, and I was famished. My attractive benefactor provided me with a steaming, delicious supper of hominy, bread, coffee, and stewed meat. I particuarly enjoyed the tender, tasty meat, which I assumed to be veal.

As I was finishing up the last remnants on my plate I unexpectedly found a long black hair in the stew. This untimely discovery, however, in no way detracted from my enjoyment of the meal, since my life in the open had dulled my aesthetic sense to such mishaps.

It was dark by the time I finished eating, and, my appetite finally appeased, I began wondering where I was going to spend the night. As I got up from the table, the Indian woman answered this question by pointing to a comfortable looking bed in a corner of the room.

After clearing the table, Mrs. Pusley and her daughter went outside, apparently to sleep in one of the other cabins. I immediately crawled into the bed in the corner, still wearing my wet underwear, and was soon asleep.

Early the next morning after a refreshing sleep, I dressed and went outside to catch my horses. On my way out to the corral I noticed a fresh skunk hide hanging on the side of the cabin. I recalled the black hair which I had found in my stew, and, as a revelation, I realized that the savory meat I had feasted on was none other than skunk or pole cat.

Sore from my all-day excursion on the bony horse, I fashioned a saddle out of an old gunny sack that I borrowed from my benefactor. I filled it with leaves and sewed up the open end with sticks. After laying this improvised saddle on the sorrel, I made some stirrups out of hickory bark, and tied one on each end of a long strip of bark. I then hung this strip of bark over the sack of leaves so that the stirrups dangled at the horse's sides.

Being unable to mount in the usual manner without pulling off my unique riding gear, I led the sorrel up to a stump and jumped on to my burlap saddle. The stirrups were a trifle short for me, but at least it beat riding bareback—especially after my previous day's experience.

Thanking the Widow Pusley I started out on my return trip to Stonewall, driving the thin horse ahead of me. I made such a ridiculous figure sitting there on the stuffed gunny sack with my toes sticking in the bark stirrups that my Indian hostess and her daughter could not refrain from laughing as they watched me ride away.

Late that evening as I approached Stonewall, I met my partner and some Indians who were out looking for me. They were afraid that I had been bushwhacked and robbed.

After a few days recuperation from this misadventure, my companion and I continued southward across the Red River into Texas, looking for cattle to buy. The farther south we traveled, the poorer became the quality of the cattle. After going nearly as far south as Austin, Texas, we decided to return to Indian Territory, where the cattle were of a better grade than the Longhorns.

These Indian cattle did not have as long horns as the Texas cattle and were known as Short-horn Durhams. The cowboys who drove the Durhams up the trail were called "Shorthorns" and were not considered quite as hardy and reckless as the more colorful men who herded the wilder and hardier Texas Longhorns.[3]

After re-crossing the Red River back into the Chickasaw nation, we made camp near Tishomingo, where we remained until early in April. While there we scouted around and finally made arrangements to buy several hundred head of Durham cattle from two Indian brothers, who had a ranch near Stonewall, located thirty miles north of Tishomingo.[4]

One Sunday morning we started out from Stonewall to wind up the deal. We rode through the canebrakes over to the camp where the Indian brothers lived with their families. There we found the wives and children of the two cattle ranchers wailing and moaning beside two newly made graves. Around each grave was a small log enclosure covered with a shingled roof, which type of internment was typical among the Chickasaws. We were informed by the grieving relatives that the brothers had been bushwhacked and killed the night before while returning from what the Indians called a "frolic" down on the Red River.[5]

We left the mourners, but returned several days later at a more appropriate time to do business. Then, we paid the widows and gathered our cattle. We held them for several days at Stonewall, where we were joined by three other trail drivers who wanted to make the trip north with us. All-told we had a total of about six-hundred head of Shorthorn Durhams, including steers, cows, and calves which had been purchased in the southern part of Indian Territory and northern Texas.

Among the three newcomers who joined forces with us was a young easterner of twenty-one by the name of James Braidwood. He had come West that winter from Albany, New York, accompanied by his mother, sister, and brother. The family had located a claim near Winfield, Kansas, and Jim had come south into Indian Territory to purchase about sixty head of Durham-shorthorn cows from the Chickasaw Indians to stock the new ranch. He had a polish about him seldom seen on the frontier and was inexperienced in the rough and ready ways of the West. However, he took all the hardships good naturedly, tried to do his part, and soon won the respect and friendship of everyone in the group.[6]

That spring of 1871 my four fellow trail drivers and I started north from Stonewall with our mixed herd. We pointed our cattle toward the South Canadian River, intending to strike the Black Dog Trail—a little-known trail made during the Civil War and named by an army officer.[7]

The long horned herds from Texas began splashing their way across the Red River into Indian Territory right behind us. Most of them were on their way to the old Kansas-Pacific railhead at

Abilene, Kansas. These herds were much bigger than ours, averaging from 1500 to 2000 head, many of which consisted entirely of steers from three to ten years old. It took about a dozen riders, together with a trail boss and cook, to manage each herd.

At break of day these Longhorns were moved off the bed ground, the last of the three relays of night guards starting them out before being relieved by the day herders after they finished breakfast. The cattle were grazed along for an hour or two in the early morning and then were swung slowly into the trail. Two riders, known as the points, rode on either side of the leaders to guide the advance. Several hundred yards behind the points came two other riders on each side of the herd, known as the swing, and behind the swing two or three hundred yards rode the flank, and finally drawing up the rear of the herd were several riders called the drag. A short distance behind the drag came the remuda, consisting of replacement horses in charge of the wrangler. Each trail driver usually had four or five horses in his string, and he would ride a different horse each day.

The chuck wagon, driven by the cook, customarily went on ahead in order to have the meals ready at the noon and evening stops, made at water holes designated by the wagon or trail boss. The chuck wagon not only carried grub, such as flour, bacon, sugar, and coffee, but it also contained each cowboy's blankets and his sack of plunder, consisting of his extra clothing and personal belongings.[8]

Well grazed and watered, a big herd of cattle would lie quietly for about half the night. Then they would get up and lie down again, generally on the other side. The two night guards rode in a circle about four rods from the sleeping herd, usually moving in opposite directions. Those not on guard duty would each sleep on his two blankets with a folded wagon sheet pulled over him so that he could have some protection from the ground below and from the rain which might fall from above. Coats and boots served as pillows, and the trail drivers slept in their clothing worn during the day.[9]

Our outfit followed this same general pattern in conducting the drive northward with some minor modifications due to the comparative smallness of our herd.

The spring of 1871 was unusually rainy, and the rivers and creeks

Herd of Longhorns on Chisholm Trail in 1871. *Photo courtesy of Denver Public Library Western Collection.*

were on the rampage. The South Fork of the Canadian was twenty-seven feet deep in its channel and three or four miles wide, covering the surrounding territory with from six inches to four feet of water.[10]

There were about 150 head of calves in our bunch, and they were very difficult to drive across streams of any kind, let alone rivers at flood stage.[11]

As the bawling cattle splashed through the shallow water toward the main channel of the South Canadian, the leaders unexpectedly stepped into a concealed arroyo, filled with running flood water. The surprised animals plunged down head first out of sight and then emerged, swimming frantically.

Since the submerged gulch was hidden in the timber, those of us coming up from behind were not aware of the trap until we stepped into the deep water.

James Braidwood, who was the best swimmer in the group, made the treacherous crossing a little easier than the rest of us. Although thrown clear when he and his horse went under, he swam over to the struggling animal when it came to the surface and pulled himself on in back of his saddle. He was the only man who reached the other side still mounted. He did not even lose his inseparable, funny little flat cap, which he had brought with him from back East and which we all made so much fun of.

When my turn came, I was dragging along a stubborn calf at the end of a rope through the shallow water. Suddenly the sorrel horse I was riding turned a somersault into the bottomless, riley water. I fought my way to the surface and looked around. My horse bobbed up out of the water within reaching distance; so I grabbed him by the mane, and he dragged me and the calf across the water-filled gully.

On reaching the other side I freed the frightened calf and was getting ready to mount when I saw another horseman plunge into the concealed channel and disappear. When horse and rider reappeared in the swift current, they were too widely separated for the man to grab on to his horse as I had done. The trail driver was an elderly cattleman whom we called "Old Man Robinson." He always wore a small derby hat, which was as much out of place on the trail as was Jim Braidwood's cap. Robinson had a few cattle in the herd, which he was taking to Caldwell, Kansas.

Robinson couldn't swim; so, in desperation, he frantically caught hold of a piece of passing driftwood which barely held his face above the surging water.

Seeing me standing there in water up to my knees, the old man began sputtering, "Hulp! Hulp! Hulp!" as his head, still wearing the unattachable derby, bobbed in and out of the raging stream.

As the drowning man swept by, I hurled my rope out to him. It was a long throw, but, fortunately, it landed within easy reach of the floundering cattleman. Robinson immediately let go of the floating log and seized the rope, going under as he did so. He hung grimly on, and I pulled him to safety.

In spite of the near tragedy of the situation, Robinson was such a soaked, indignant little old man as he came spluttering up out of the water with the ridiculous looking derby perched on his head that I couldn't help but laugh. This made the old gentleman even more indignant.

"What's so damned funny!" he roared, spitting water out of his mouth. "What's so damned funny about seeing a man drown in the Canadian River?"[12]

I didn't blame him for being mad at me—even though I had just saved his life. It was all part of the day's work.

FOOTNOTES

[1]C. W. Shores, "Eating Pole Cat," original manuscript, Denver, Colo., Jan. 20, 1928, p. 2. In possession of Western History Dept. of Denver Public Library.

[2]*Ibid.*, pp. 2-3. Also, see C. W. Shores, "Going in the Cattle Business," original manuscript, Denver, Colo., pp. 3-4-5. In possession of Western History Dept. of Denver Public Library.

[3]C. W. Shores, "A Stampede of Longhorns in 1871," original manuscript, Denver, Colo., Dec. 22, 1927, p. 1. In possession of Western History Dept. of Denver Public Library.

[4]Shores, "Going in the Cattle Business," *op. cit.*, p. 5.

[5]*Ibid.*, pp. 5-6.

[6]C. W. Shores, "The Drowning of James Braidwood in the Creek Nation," original manuscript, Denver, Colo., Dec. 21, 1927, p. 1. In possession of Western History Dept. of Denver Public Library.

[7]*Ibid.*, p. 2.

[8]Wm. MacLeod Raine, and Will C. Barnes, *Cattle,* Doubleday, Doran and Company, Inc., Garden City, New York, 1930, pp. 77-79.

[9]Andy Adams, *Log of a Cowboy,* Houghton Mifflin Co., 1903, p. 26.

[10]Shores, "The Drowning of James Braidwood," *op. cit.,* pp. 2-3.

[11]Shores, "Going in the Cattle Business," *op. cit.,* p. 7.

[12]Shores, "The Drowning of James Braidwood," *op. cit.,* p. 4. Also, see "Going in the Cattle Business," *op. cit.,* p. 7.

Chapter VI

The main channel of the South Canadian was in places twenty-seven feet deep, but we managed to swim our herd across without mishap.

One of the biggest problems in crossing a rampaging river was to get our chuck wagon across. We had an old southern-made wagon, built out of bodock timber, with very high wheels, and drawn by a yoke of oxen.[1]

In most cases when the streams were up and there was no convenient bridge, ford, or ferry, we lashed a big cottonwood log to each side of the wagon to keep it afloat. Then, several of us would tie our ropes to the wagon, and with the other ends dallied to our saddle horns, we would help the oxen pull it across. Occasionally the wagon overturned in the swift current, losing much of its contents, but usually we got it over without serious trouble.[2]

As my four comrades and I crept northward up the Chisholm Trail with our 600 head of mixed cattle in that spring of 1871, we could look back from rises in the land and see gigantic herds heading north in every direction. Most of them were Texas Longhorns on their way to the railhead at Abilene, Kansas, the capital of the cattle trade. Due to the good prices of beef in the preceding year, more cattle were moved up the trails from Texas during 1871 than in any other year of the great cattle drives.

After passing through the Chickasaw and Choctaw nations in

present Oklahoma, my fellow trail drivers and I came to the town of Okmulgee, which was the capital of the Creek nation. From here we continued due north along the Black Dog Trail, which crossed the Arkansas River at a place called Gano's Ford.[3]

Like the South Canadian, the Arkansas was a mighty river, violent and turbulent in its spring run-off. A group of Creek Indians were camped near Gano's Ford to assist trail drivers cross the swollen stream for pay. The Indian ponies were good swimmers and trained for this type of work. Their manes were roached (cut short) except for a lock of hair on the withers, which the Indian riders could hold on to when swimming the river.[4]

I, who had been chosen as trail boss of our herd, made arrangements with five or six Creeks to help us get our bunch across the ford. I agreed to pay the Indians two dollars apiece, providing that the crossing was successful. If unsuccessful, I made it clear that I wouldn't pay them anything. I had been told that this sort of a bargain was the only way to get the Indians to do their work efficiently.

It took a lot of luck, as well as know-how, to get a bunch of cows and calves across a flooding river. The crossing should be made at a time of day when the sun was not shining in the cattle's eyes. Also, before making the approach, the herd should be well grazed and beginning to want a drink of water.

After these basic essentials were taken care of, I gave the signal to start. The Indians, who had been hired to help us, were stripped down to their breech-clouts and carried sticks three or four feet long. They had tied their shirts to the ends of these sticks, and they waved them around at the cattle to help shoo them into the water. With the help of the Creeks, the herd plunged into the roaring river and began swimming. The yelling riders, occupying strategic positions, grabbed their mounts by the mane or tail and jumped in also. Everything appeared to be working smoothly, and it looked as if we would make the crossing without difficulty.

However, when the cattle reached the middle of the torrent, the calves, which were always the biggest problem in such an undertaking, began to turn around and swim back the way they had come. The Indians and trail drivers swam their horses in front of them in a desperate effort to turn them toward the farther shore. A few were headed, but others sifted through the line of horsemen. As more and more of the calves started back, their mothers also began to follow. Before long the entire herd had balked, and we were forced to give up the struggle and swim back with them.

It hadn't rained for several days, and the Arkansas was beginning to fall rapidly. So, we decided to lay over for ten days or two weeks until the river was low enough for the older cattle to touch bottom most of the way across. During this wait we cut jack oaks and used these little trees to make a long narrow chute to the river's edge.

I paid off the Indians who had helped in the attempted crossing although according to our agreement I was under no obligation to do so. However, they had worked hard and earned their pay, even though their efforts had failed to get the cattle across.

When it looked as if the river had fallen sufficiently for a more successful try, I hired the same five or six Creeks to help us again. They caught their horses, stripped down, and once more tied their shirts to the end of long sticks. However, after the cattle had been gathered and were being driven through the jack oak chute toward the river, the Indians unexpectedly rode over to a shady tree and dismounted.

I galloped over to them and cried, "What's the big idea?"

"Want more money," one of them answered. "No help unless get more money."

Too late, I now realized the bad psychological effect of having paid them the first time. As much as we needed their help, their tactics so prejudiced me against them that I said angrily, "If that's the way you feel, we'll try and cross without you."[5]

We hurried the cattle through the chute, hoping that their momentum would carry the herd into the water. One old blue stag took the lead and leaped into the river. In every bunch of cattle there are a few who invariably move to the front and maintain a lead on the trail, across rivers, and in stampedes. They are the real leaders of the bovine world.

This blue stag or bull was one of the leaders in our herd. After jumping into the river, he waded out to deep water in the middle of

Herd of cattle crossing river on trail drive. *Photo courtesy of Denver Public Library Western Collection.*

the channel and unhesitatingly swam across to shallow water, where he stopped on a sand bar and looked back.

The rest of the herd followed reluctantly while we urged them on. When the leaders came to the high water, which was about ten or twelve feet deep, a few old cows seeing the blue stag on the other side started swimming toward him. Others followed, and it looked as if we had it made.

I was riding on the lower side of the herd through the deep water to keep the cattle from drifting too far down the current. Shortly before riding into the river, I had temporarily exchanged my sorrel for a larger horse, which had been represented by his owner to be a first-class swimmer.

He proved to be over-rated. When I spurred him into the deep water, he sank like a rock. When he finally emerged, I grabbed him by the tail. By the time I got organized, however, the cattle in the lead had drifted down with the stream and were beginning to turn back. Soon the whole herd was milling. Not anticipating any serious trouble, we had not stripped ourselves for swimming, and our soaked, heavy clothes made it difficult for us to maneuver around in the water.

To further complicate matters, one of the resentful Creek Indians, who had gone on strike, swam his horse across the channel and tried to drive back the blue stag which was standing on the other side of the river. I heard my companions yelling at the Indian to leave the bull alone, but he paid no attention.

Exasperated, I yelled, "Lay off that bull, you low-down, yellow-bellied rat!"

The insult apparently got under his hide, for he looked up to see who had spoken. He eyed me intently for a moment and then swung his horse about and rode away.[6]

Once the cattle started to mill, our cause was lost, and again our attempted crossing resulted in failure, much to the delight of the watching Indians.

Believing that the water might be shallower farther downstream, I chose James Braidwood, the best swimmer in the group, to help me investigate. The river was full of deep water holes, and the quicksand rolling into them caused large riffles to form on the surface, making the water very rough.

Jim and I removed our clothing and waded out into the roaring stream. I noticed with some amusement that he had neglected to remove his funny little cap that he had acquired in the East and wore constantly. With the reckless courage of youth, Braidwood ran into the rippling, muddy current and began swimming with abandon as if he were having a lot of fun.

Not being the swimmer that my companion was, I proceeded more cautiously. I waded slowly out into the treacherous water, feeling my way along with a ten-foot pole in order to avoid stepping suddenly into some deep hole full of moving quicksand. As I worked my way along, through the corner of my eye I occasionally caught glimpses of Braidwood's cap bobbing up and down below me as Jim swam gracefully along.[7]

After satisfying myself that I had found a good fording place where the herd could be taken across with a minimum of swimming, I started wading back, the raging water surging around my face and neck. In the distance I could still see my young friend's cap traveling farther and farther downstream as if drifting somewhat with the current.

As I approached the shore, I could faintly hear several of my comrades calling to me. However, the din of the river made it impossible to distinguish what they were saying. It was only after I struck shallow water that I could make out enough of what was being said to realize that Jim Braidwood was in serious trouble.

His cap was still visible far below, moving with the rapid current. I splashed to dry land as fast as I could run, and, still naked, jumped on one of the Creek ponies which I knew to be an expert swimmer. By this time Braidwood's cap had disappeared under the water. When it did not return to the surface, one of the trail drivers, who had accompanied the youth from Winfield, Kansas, sat down on a rock and cried like a baby.

I galloped madly down the shoreline, the vines and briars scratching a sheet of blood on my bare legs. When parallel with the spot where I had last seen the cap, I guided the Indian pony into the river. He hesitated a moment and then plunged in, swimming like a veteran. I rolled off into the water, holding my well-trained mount by a lock of hair on his withers. When we reached the other side of the channel near where Braidwood had gone under, I waded around in water up to my shoulders vainly looking for any sign of the missing trail driver.

Following my example, the others—cowboys and Indians alike—joined in the search. The Creeks, using poles, pushed their little flat boats back and forth in the wide channel, feeling for the body on the bed of the river. One of them told me that the quicksand moving near the bottom of the stream had probably rolled Braidwood into some deep hole and gradually buried him.

During the frantic hunt, some of the cattle drifted down along the river bank and trampled Braidwood's and my clothes into the river. I lost many personal possessions which I had in my pockets, including a pocket knife, a key to an old trunk in the chuck wagon, and a Masonic pin which I had carried for many years.

Jim Braidwood was never seen again, and those of us who had come up the trail with him felt a great personal loss at his death. I was so shaken by the sudden tragedy that I have never completely got over it, always feeling that I was somehow to blame. Furthermore, the drowning of so powerful and skilled a swimmer before my eyes caused me to lose confidence in my ability to take care of myself in the water. From that time on whenever I waded out into a stream and felt the roaring, riley water rushing around my chest and shoulders, I would nearly panic as I imagined death reaching out for me as it had for Braidwood.[8]

The highest tribute that a trail driver could pay to another man was, "He will do to cross the rivers with." Literally, the expression meant that the cowboy referred to was one who could be depended upon to do his part in meeting the perils of driving a herd of wild Longhorns across a raging river—one of the most severe tests of courage and skill which could confront an early-day cowpuncher. Symbolically, this token of respect came to mean a man who could be relied on to manfully do his part in meeting any emergency or crisis.

Although Jim Braidwood was an easterner unfamiliar with the

rough ways of the West, we who rode with him will always remember him as "a man who will do to cross the rivers with."

FOOTNOTES

[1]C. W. Shores, "The Drowning of James Braidwood," original manuscript, Denver, Colo., Dec. 21, 1927, p. 2. In possession of Western History Dept. of Denver Public Library.

[2]Wm. MacLeod Raine and Will C. Barnes, *Cattle,* Doubleday, Doran & Co., Inc., Garden City, N. Y., 1930, p. 87.

[3]Shores, "The Drowning of James Braidwood," *op. cit.,* pp. 1-2.

[4]*Ibid.,* p. 4.

[5]*Ibid.,* p. 6.

[6]*Ibid.,* p. 7.

[7]*Ibid.,* pp. 8-10.

[8]*Ibid.,* p. 10.

Chapter VII

The hunt for Jim Braidwood's body continued for several days, but the Arkansas River refused to give up its tragic secret. In the meantime, the swollen stream was dropping a little each day so that when we finally gave up the search and again started north, our herd was driven across without further mishap.

It was late afternoon when we got our mixed herd of six hundred head of cattle on the other side; so we made camp for the night only a short way from the river, prepared to get an early start in the morning.

That evening before dark I hired a Creek Indian to take me back across the Arkansas on his flat boat in order to take one last look for my lost clothing, which the cattle had trampled into the mud and water on the day Braidwood drowned. I didn't mind losing the clothing so much, but there were personal belongings in the missing apparel that couldn't be replaced, including the key to a trunk in the chuck wagon and a Masonic pin which I had worn for years.

While I was digging around in the bank of the river looking for some sign of the clothing, I suddenly noticed an Indian stealthily moving off to one side in a parallel course with me. He was carrying a muzzle-loading rifle and advanced from one bush or tree to another, apparently intending to shoot me from ambush. I was wearing a small six-shooter, but it was not big enough to be of much protection against a man armed with a rifle. I immediately forgot about the lost clothing and hurried back up the river where some Creeks were lounging under a tree.

"Why is that fellow over there in the brush following me?" I asked.

No one volunteered any information at first, but after more persuasion one of them explained that he was the man whom I had called a low-down, yellow-bellied rat several days previously.

I remembered him then. He was the Indian who had tried to drive the old bull off the sandbar back toward the milling herd in order to block our second attempt to cross the Arkansas. He hadn't paid any attention to the other trail drivers who shouted at him to leave the blue stag alone. Then, I had lost my temper and called him every name in the book. This stopped him. He looked angrily at me and rode away. Apparently ever since that time he had been awaiting an opportunity to bushwhack me.

After learning that I was the potential target of a bushwhacker, I decided to get back to my camp as soon as possible. As I returned to the boat, a group of drunken, yelling Indians gathered around me. I was surprised at this hostile reception, but I was informed later that the Creeks were having what they called a "ball play." When these games were held, whiskey smugglers came into the region to sell fire water to the Indians during the celebration. I had seen two men ride past our camp that afternoon each carrying a jug of whiskey in a sack tied to the back of his saddle.

The Creeks who surrounded me were in a wild, riotous mood. Several squaws, fearing that I might be killed, tried to pull their intoxicated spouses away. I knew that I was in grave danger and kept my little six-shooter out of sight for fear it might arouse them all the more.[1] However, by keeping my mouth shut and accepting quietly their threats and insults, they finally allowed me to be transported across the river to my camp.

The next morning my remaining three associates and I started north again with our herd, which we intended to divide up just over the Kansas line and each go his respective way. I was taking my cattle to the railhead at Abilene to sell.

After Braidwood drowned, we were short one man and had to

double up on our work. We took his cattle and horses along in order to turn them over to his family near Winfield, Kansas.

The Osage Indians, who resided in the northwestern part of Indian Territory in present Oklahoma, had the reputation of being more hostile and troublesome to trail drivers than the other tribes. The Creeks had told me that a large band of them was camped on Hominy Creek along the Black Dog Trail, which we were following.

To avoid these unfriendly Indians, we left the trail and crossed Hominy Creek six miles below their camp. We then circled around and picked up the Black Dog Trail again some miles to the north of this warlike band.

Late that afternoon I rode on ahead of the herd to where the cook was preparing supper beside the chuck wagon. I dismounted and helped with the meal. While we were working, the cook suddenly exclaimed, "For Pete's sake, look what's comin'!"

I was parching coffee at the time, but I looked up to see a large number of Indians riding single file toward us. When the first one rode into our camp, he swung his arms in a wide sweep behind him and grunted, "Osage, heap come!"

Then, he began riding over the mess outfit, begging, "Give me some money."

"Ain't got any," I answered.

"Give me some whiskey."

"Ain't got any."

"Give me some tobacco."

"Ain't got any."

As the other Osages filed in, they followed this same procedure, trampling anything in sight and getting more and more belligerent. The cook and I grabbed the cooking utensils and placed them under the wagon. Some of the Indians even arrogantly tried to guide their horses into us.

While all of this commotion was going on, our herd began coming into view. I was afraid that the Indians would molest the approaching cattle, but, luckily, they finally rode away for the time being without causing any more trouble.

After the cattle were grazed and watered, they were bedded down for the night, and the first guard went on duty. Even though the weather was clear and pleasant, we kept constantly on the alert, fearing that the Indians might return under cover of darkness. The night guard kept riding around the sleeping herd, occasionally whistling or singing softly. This seemed to have a soothing effect on the cattle.

At midnight I relieved the night herder. As I circled the herd, I could hear the cattle chewing their cuds and grunting and blowing over full, contented stomaches. Tired from the long day's ride and having slept very little for fear of an Indian raid, I grew very sleepy and felt like dozing off in the saddle, knowing that my well-trained horse would continue the slow, sentinel-like pace without any urging. However, I did not dare relax because I felt certain that sooner or later the Osage Indians would be back to cause trouble.

About two o'clock I started breakfast so that our outfit could eat and get started at the first break of day, since we wanted to get out of Osage territory as quickly as possible. After breakfast was ready, I awakened the others. We ate hastily and packed away the blankets and cooking utensils in the chuck wagon. Our mounts were saddled and the extra horses tied to the back of the wagon. By the time these chores were done it was light enough to travel; so we pushed the cattle off the bed ground and drifted them up the trail.

We had hardly started when, sure enough, the Indians came riding up, several hundred strong. They formed a half circle around the herd, the chuck wagon, and ourselves and pushed our entire outfit back to their agency headquarters several miles away.[3]

The Quaker agent had no control over the mob, and he was as frightened as we were. The Indians were rough and insolent. They kept asking us for money for the privilege of driving cattle through their country.

"We have no money," we kept telling them.

"Then, give us some beef," an Indian spokesman would answer through interpreters.

We, of course, refused to give them any beef.

While bargaining, they kept running their horses against us and the agent. Occasionally, they threatened to cut out some of our cattle and butcher them.

"Gentlemen," the terrified agent finally shouted to me above the tumult, "if thee have any money at all, please give the Indians some. It will save thee trouble and me too."[4]

The situation was rapidly becoming desperate. One of the cowboys called over to me, "Say, Doc," he yelled, "Jim Braidwood had a little money in that old trunk in the chuck wagon. Let's give 'em that."[5]

The key to the trunk had been lost with my clothes in crossing the Arkansas, but I broke it open with an axe and found the drowned man's pocketbook, which contained fourteen dollars in bills and fractional currency. The only coin was an old siver ten-cent piece, which Braidwood apparently kept for good luck, since silver was very uncommon in the region at that time.

I gave all of the paper money to the agent to pay off the Indians, but I did not take out the ten-cent piece. A fierce-looking Osage, who was sitting on his horse beside me watching the transaction, noticed the coin and thrust his lance through the pocketbook, knocking it out of my hands. He then leaped off his horse and retrieved the pocket piece.

The lance which the Indian carried was about eight feet long with a steel blade at the end. These lances were issued to the Indians by the government to use in hunting buffalo.

The dead man's money seemed to satisfy the Indians, and we were permitted to resume our way. The agent offered to send an Indian escort along with us for an additional fee in order to prevent further interference. However, we declined the offer since we would rather take our chances than do any more bargaining with the Osages.

One morning two or three days later the herd, as usual, was drifted off the bed ground. As the cattle grazed slowly along, the cook, who was a big fat fellow by the name of Quigg, completed his chores and drove the wagon around in front of the herd into the trail. The cattle, smelling the fresh tracks of the oxen, which were moving along ahead of them, swung in behind and began following.

As Quigg drove placidly along, he suddenly espied a group of Indian horsemen approaching. One of them galloped up to the chuck wagon and covered him with a big cap and ball six-shooter. Quigg pulled the oxen to a stop.

I was helping with the drag at the time, but seeing what was happening, I galloped around the herd toward the chuck wagon. As I rode up, the Indian turned and leveled his gun at me. I drew my six-shooter also, and the two of us sat there on our horses for a few tense moments looking into the gaping muzzles of each other's guns. Finally the Indian lowered his outmoded pistol and held it down against his horse's neck.

"You got any money?" he asked.

"No," I answered, now accustomed to the begging routine of the noble redman.

"Give us some tobacco."[6]

"I have no tobacco."

As the other ten or eleven Indians came forward and surrounded Quigg and me, I yelled for my companions to come over. After the loss of Braidwood, we were shorthanded with only two riders besides me and the cook.

The Indians circled around us four white men asking for money, tobacco, whiskey, beef, coffee, flour, sugar, and salt. When we refused to give them any of these items, they tried to cut out a steer or a dry cow and appropriate it. Each time they rode into the cattle and started to work out a beef, we would gallop our horses against the intruders, allowing the beef to run back into the herd. The Indians repsonded by running their horses into us.

These rough tactics went on for some time before the Indians realized that we couldn't be bluffed. Finally they all rode away except one. He was an old Indian and very large.

"Give me some tobacco," he presisted, undiscouraged by the previous failures.

One of the cowboys by the name of Frederick tried to throw a scare into the old fellow. Pulling out a cap and ball navy six-shooter, he jabbed the barrel into the Indian's portly stomach and said, "You go!"[7]

The Indian sucked his stomach away in but didn't show the least sign of fear. Frederick cocked the trigger and repeated the order. However, except for pulling in his stomach, the Indian paid no attention to this show of force and kept right on asking for whiskey, tobacco, beef, and coffee.

As the exasperated, flustered cowboy kept poking his cocked gun into the mid-section of the unconcerned Indian, saying, "You go!" You go!" I became fearful that the trigger might accidentally be tripped.

"Cut it out, Fred," I said. "He's not afraid of you, and if you should happen to shoot that Indian, we'll lose everything we got on earth, including our lives. You'd better lay off."[8]

Frederick reluctantly holstered his gun, and we mounted our horses and left the courageous old Indian standing there with a faint smile on his lips. Even though he hadn't obtained what he wished, he—and not us—had won the moral victory.

FOOTNOTES

[1]C. W. Shores, "The Drowning of James Braidwood in the Creek Nation," original manuscript, Denver, Colo., Dec. 21, 1927, pp. 11-12. In possession of Western History Dept. of Denver Public Library.

[2]*Ibid.*, p. 12.

[3]*Ibid.*, p. 13.

[4]*Ibid.*

[5]*Ibid.*, p. 14.

[6]*Ibid.*, p. 15.

[7]*Ibid.*, p. 16.

[8]*Ibid.*

Chapter VIII

As my three fellow trail drivers and I neared the Kansas line on our journey north up the Chisholm Trail with our herd of cattle, we hoped that our encounters with unfriendly Indians were over. However, we were still in Indian Territory, and anything could happen.

One evening while we were camped on the Caney River, several Indians who could speak a little English rode up and dismounted to visit with us. I was scheduled to relieve the night herder at midnight; so I turned in earlier than the others, who continued to talk and spin yarns with our uninvited guests.

I got my two blankets out of the chuck wagon and laid them on the ground under a canvas, which we had stretched out over a long pole, one end of which lay on a high back wheel of the wagon, while the other end rested on a pair of crossed sticks driven into the ground.[1] This improvised tent was open at both ends but provided a little shelter.

The Indians and my companions kept visiting and laughing until it was about time for me to go on night duty. Their conversation kept me awake; so when I got up at midnight, I was extremely tired and sleepy. The Indians had left perhaps a half-hour before, and my three comrades were snoring peacefully beside me under our canvas roof.

After saddling my horse, which was staked out nearby, I rode over to the sleeping herd. The night guard whose place I was taking exchanged a few words with me, and rode away to get a couple of hours of needed sleep before we hit the trail.

It was a clear, moonless night, and the cattle were unusually quiet. I could hear a few of them chewing their cuds and grunting contentedly over well-filled stomachs. Since a third of our bunch consisted of cows with calves, our cattle were less easily disturbed and less likely to stampede than a herd composed entirely of steers. Nevertheless, as trail boss, I had repeatedly warned my fellow riders never to take any chances when on night duty. I told them that if at any time they were unable to stay awake to be sure to awaken me and I would stand their shift for them.

This night the situation was reversed. I was the one who was unable to stay awake, and if I was to follow my own advice, I should awaken one of my companions to relieve me. However, they too had been up late talking with the Indians and had just recently retired. Under the circumstances, what I should have done was to stick it out for an hour and then awaken the next shift—even if it would have lengthened his guard duty.

Instead, I decided to take a chance and sneak in a short nap. Although pitch-black, the night was clear and quiet. The cattle were as contented as I had ever seen them, and the chances of a stampede seemed very remote.

Temporarily abandoning my charges, I rode back to the wagon. Quietly unsaddling my horse so as not to disturb my unsuspecting buddies, I tied him with a lariat to the wagon tongue. Then, using my saddle blanket to cover me, I stretched out on the ground and was soon asleep.

I was awakened suddenly by the thunder of hoofs. I leaped to my feet with the sickening realization that the cattle were stampeding. My frantic horse lunged against the lariat rope, snapping it in two and nearly upsetting the chuck wagon. The pole over which the canvas was draped dropped to the ground and the improvised tent collasped on my sleeping comrades. Before I could stop him, my horse galloped away with the other horses, which had also broken their stake ropes in the turmoil.

The three cowboys crawled out from under the canvas and looked about in astonishment. "What the hell has happened?" one of them yelled at me above the awful din.

Sheepishly I admitted that I had committed the unforgiveable sin of going to sleep on guard duty, and did not know what had aroused the cattle.

The loud rumbling of the galloping herd grew less and less distinct until it vanished altogether, and the four of us stood there helplessly, not knowing what to do. There can be nothing more frustrating to a group of cowboys than to be caught on foot during a stampede. Talk about getting caught with your pants down! We were caught with our pants completely off!

"It's all my fault, fellows," I said, breaking the tense silence. "I did the very thing that I've always warned you never to do. But the only course we can take now is start out after the sons of guns on foot and pray for some kind of a break."

Without further comment, we set out after the stampeding cattle and horses, which, according to the noise, had run down the shoreline of the Caney River. Each of us carried a bridle and a rope on the outside chance that one of our horses might slow down and stop to graze. We all knew that sooner or later the horses and cattle alike would head back for their home ranges hundreds of miles away, and our only chance was to catch them before they really got going. Without mounts we had no chance of recovering our lost herd, but we kept walking doggedly on down the Caney River in the pitch-black night, hoping for a miracle. If we could not catch a horse, each of us knew that our entire investment would be a total loss, because our cattle were too wild to do anything with on foot.

In spite of the predicament I had put us all in, not one of my companions uttered a word of criticism or complaint. They all knew that if I had been on the job, the stampede and loss of our cattle and horses would probably never have occurred. At worst there would have been one man on horseback to help out in the recovery.

However, so close did men become during their weeks and months together on the trail that when misfortune struck, regardless of the cause, they stuck together with a tolerance and loyalty that I have never seen surpassed anywhere. Like any close-knit family, they had their differences, but in the clutch they stood shoulder to shoulder, presenting a solid and united front.

One point in our favor was that our cattle had traveled several hundred miles up the trail togther and had never stampeded before. Consequently, they were accustomed to staying in one bunch and might not split up and scatter, which catastrophe would make our job infinitely harder.

We had progressed down the river about four miles when day started to break through the dark night. As it grew gradually lighter, in the distance we could see the drags of the stampeded herd. The cattle seemed to have quieted down after their initial scare and were spread out along the river grazing. Fortunately, force of habit had kept them together, and they had not split up and gone in different directions as we feared.

Our horses had mingled with the herd and were also grazing before continuing on toward their home ranges. However, catching these loose horses presented a real problem, especially without a bucket of oats to lure them to the rider.

One of them was a sort of pet and less spirited than the others. After long and patient effort we eased him out of the herd and formed a circle around him. While we tried to hold him in this makeshift corral, his owner slowly approached the skittish animal, talking quietly to him all the while. After several unsuccessful attempts, he finally got close enough to catch him, first putting a rein over the pony's neck and then putting on the bridle. Things had begun breaking our way.

After catching a horse, it was now only a question of time until we got the situation under control. Riding bareback, the cowboy circled around the grazing cattle and horses, bunching them in a small area. While those of us on foot held bunch, he then rode quietly into the herd and, with a skillful flip of his rope, tossed his lasso around the neck of another horse. Before long all four of us were mounted. I held the cattle while the others rode back to the chuck wagon to get their saddles. When they returned, I followed suit.[2] It took us all day to round up the strays and work the cattle back to our camp along the Caney River.

This was our first stampede, and we could think of no reason for

Indians appropriating stray cow in northern Oklahoma. *Photo courtesy of Denver Public Library Western Collection.*

the herd's unusual behavior. It was not until several days later that we met a friendly Indian who informed us what had scared the cattle. He said that the Indians who had come into camp and visited with us on the night of the stampede were responsible for the trouble. After leaving our camp shortly before midnight one of them had tied the end of his rope to an old dried-up cowhide. Then, running his horse at full speed, he dragged the loudly rattling hide alongside the sleeping herd. This frightened the cattle and caused the stampede.

This maneuver was a common practice among Indians. They did it not only out of a spirit of deviltry but also to appropriate any strays which the trail drivers might fail to find after the stampede.[3]

This account of how our Indian visitors had frightened our cattle while I was asleep on guard duty did not increase my love for Indians. The entire episode was an exceptionally sore point with me, and I didn't even like to talk about it.

So, as a result of this experience with apparently friendly Indians, I was not in a particularly cooperative frame of mind when another group of jovial Indians came riding into our camp one noon a short time later. I had just finished oiling my .50-caliber Spencer carbine with bacon grease and laid it out in the sun to dry, while I crawled under the chuck wagon within reach of the rifle to take a brief nap.

I had hardly fallen asleep when I was awakened by the yelling of Indians. I looked up startled, expecting to see a war party. However, our visitors were in a friendly though arrogant mood. I watched them ride around to each of my companions saying, "How! How! Shake hands with chief."[4]

After the chief had shaken hands with my three associates, the group of newcomers started over toward me. As they approached, I reached out from under the wagon and pulled the Spencer rifle up to my side, quickly slipping five cartridges into the magazine and snapping one in the chamber.

"How!" one of the Indians said, getting off his horse and looking under the chuck wagon. "Come out and shake hands with chief."

"Come and get me," I said threateningly, holding my gun in readiness. I admit that I was being a little unreasonable, but after all the difficulties Indians had caused me on this trip north, I didn't want to have anything more to do with them for a while.

Finally, the group rode away, somewhat puzzled that their friendly entreaties were not accepted by the crochety cowboy under the wagon.

That evening we bedded our cattle down near the Kansas line about thirty or forty miles south of Winfield, Kansas, where James Braidwood had lived with his mother, brother, and sister on their little claim. He had a horse and about fifty or sixty head of cows in the bunch with which he planned to stock his ranch.

Early the next morning I started out for Winfield to inform Jim Braidwood's family about his death. Arriving in town about noon I inquired where the Braidwoods lived. I was told that a doctor who lived several miles from town was acquainted with them and could give me the desired information. I located this doctor who said that the Braidwood family had gone to church but would be home soon. Since days were all more or less alike on the trail, I had lost track of the day of the week and didn't know until then that it was Sunday.

The doctor instructed me how to find the Braidwood claim, and I rode over to the little ranch which Jim had so often told me about. There was a lump in my throat as I rode up to the house. It all made Jim seem very close. Although he hailed from the East, Jim Braidwood was one of the best friends I ever had, and "a man who would do to cross the rivers with."

The Braidwood family had not as yet returned from church; so I unsaddled my horse and staked him out nearby. Then, I lay down on my saddle blanket in the shade of the house and immediately went to sleep. I had only been averaging four hours sleep a night, and I always took advantage of a break in the day's activities to get in a little shut-eye.

I was awakened a short time later when the family arrived home, accompanied by the doctor who had told me where they lived. He introduced me to Jim's mother, sister, and brother. I then had the unpleasant task of telling them that Jim was dead. As quickly as I could, I told them how he drowned in the Arkansas River while

Cutting out Jim Braidwood's cattle to take across Kansas line. *Courtesy Denver Public Library Western Collection.*

helping me find a fording place to take our herd across. They took the bad news very hard, especially the mother and sister.[5]

I went on to say that Jim had a horse and about sixty head of cattle in our outfit, which was now camped just below the Kansas line. It was against the law to drive Texas or Oklahoma cattle into Kansas between the months of April and November. These cattle, while immune to what was at that time called Spanish fever, carried ticks which dropped off and spread the disease among Kansas cattle, which were very susceptible to it. We then believed that Spanish fever was spread by mere contact with infected animals.

Jim Braidwood's brother and the doctor agreed to ride back to camp with me and help smuggle Jim's cattle and horse across the Kansas line. I said goodby to Jim's tearful mother and sister, and we set out for the herd. Upon arriving, the Braidwood cattle were cut out and I helped drive them into Kansas. Before parting, I told Braidwood and the doctor to represent their cattle as coming from Arkansas, which was free from Spanish fever and not subject to the Kansas quarantine regulations.

My three companions and I then continued westward in Indian Territory for another few days before pushing our herd north into forbidden Kansas territory south of Wichita, which town had just recently been established. There were fewer grangers, or farmers, this far west and, consequently, less danger of being caught violating the quarantine law.

All things must come to an end; so south of Wichita my three comrades and I cut out our respective cattle, and, hiring extra cowhands from the new town, we bid each other a goodby and went our respective ways to different destinations.

Although it was done casually, saying goodby to my three fellow trail drivers was one of the hardest things that I've ever done. Several months of going through hell and high water together on the old cattle trail had made us closer than brothers. Yet, as we parted on our respective ways, we realized that our paths would probably never cross again. They never did. Such was the way of life then, as it is today.

FOOTNOTES

[1]C. W. Shores, "Cattle Stampeded by Indians on the Caney River," original manuscript, Denver, Colo., Dec. 24, 1927, p. 1. In possession of Western History Dept. of Denver Public Library.

[2]*Ibid.,* p. 3.

[3]*Ibid.,* pp. 3-4.

[4]C. W. Shores, "The Drowning of James Braidwood in the Creek Nation," original manuscript, Denver, Colo., Dec. 21, 1927, pp. 16-17. In possession of Western History Dept. of Denver Public Library.

[5]*Ibid.,* p. 18.

Chapter IX

Because so many cattle were driven up the trails from Texas during 1871 to the railhead at Abilene, Kansas—the capital of the cattle trade—prices were low and buyers scarce. Many drovers, including myself, who had planned to sell our herds at Abilene to be shipped to the eastern markets, decided to hold our cattle until the following year, gambling on a better price in the spring of 1872. Most of these hold-over cattle were drifted west and wintered along the Solomon, Saline, and Smoky Hill rivers. I pastured my small herd of 300 head a little farther west in the brakes of the Saline and Smoky Hill rivers fifteen miles north of Fort Hays.[1]

My cattle were the first to arrive in this region, and the grass was plentiful. Buffalo, elk, and black-tailed deer abounded. The country was cut by many deep canyons extending to the Saline River. Sparkling streams ran down most of these canyons, and I staked out a claim near a little creek in one of these picturesque valleys. Twelve miles farther down the Saline I also established another camp, excavating a large dugout for shelter. I grazed my herd near the upper camp during the summer, and made the dugout at the lower camp my headquarters during the late fall and winter.[2]

One afternoon during that summer of 1871 I was returning to my upper camp after a day's ride when I came upon a large herd of elk. They were moving across the wide Saline Valley toward the north side of the river. I made a rough count of 114 head in the bunch, many of which were calves. I decided to catch one of the calves and bring it back to camp with me.

I unfastened my lariat and gave chase. At sight of my approach the startled herd began bounding ahead, leaving the calves and one ancient bull in the rear. This bull was so old that he had not shed all of his last winter's hair, which bristled out in faded color on his hips and back. His horns, which had not developed propertly, were mere stubs not over a couple of feet in length. As I galloped past the sluggish beast, I poked him in the ribs with the muzzle of my Ballard rifle. He blatted and stopped.[3]

It was hot, and the elk did not run very far before most of them had their tongues hanging out. When I drew up beside one of the bigger calves, I roped it around the neck. The calf wouldn't lead but pulled back and fought the rope every step of the way. I dragged and pushed him along by turns, but the progress was so slow that I finally laid the calf across the front of my saddle and carried him until within a few miles of camp. I lifted him off and tied him there to a big bush. I rode on into camp where I yoked two oxen to a wagon and returned to haul the calf the remaining few miles. I staked him out near the creek which ran by my tent. He drank thirstily and lay down. The next morning when I went over to see how he was coming along, he was dead. Apparently he had got hurt internally while being packed on my horse and drank too much water.

The small timbered gulches which ran into the canyon where I had my summer headquarters were good places to hunt elk. I was fond of elk meat, and whenever I got low on grub, I would go hunting up these draws. On these occasions I had difficulty keeping at home an old one-eyed mongrel dog, which had strayed into my camp that summer and adopted me. He followed me around like a shadow, but because he was an overzealous barker and would chase after game without my consent I didn't like to take him hunting.

One morning before starting out on an elk hunt, I tied my eager friend up to a tree with a big rope. After he was firmly fastened, I mounted a small, white pack mule and set forth in search of a yearling elk. I had not gone far when the one-eyed dog unexpectedly came bounding up to me with his customary enthusiasm. Apparently he had freed himself by chewing through the big rope which held him prisoner.

I soon put a damper on his unwarranted zeal. Taking the strap off my Ballard rifle, I hogtied my ardous friend so tightly that he could barely move. Convinced that the worthless creature was well taken care of, I again mounted my mule and continued on to the nearest promising gulch.

I had just turned up this forested draw, which was a favorite hangout for elk, when an expectant yelp brought me up with a start. I whirled around and, to my dismay, there was the zealous old dog, wagging his tail vehemently. He had chewed the gun strap in two and worked himself free.

I had about decided to give up the hunt and return to camp when I thought of the large burlap sack under my saddle blanket. I pulled off the saddle and removed this gunny sack from the mule's back.

Although the dog was big, I managed to squeeze him into this old bag and tie a string firmly around the top. Having thus once more restrained my eager friend, I resaddled and rode up the draw, leaving my nemesis leaping around in the burlap covering like a chicken with its head cut off.

Before reaching a little grove, which was a likely stomping ground for elk, I dismounted and crawled quietly up to it. As I had anticipated, a bunch of elk were grazing in the shelter of the trees. I raised my rifle and took aim at one of the yearlings. Just as I fired, I heard a loud bark, and the one-eyed monster came rushing past me after the startled elk, baying like a bloodhound. Fortunately, my first shot had found it mark, and the yearling buckled over and fell dead with a bullet through his heart.[4] In spite of the mongrel's Houdinic powers, that was one day he failed to spoil my hunt.

Not long after this episode I was riding over on Elm Creek about twenty-seven miles from my summer place when I came upon a family camping there about four miles from the present town of Stockton. I stopped for a few minutes to pass the time of day, and this was the beginning of a friendship which has lasted all of my life. The family consisted of a Mr. and Mrs. Taylor and their two young sons. One of the sons was Ed Taylor, who many years later was elected to Congress from Colorado's Western Slope. He served in this capacity for more than thirty years.[5]

On my return trip home after meeting the Taylors I sighted a small herd of two or three hundred buffalo on Paradise Flats—a high, rolling country. I set spur to my horse and galloped toward them, intending to kill one and bring home some fresh meat. As I pulled up alongside the rear of the stampeding herd, I raised my single-loading Galagher rifle and took a shot at a yearling. The bullet did not hit a vital spot, and the young buffalo kept right on running. Placing my tied bridle reins over the saddle horn, I broke open the rifle at the breach, removed the spent shell, and shoved in a new cartridge.

While reloading, my horse slowed down somewhat, and the herd pulled ahead of me. They were running at top speed down a draw, and as I began closing up the gap between us, I noticed that the buffalo in the lead were dropping out of sight. Too late I discovered that they were jumping down a five or six foot ledge in the draw. I let go of my rifle, and pulling back on the bridle reins with both hands, I stood up in my stirrups to brace myself for the fall.

The galloping horse, which was moving too fast to stop quickly enough to avoid the drop, leaped out into empty space and landed with a loud grunt on solid ground. The terrific impact caused both stirrups to break off, and I was thrown off. I dazedly got to my feet and gathered up my rifle and stirrups. The horse's back was so badly injured that I did not remount but led him the twelve or fifteen miles back to camp. After arriving, I removed the saddle and staked the horse out down by the creek, where he died within a few hours.

During the fall of 1871 the buffalo, which were abundant along the Saline River, began mixing with my cattle at night. To prevent this, I and two cowboys, who were working for me at the time, built a log corral, and each evening we rounded up the cattle and put them in this corral where they were held until morning.

One evening after corraling the cattle, I caught three yoke of oxen which I chained to the wheels of a wagon, intending to set out for Hays City early the next morning to get some supplies. During the night my two cowboys and I, who were sleeping in the dugout at my lower camp near the corral, were awakened by a loud commotion and the terrified bellowing of the chained oxen.

I grabbed an old Spencer Carbine and rushed outside. In the moonlight I could see what was happening. A gigantic buffao bull had attacked the three yoke of oxen and was alternately butting one yoke after another into the air as far as the rattling chains would allow. I shot the huge buaffo through the side, and he ambled away into the night. The next morning I found him lying dead a short distance away.[6]

In November I left one man at my winter headquarters to keep an eye on the cattle, while I and three other men rode twelve miles up the Saline to the summer camp to begin construction of a cabin. A few days later on November 17th a howling blizzard struck the region about midnight. My three companions and I were sleeping on the short buffalo grass with a large canvas wagon cover spread over our blankets.

The wind, which reached hurricane velocity, hurled sleet and rain into the inadequate covering. When the moisture began seeping through the soaked canvas and blankets, everyone except me abandoned the uncomfortable bed and sought protection in the thick brush and timber along the banks of the creek. The savage, whistling wind was blowing so hard that it took the shivering men some time to get a fire started. Then, they hastily threw up a make-shift shed out of some lumber which had been plied nearby for construction of the cabin.

At daybreak I, badly chilled, crawled out of the cold, drenched bed and joined the others, carrying the soaked canvas and blankets along with me. It was snowing hard, and the gale took my breath away whenever I faced it. Fortunately, my companions had a big fire going under the improvised shelter, and after putting the canvas and blankets in a dry place beneath the pile of lumber, I moved up close to the roaring flames in order to thaw out a little.

My favorite horse—a sorrel pony which I had bought from a Choctaw Indian in present Oklahoma, was picketed out in the storm with a rope tied to the horns of a big buffalo skull. But it was so intensely cold and the snow was blowing with such tremendous force that to leave the protection of the fire and shed in order to

Herd of cattle threatened by blizzard. *Photo courtesy of Denver Public Library Western Collection.*

free my horse would have been suicidal.[7] So, as much as I hated to leave him staked out in the blizzard, there was nothing that I could do about it. It was either him or me.

The four of us remained in our shelter all during the day, cutting up the stacked lumber for use as fuel to keep the fire burning. We had grub and coffee, which we cooked and boiled over the open flame. That night before turning in we banked up a big fire, believing that it would last until morning. However, the storm grew worse during the night, and the groaning wind whipped snow under the shed, putting out the fire.

I was the first to arise that morning, since I had been the last to get up on the preceding day when the blizzard struck. I, like the others, had slept with my clothes on; so all I had to do to finish dressing was pull on my boots. But they were frozen stiff, and I couldn't get my feet into them.

"Take my boots, Doc," one of the men called over to me from his blankets. "They're bigger than yours."

The man who spoke was an elderly gentleman by the name of Parrott. He had gone to college for a short time, and, unlike most frontiersmen, seldom swore, believing it to be unworthy of a college man.

In spite of their larger size, I couldn't get into Parrot's frozen boots either; so after building a fire, I placed both pairs beside it to thaw them out. By the time I had prepared breakfast, the boots had become more flexible, and I was able to get mine on. However, I noticed, to my dismay, that one of Parrott's boots had been put too near the fire, and the grease was frying out of it. I immediately set it off to one side and proceeded to eat my breakfast.

After eating, I awakened the others to tell them that their breakfast was ready, and crawled back into my blankets to get some more sleep. The blizzard had not abated, and there was nothing to do but wait in our shelter until it was over.

As I lay there, I heard Parrott mumbling something about his shrunken boot.

"What the devil is the matter with this boot, anyway?" he said aloud to himself. "I've always been able to get it on before."

He kept trying unsuccessfully to pull it on, and finally, in exasperation, he began swearing softly to himself. He was not accustomed to using profane language, and I had difficulty to keep from laughing out loud as I lay there pretending to be asleep.

Parrott eventually had to cut open the front of his boot with a butcher knife in order to get it on. I never told my friend what had happened to his mutilated boot, but every time I looked at it, I had a twinge of conscience.

FOOTNOTES

[1]C. W. Shores, "Autobiography of C. W. Shores," original manuscript, Denver, Colo., Jan. 17, 1928, p. 46. In possession of Western History Dept. of Denver Public Library.

[2]C. W. Shores, "Killing Three Buffalo with a Gun that had a Broken Mainspring," original manuscript, Denver, Colo., Mar. 10, 1927, pp. 4-5. In possession of Western History Dept. of Denver Public Library.

[3]C. W. Shores, "Jack Johnson's Gang," original manuscript, Denver, Colo., Jan. 19, 1928, pp. 1-2. In possession of Western History Dept. of Denver Public Library.

[4]*Ibid.*, pp. 2-3. Also, see C. W. Shores, "A Crafty Old Dog With One Eye," original manuscript, Denver, Colo., April 25, 1929, pp. 1-2. In possession of Western History Dept. of Denver Public Library.

[5]C. W. Shores, "A Story of Trying to Kill Buffaloes," original manuscript, Denver, Colo., Mar. 10, 1929, pp. 1-2. In possession of Western History Dept. of Denver Public Library.

[6]Shores, "Jack Johnson's Gang," *op. cit.*, p. 3.

[7]Shores, "Killing Three Buffalo with a Gun that had a Broken Mainspring," *op. cit.*, p. 1.

Chapter X

The blizzard which broke out on the Kansas plains November 17, 1871, lasted four days and nights, and man and beast alike suffered untold hardships. Thousands of cattle which were being wintered in the area froze to death. Hundreds of horses perished where they had bunched under bluffs and cliffs to seek some protection. Unlike cattle, which will drift with a storm, horses stop at the first shelter they come to. In severe blizzards their chances of survival would be better if they kept moving like cattle.[1]

When the storm subsided, I went in search of my sorrel horse which I had picketed just before the cataclysm to a large buffalo skull. During the blizzard he had dragged the heavy skull down into the brush where the rope had become so entangled that he could go no further. He had eaten down most of the brush around him, which kept him from starving to death. However, he was so chilled from his long exposure that he never was worth anything again.

Many freighters, cowboys, and hunters lost their lives in the storm. One bull train, consisting of twelve big freight wagons loaded with cord wood, was camped six miles south of Fort Hays when the blizzard hit about midnight. They were returning to Fort Hays from Camp Supply or Fort Dodge. Although the wagons were full of wood, which the bullwhackers had picked up about forty miles to the south on Walnut Creek, none of the twelve men were able to get a fire started in the terrific gale. In desperation, they started back on foot toward a combination ranch house and store six miles south on the Smoky Hill River, where the proprietor carried groceries, supplies, and whiskey for the neighboring ranchers. Only two of the bullwhackers arrived. The others froze to death.

On that fateful day a seventeen-year-old boy was on his way to Paradise Creek with a chuck wagon and team of mules. He was carrying some blankets, grub, and cooking utensils for several cattlemen who had gone ahead to meet him there with a small herd of cattle. It was about thirteen miles from the Saline River to Paradise Creek, and the boy was midway between the two streams when night came on. Although he had originally intended to drive all the way to his destination that evening, it became so dark that he decided to stop and continue on at daybreak when he could see where he was going. So he unhitched his hobbled mules and crawled into some blankets inside the wagon.

The storm came roaring down upon him in the middle of the night, and it was not long before the driving sleet was blowing through the cracks and openings in the wagon, soaking the blankets. Trembling with cold, the youth finally abandoned the wagon, and drifted south with the storm toward the Saline River in search of shelter.

Since his boots were too frozen to get on, he trudged along in what was then known as California socks. These consisted of any kind of cloth—cotton or woolen, flour sacks or shirt tails—about two feet square which were wrapped around the feet by lapping over the corners and tying at the instep. Since real socks were scarce throughout the frontier at this time, California socks were used by most pioneers of the early West.

When the boy came to the frozen Saline River, he traveled downstream on the ice, hoping to run across someone's camp. Becoming thirsty, he broke the ice by stamping on it with his benumbed heels, getting his feet wet. Caked ice formed on the soaked cloth around his frozen feet, but he could not feel it. His legs were so paralyzed with the cold that he felt as if he were walking on wooden stilts.

Late the next day he stumbled into a camp where some cattle drovers were waiting out the storm. How the boy managed to keep going for so long a time through such a raging blizzard was something I never could quite understand. It was a magnificent feat of human endurance against the raw elements.

Seeing the youth's desperate plight, the cattlemen hauled him by wagon to the railroad twenty miles away. Here he was placed on a train and rushed to a hospital in Salinas, Kansas. Both of his legs had to be amputated, and he died soon afterward. His heroic struggle had been to no avail.[2]

Such tragic events were commonplace in western Kansas during this awful blizzard. A number of wolf hunters, who were out poisoning wolves for their hides west of my lower camp where there was little wood to burn, froze to death during the storm.[3]

Also, among the casualties was one of my cowboys, who had been left at the lower camp to look after the cattle, while the rest of us worked on the new log cabin at the upper camp. Not wanting the drifting herd to get away from him, he had caught his horse and rode along behind them with the storm howling at his back. I did not find his body until the following spring about fifteen miles from the dugout. His saddle horse lay nearby. The wolves had gnawed on the man's face and hands and eaten part of the horse.[4]

That winter of 1871-72 was so severe in western Kansas that most of the cattlemen who wintered their herds along the Solomon, Saline, and Smoky Hill rivers were unable to gather in the spring more than ten percent of the cattle and horses they had turned out. One outfit, which held over 4,000 Longhorn steers, lost all but one hundred head.

During the storms the cattle drifted south from stream to stream as far as the Arkansas River. It is estimated that about 200,000 cattle failed to rough it through that terrible winter in Kansas. Of these about half were skinned out in the spring and their hides shipped east to tanneries.[5]

I was more fortunate with my cattle. Unlike many of the Texas cattle and horses which were thin after their long trip up the trail late that summer and fall, my herd arrived at its destination early in the summer and had waxed fat on the rich buffalo grass along the Saline River before winter came. Consequently, they were in top condition and better able to withstand the unfavorable weather.

Also, unlike the thin Longhorn cattle and Texas cow ponies,

Blizzard in western Kansas during winter of 1871-72. *Photo courtesy of Denver Public Library Western Collection.*

which died like flies during the blizzard, the buffalo, elk, and deer in the region were in good enough shape and sufficiently acclimated to the weather to survive, although they suffered greatly. The November storm had driven them down out of the higher country with their backs and necks covered with ice and snow. They were so sluggish from the four-day ordeal that they were easily killed by hunters.

For example, shortly after the storm two farmers riding old plow horses followed a bunch of elk and wantonly shot twenty-seven of them. The elk were in such a dazed, stupified condition that they refused to run away. The farmers hauled three or four to their cabins and left the rest lying there on the snow to be eaten by wolves.[6]

Immediatly after the blizzard my three employees and I rode down to the lower camp to see how my herd had fared. The cattle and cow-herder were missing, their tracks covered by the drifting snow. We rode southward and finally found my cattle and horses which, because of their good condition, had weathered the storm in fair shape. The herder, however, was missing, and, as I mentioned before, we were unable to find his body until spring.

A few days after we had gathered the cattle and driven them back to camp, a former bullwhacking partner of mine by the name of A. E. Buddecke unexpectedly rode in from Fort Hays to see me. Among other journeys Buddecke had accompanied me on the round trip from Fort Hays, Kansas, to Camp Supply, Oklahoma, on my last freighting expedition a year ago. He was still in the business. I was delighted to see my old friend again, and we reminisced about our experiences together.

During the conversation, he said, "Doc, I understand that there's quite a few buffalo around here. How about gettin' me a piece of meat to take back to Fort Hays?"[7]

Early that morning I had noticed a small herd of buffalo along the Saline about a half-mile from our dugout. So, I got my Spencer carbine, and we walked up the river, hoping to run across them. We soon saw the herd in the distance, bunched up with their shaggy heads drooping in a dazed condition. Their long manes and hair were still caked with ice and snow, especially on the larger animals.

It was very cold, and my fingers became numb in my gloves as we

A. E. Buddecke "Uncle Bud." Built 2nd store in Montrose. Early-day freighter and bullwhacking associate of "Doc" Shores. *Photo courtesy of Tom Reeves.*

crawled up a rocky draw toward the unsuspecting buffalo. When we got within shooting range of the sluggish animals, I rested my rifle on a rock along the edge of the arroyo, which was nearly level with the herd. I removed my gloves and snapped back the hammer with cold, awkward hands before taking aim. As I did so, the mainspring broke, leaving the hammer unconnected to the trigger.

"Well, there goes our fresh buffalo meat," I said, showing my friend what had happened to the gun.

Buddecke looked so disappointed that I decided to try out an experiment.

"Since the hammer won't fall when I pull the trigger," I said, "take this rock and hit down on the hammer as hard as you can when I tell you to. That might explode the cartridge."[8]

I steadied the rifle on a boulder and sighted down the barrel at a fat young cow just back of her left shoulder.

"All right," I said, holding the stock tightly up against my shoulder, "give her hell!"

Buddecke slammed the rock against the hammer, and the gun went off. The cow staggered ahead for a foot or two and then crumpled over on her side.

"Let's try it again," I said, hastily reloading and taking aim at another cow. Once more Buddecke struck the hammer when I gave the signal, and another buffalo tottered forward a few steps and fell dead.

We shot at a third buffalo in the same way, but the bullet apparently hit a little further back of the shoulder than intended, for this cow moved at least a hundred yards before she finally lost her footing and went down in a heap.

Taking an ax and butcher knife, I started down to dress out my three victims, while Buddecke headed back for camp to get a wagon and a yoke of oxen to haul in the meat.

Two of the fallen cows lay close to each other; so I built a fire between them so as to occasionally warm my bloody hands while I worked. I braced each one up on her back as much as possible with a forked stick. Because of the hump, it is impossible to roll a buffalo over on its back as can be done with an elk or deer. I then skinned them, removed the entrails, and quartered them. They were hog fat

—in spite of the beating they had taken from the recent storm—and would keep us in fresh meat for a long time. I cut off a goodly portion of their humps, which, strangely enough, are not bad eating, and set aside the hearts and livers to take home also.

After dressing out the two cows which were lying together, I gathered up my rifle and another armload of fire-wood and walked over to the third buffalo, which was stretched out a hundred and fifty yards away in the tall, coarse grass. When within a few feet of the animal, for some reason or other I casually tossed a piece of wood on her to make sure that she was dead. When the stick landed, she suddenly came to life. With amazing agiilty she jumped to her feet and whirled around toward me. I was so startled that I dropped my old carbine and the armful of wood and reversed my course in a panic. After establishing some sort of an unofficial world record in the fifty-yard dash, I finally got up enough courage to look behind me. The buffalo was lying dead just a step or two from where she had so unexpectedly arisen.

With trembling hands I then proceeded to build a fire near her, and by the time I had her skinned, dressed and quartered, Buddecke arrived with the oxen and wagon to carry our game back to the dugout.[9]

I have always felt that, everything considered, I really earned my fresh meat that day.

FOOTNOTES

[1]C. W. Shores, "Killing Three Buffalo with a Gun that had a Broken Mainspring," original manuscript, Denver, Colo., Mar. 10, 1927, pp. 3-4. In possession of Western History Dept. of Denver Public Library.

[2]*Ibid.*, pp. 9-10.

[3]*Ibid.*, p. 5.

[4]*Ibid.*, pp. 4-5.

[5]Wm. MacLeod Raines and Will C. Barnes, *Cattle,* Doubleday, Doran & Co., Inc., Garden City, N. Y., 1930, p. 110.

[6]Shores, "Killing Three Buffalo with a Gun that had a Broken Mainspring," *op. cit.*, p. 9.

[7]*Ibid.*, p. 6.

[8]*Ibid.*

[9]*Ibid.*, pp. 7-8.

Chapter XI

During the winter of 1871-72 while holding over my cattle until spring on the Saline River near Fort Hays, Kansas, I came in contact with several desperados who staked out a ranch claim near my camp. Three of these men—Jack Johnson, who was the leader, Gary Switzer, Johnson's right-hand man and Bill Henderson—were former bullwhackers whom I had met when I was carrying freight between Cheyenne and Denver. There were two other fellows with them—Bill Morris and Jack Eaton—whom I had not known previously. These five cattle rustlers, killers, and horse thieves became known as the Jack Johnson gang.

Because of my former association with some of these men, I helped them survey their claim in one of the big canyons which extended down into the Saline River. At the mouth of this canyon they constructed two big dugouts about twenty feet wide and thirty feet deep in the bank of the river. These underground shelters were roofed with poles on which were piled rocks and dirt, and a strong door was built at each entrance.[1]

These outlaws spent a lot of time away from their claim, showing up every few weeks with a herd of cattle or a bunch of horses, which they would pasture for a few days, and then take somewhere else. They were obviously using their claim in the canyon as a stop-over for stolen livestock. Horses seemed to be their specialty since they could be moved faster over long distances.

As I became more familiar with the gang's activities, I discovered that during the summer and early fall they stole horses in present Oklahoma and sold them in Nebraska. In the late fall and winter they reversed this procedure, rustling horses in Nebraska and driving them south to Indian Territory where they were disposed of.[2] The ranch along the Saline River served as a convenient stopping and hide-out place midway between these two fields of operation.

Jack Johnson and his men left their neighbors' livestock strictly alone. However, they occasionally picked up animals being driven through the region. One day during the summer several Mexican muleskinners rode up to my camp. They told me that their train of small Mexican mules had been stolen near Fort Hays, and they were following their tracks which led toward Jack Johnson's ranch. This region was getting a bad name because of the shady activities of the Johnson gang. The Mexicans seemed to be afraid of this unfamiliar country with its unsavory reputation; so after making a half-hearted search up several of the canyons near my place, they gave up the hunt for their mules.[3]

At another time a man from Illinois came into the country with about one hundred head of purebred cattle, which he turned out on the rich buffalo grass along the Saline to take on a good fill before selling them at Abilene. The drover turned them loose there for a couple of days unattended, and when he and his cowboys went to gather them, the herd had vanished.

After inquiring around, the drover was convinced that Jack Johnson and his fellow outlaws were responsible for the loss of his cattle. He was right in this assumption, for I found out later that Johnson and his men had taken the purebreds north to the Solomon River. There the cattle had been traded off for horses and mules, which were then driven on north to be sold.[4]

The owner of the stolen cattle was a big, impressive-looking man who talked and acted as if he could handle a desperado like Jack Johnson. He suggested to me and the other ranchers in the vicinity that Johnson should be lynched in order to put a stop to all the horse stealing and cattle rustling which was giving our area such a bad reputation. He looked like a man who meant business; so we agreed to help him whenever he gave the word.

When the outlaw leader and his men returned to their ranch along the Saline a few days later, the cattle drover passed the word around to me and four other ranchers to meet him at a designated place the next night to arrest Johnson and stage a necktie party. At the appointed time the five of us gathered at the meeting place, but the drover didn't show up. Apparently he lost his nerve at the last minute. We waited half the night for him and then finally disbanded and returned to our respective ranches.[5] This experience taught me never again to judge a man by his appearance.

A short time after this incident, another cattleman from Iowa was traveling westward south of Hays City with a small bunch of cows, which he and two young cowboys were taking to Pueblo, Colorado. While camped on Walnut Creek, the drover rode up to Hays City to see if any mail was being held for him at the general delivery office. The clerk handed him a letter, which bore the bad news that his wife was seriously sick and asked him to return home immediately.

Before catching the train that afternoon for Iowa, the cattleman hired a pleasant looking, blonde young cowboy with a freckled, honest face to guide his outfit on toward Pueblo. The youthful stranger, whom the drover had met that day in a saloon, said he knew the way to Pueblo and would be glad to take charge of the herd during the owner's absence.[6]

The young cowpuncher assigned to this responsible job was none other than Gary Switzer—Jack Johnson's right-hand man. As soon as the cattleman had departed on the train, Switzer got in touch with Johnson, and the two outlaws made their plans.

That evening Switzer rode down to Walnut Creek, where the two boys were camped with the herd, awaiting the return of their employer. Switzer told them what had happened and that he had been hired to help out in the emergency and guide them to their destination. During the night Switzer shot and killed in cold blood the two unsuspecting cowboys while they slept. Early the next morning he was joined by Jack Johnson and Jack Eaton. They herded the cattle up to their ranch on the Saline, and after pasturing them overnight continued northward toward the Solomon.

Gary Switzer, fearful of being pursued and overtaken before they could get rid of the stolen herd, insisted upon starting out each morning at break of day. Jack Eaton, on the other hand, refused to take the matter so seriously and wouldn't get up as early as his companions, thereby delaying the getaway. The high-strung, overzealous Switzer kept warning his more complacent comrade to get out of his blankets sooner or the whole bunch would be overtaken and arrested. When Eaton still continued to lie abed, Switzer shot him through the heart one morning and cut his throat with a butcher knife. He then dragged the body some distance away into the sand hills and covered it with sand. After this, there were no more delays.[7]

Early the following spring I was holding some cattle on the Solomon River when a boy who was working for me came galloping in from the sand hills. He rode up to me, and it was evident that he was pretty well shaken up about something. He looked as if he had seen a ghost. He told me that as he was riding along looking for cattle he had observed a red flannel cloth sticking out of the sand. Curious at finding so unusual an object out in the hills, he dismounted and started to pull it out into the open. To his horror he discovered a man's leg inside the rotting cloth. Too startled to investigate further, he had jumped on his horse and rode over to notify me of his grisly find.

I accompanied the youth to where the red-flanneled leg was protruding from the sand. Together we uncovered the rest of the corpse, which I recognized as the decomposed body of Jack Eaton, lying there in his long underwear.[8]

When the owner of the stolen cattle returned to Hays City from Iowa after visiting his sick wife, he was not long in finding that his cattle had been rustled and his two cowboys murdered. The drover followed the cold trail to the Johnson ranch near my place. When he learned that I was acquainted with Gary Switzer and his accomplices, he rode over to see me. He told me what had happened and offered to pay me for helping him find the outlaws. I was too busy to leave my cattle at the time since the rustlers had a two-week start, and it would be a long trail. However, I sent him to see one of the neighboring ranchers, who agreed to accompany him.

The two men took a pack outfit and rode northward. Luckily,

they ran across Switzer and Johnson near a small settlement just north of the Nebraska line in the Sappa Creek country. The rustlers were returning to their claim on the Saline after having traded the cattle for horses and mules and disposing of the latter farther north at a goodly profit.

The cattleman told his tragic story to the settlers of that region, and a posse was organized which arrested Switzer and Johnson as they slept in their camp. Since no jail was available, they were shackled together and held in a nearby cabin under guard. After a short consultation the posse decided to hang the two rustlers without more ado.

"We're gonna string you up," one of the posse leaders said to the outlaws, "but before we do, we'll give you each time to write any last letters."

"I'd like to write a note to my wife in Colorado Territory," Johnson said, accepting the pencil and paper offered him.

"I don't have no friends to write to," Switzer said, "but I'd like to make a last request."

"What is it?"

"I'd like to have my horse delivered to a man by the name of Jim Stevens. He's a rancher who lives on the Saline River near Fort Hays. He lent the horse to me."

"Most likely you stole it," someone commented with a laugh.

While Jack Johnson was composing a farewell message to his estranged wife, a woman unexpectedly entered the cabin. She was tall, middle-aged, and handsome. Surprised at her sudden appearance, the crowd quieted. I don't remember now just who she was, but she held a position of great respect in the community. Everyone listened as she began speaking in a loud clear voice.

"Gentlemen," she in effect said, "as you all know, it has been a long, hard fight to bring law and order to our little community, and I don't want to see you in a moment of passion go back to the old days of violence and bloodshed, which brought us all so much suffering. I can well understand the indignation you feel about the crimes that these two worthless wretches have committed, but if you take the law into your own hands and hang these men in cold blood—even if they may well deserve it—you will be putting both yourselves and your community on the same level as they are. I plead with you to turn these prisoners over to the proper authorities and let the law take its course."[9]

If a man had spoken these words, this angry group of hard-eyed frontiersmen would have laughed him out of the place, but coming from a woman, the plea saved the outlaws' lives. Never underestimate the power of a woman.

Lawmen from both Nebraska and Kansas were summoned. Jack Johnson, who was wanted in both states for horse stealing, was retained in Nebraska to stand trial. He was convicted and taken to the penitentiary, where he served two or three years.

Sheriff Camerin and his deputy, Frank Sheppard, rode up from Fort Hays to get Gary Switzer. He also was wanted in both states for rustling, but since his killings had occurred in Kansas, he was released to the Fort Hays officers to stand trial in that state for murder.

On the way down the two Kansas lawmen and their prisoner stopped for the night near a small settlement called Bull City on the South Fork of the Solomon River. They unsaddled their horses and made camp.

After supper Gary said, "I didn't water my horse before staking him out. May I take him over to the town well and give him a drink?"

"Sure," Sheriff Camerin replied, "but we'll go with you."

Switzer untied his pony and led him over to the well, which was located on Main Street in the middle of town. He pulled up a few bucketfuls of water from the well and poured it into the wooden watering trough. As the horse drank under the watchful eyes of the officers, Switzer suddenly let out a yell and leaped on the startled pony, which started off on a dead run.

The surprised lawmen jerked out their six-shooters and kept shooting at the outlaw until he disappeared over the hill. Then, hastily saddling their own mounts, they galloped off in pursuit. Switzer was riding the fastest horse and made his escape. [10]

A day or so later I happened to be riding along the Saline River when I noticed smoke curling out of one of the Johnson gang's dugouts. Since nobody had been around there for quite some time,

I rode over to investigate. The door to the dugout was open; so I dismounted and walked in. Gary Switzer was sitting there baking a pone of corn bread in a dutch oven. He looked up in surprise as I entered.

"Oh, hello, Doc," he said, "you gave me a start, walkin' up so unexpected-like. Sit down and have a bite to eat."

I sat down on an old rickety stool, and Gary fixed a pot of coffee.

After exchanging a few pleasantries, he said, "I wonder if you'd keep an eye on the bread while I tend to my horse. I'll be back in a minute."[11]

I took the corn bread out of the oven when it was done and set the pan on the table. After waiting for another fifteen minutes I walked out to the barn to see what was holding up my host. Gary and his horse were both gone. I never saw him again. He was shot and killed a year or so later in Dodge City by a vigilante committee.

After Jack Johnson had served his short prison term in Lincoln, Nebraska, he came back to his ranch, which adjoined mine. I saw him several times before he sold out and left the country. He told me about Gary killing the two young cowboys on Walnut Creek while they slept and also about his shooting and cutting the throat of Jack Eaton because he wouldn't get up early enough in the mornings.

All of the Jack Johnson gang met with violent deaths. Jack Johnson was killed in a dance hall at Camp Supply, Oklahoma, by a member of his own gang—Bill Henderson—during a dispute about some horses they had stolen. He was taken out in the hills, where he was buried in a lonely grave. His brand O< (O K connected) was burned on his wooden tombstone as the only mark of identification.[12]

Bill Henderson was hung along the Pecos River in Texas, and Bill Morris—the last surviving member of the gang—was shot down on the Ocatay in New Mexico. So, they all died violently—a fitting reward for their careers of crime.

The Johnson gang were by no means the only badmen I came in contact with during my sojourn on the Saline. During the summer of 1871 while I was living at my upper or summer camp, two disreputable looking horsemen came by driving a bunch of mustangs. Since it was about dinner time, I invited them to stop and eat with me. After finishing the meal, we visited for a short time, and then they continued on their way, heading northward.

Later that afternoon Sheriff Camerin and Deputy Sheriff Frank Sheppard of Hays City rode up. They asked me if two men had ridden by with a herd of horses. I told the officers about my guests. I then learned that they were two of four men who had stolen a lot of horses from the Cheyenne Indians farther south.

The lawmen overtook the two rustlers in the hills just south of Stockton, Kansas—forty miles north of Hays City. As soon as the officers were within rifle range, they jumped off their horses and began shooting at the outlaws, who returned the fire. In this exchange of shots Sheriff Camerin and one of the horse thieves were killed.[13]

The surviving horse thief got away, and the next day he rode into Stockton, where he bought a quart of whiskey. As he was leaving town still carrying the half-empty bottle, a buffalo hunter from Paradise Creek recognized him from the deputy sheriff's description. He took a shot at the rustler, the bullet searing through his face. The wounded outlaw galloped on to the town of Kirwin, about eighteen miles northeast of Stockton. By the time he arrived his face was hurting so badly that he could not ride on any farther. So he gave himself up. However, before his trial he broke jail and escaped.

Sheriff Camerin's body was hauled in a buckboard wagon back to Hays City where he was buried in the boot hill cemetery among the good and the bad. In the Old West those who lived by the gun usually died by the gun, be he peace officer or outlaw.

FOOTNOTES

[1]C. W. Shores, "Jack Johnson's Gang," original manuscript, Denver, Colo., Jan. 19, 1928, p. 1. In possession of Western History Dept. of Denver Public Library.

[2]*Ibid.*, p. 7.

[3]*Ibid.*, p. 4.

[4]*Ibid.*

[5]*Ibid.*, p. 7.

[6]*Ibid.*, pp. 4-5.

[7]*Ibid.*, pp. 7-8.

[8]*Ibid.*, pp. 6-7.
[9]*Ibid.*, p. 5.
[10]*Ibid.*, p. 6.
[11]*Ibid.*
[12]*Ibid.*, p. 8.
[13]*Ibid.*, p. 10.

Chapter XII

Early in the spring of 1872 I rounded up my small herd of about three hundred head of mixed Durham Shorthorns, which I had brought up the Chisholm Trail the preceding summer and wintered on the Saline River near Hays City, Kansas. Accompanied by two hired cow-hands, I started north with the intention of selling my cattle to Indian traders away up on the Missouri River in northeastern Nebraska.

We went equipped with a remuda of eight or ten horses and a chuck wagon drawn by a yoke of oxen. The herd drifted right along, hunting for the fresh, green grass, which was beginning to emerge.

Our most difficult problem at the outset of our long journey was in crossing the swollen rivers in spring flood. These included such formidable streams as the Solomon and Republican rivers in Kansas and the Platte and Loup Forks in Nebraska.

We crossed the Platte near Fort Kearney. The ford had been marked by willows, twelve or fourteen feet long, stuck about fifty feet apart in the sandy bed of the roaring river.

The cattle made it over all right, and I hired a rancher with a buckboard wagon and a span of long-legged horses to haul over our supplies and grub. The current was so swift that it kept swinging the rear end of his wagon downstream. However, the teamster and horses knew what they were doing and reached the other side with everything intact. Our yoke of oxen were then driven across with the empty chuck wagon, where the grub, blankets, and cooking utensils were transferred to it from the buckboard. The river was rising so rapidly that when the rancher returned, the willows, which marked the ford, were nearly covered by the high water.[1]

Farther north in the Loup Fork country we encountered a lot of hard rain storms with much thunder and lightning. We got very little sleep during this part of the journey, having to keep continually on the alert for stampedes. Whenever possible, we took naps during noon camp to make up a little for our loss of sleep during the night.

One threatening night while camped between the North and Middle Forks of the Loup River, I was standing watch while my exhausted young companions were taking a needed nap after having been up off and on most of the night. I started a fire by the chuck wagon, and fifteen or twenty minutes later put some eggs in the red hot ashes to roast. After riding around the restless herd a few times, I dismounted and picked up a stick to scoop out the cooked eggs.

As I was doing so, the dark night was suddenly illuminated by a huge bolt of lightning, immediately followed by a tremendous clash of thunder. Then all hell broke loose. The night came alive with a bombardment of one thunderous lightning flash after another. Sheets of rain poured down from the heavens, which seemed to be falling apart in the deluge.

Before I could recover from the holocaust which engulfed me, the ground began rocking with another more awesome sound—the ominous rumble of many hoofs. The herd was stampeding!

This sickening realization awakened me from the momentary terror which paralyzed me. While I was helpless against the elements, I could do something about the cattle.

I jumped on my frightened horse and galloped at break-neck speed alongside the terrified cattle. The lightning was striking all around me, and once it hit so close that my horse fell on its knees from the concussion, skidding on the muddy ground. I managed to hang on, and when my trembling mount finally regained his feet, I raced him up near the front of the herd.

Drawing my six-shooter, I began shooting it into the air and yell-

Stampede during storm. *Photo courtesy of Denver Public Library Western Collection.*

ing like a maniac in a desperate effort to turn the leaders and get the cattle moving in a circle. This was a slow process, and when I finally turned the lead and had the herd milling, the storm was subsiding. By daylight when my two cowboys found us, the cattle were grazing peaceably, the sudden cataclysm apparently forgotten.[2]

Late the following Sunday morning we came to the North Fork of the Loup. Just north of the river was a town then called Dengebrog, which was inhabited by people of Danish descent. There was a bridge across the river leading to the settlement, and rather than ford our herd over the rampaging stream, we drove them toward this convenient crossing.

As we neared the bridge, a number of people, dressed in their Sunday finery, also approached, apparently on their way to church. Since our cattle were unaccustomed to seeing people on foot, the leaders began stopping and eyeing the colorfully dressed crowd fearfully.

To avoid a stampede, I galloped on ahead and asked the group to go back some distance from the road until I got my cattle across the bridge. They agreeably complied, and the chuck wagon, pulled by two burly steers, was driven ahead to get the spooked cattle to follow.

The herd began hesitantly to follow the two oxen, and soon the cattle were stringing out nicely over the narrow bridge. As the drag came up, the townspeople, believing that all danger was past, started walking up from behind.

Seeing them approach, the cattle in the rear started to run. In a few minutes the entire herd was in a panic, stampeding past the lumbering chuck wagon and thundering into the main street of town.

Through the dust I saw a woman pushing a baby buggy across the street directly in front of the charging herd. As the cattle rushed by her, some of them snorted and tossed their heads as if preparing to gore her. I galloped up as fast as I could, expecting to find the carriage, woman and baby lying on the ground, trampled and torn to pieces. However, miraculously they all had escaped unscathed, although they were covered with dirt, and the woman was crying.

After getting the cattle stopped and quieted down outside of the town, I returned to make my apologies. The furious residents crowded around me, and I had to talk fast to keep from being lynched. I eventually got them calmed down, and they allowed me to continue on my way.[3]

We drove the herd in a northeasterly direction toward Cedar River on the Pawnee Indian Reservation. Upon nearing the river, I rode on ahead to look for a crossing. While searching for an indication of a shallow place in the deep water, I noticed a riffle on the otherwise quiet surface of the stream. Since this was evidence of a good ford, I spurred my horse into the riffle. Although the water was not deep here, the river bed was full of quicksand, and my mount sank down in it up to his belly. In struggling to free himself, he fell on his side, imprisoning my leg. As he splashed around trying to regain a foothold, I had difficulty keeping my head above the riley stream. Each time I took a breath, I swallowed great gulps of sand and water. Fortunately before I drowned, my horse finally got to his feet and backed out of the treacherous mire. I rode a mile or so farther upstream where I found a deeper but more favorable crossing.[4]

When seven or eight miles from the Missouri River in northeastern Nebraska, we came to a long ridge situated between two streams, one of which was called Bazelle Creek. We followed this ridge down to the Missouri, where we made camp.

There was a little trading post several miles up Bazelle Creek, and after getting settled I rode up there to get some coffee and bacon. When I arrived, there was a band of Ponca (pronounced Punkaw) Indians galloping their horses around and acting very excited. They were all painted up, and carried guns and bows and arrows as if they were getting ready to go on the warpath.

"What's all the excitement about?" I asked the proprietor of the trading post, whose name was Westerman.

"A bunch of Brules Sioux warriors rode down that ridge up yonder just a little while ago." He pointed toward the long, narrow ridge several miles away which my outfit had recently come down on our way to the Missouri.

The trader explained that the Brules Sioux were enemies of the Poncas and frequently made raids on them, running off their cattle and horses.

Trailing cattle to the Missouri River in 1872. *Photo courtesy of Denver Public Library Western Collection.*

"I just came down that ridge with a bunch of cattle," I said. "The herd was strung out about half a mile, and the Poncas must have mistaken them in the distance for Sioux horsemen."

Westerman had a difficult time explaining to the young warriors through an interpreter that what they had seen on the ridge were not their ancient enemies but only a small herd of cattle.[5]

My two cowboys and I held the cattle at the mouth of Bazelle Creek for several days, letting them rest and take on a good fill after their long journey.

Late one afternoon about four o'clock I started out on horseback for Yankton, South Dakota, forty-five miles distant, to find a buyer for some of my cattle. I only wanted to sell a few beef cows at the time in order to pick up a little cash to purchase some provisions. The cattle were putting on weight each day, and I intended to pasture them on the plentiful buffalo grass for a couple of weeks before disposing of the main herd.

I rode until about midnight. Then I staked out my horse and lay down under a tree. That morning I continued on down the Missouri to Yankton, where I soon located a man who wanted to buy a few head of beef.[6]

When I returned to camp with the prospective buyer, I learned that the herd had stampeded during a hard rainstorm and fifteen head were still missing. After cutting out several fat, dry cows and helping the buyer from Yankton get started on his way with them, I went in search of my lost strays.

Since cattle will return to their home ranges if given the opportunity, I rode back the way we had brought them. Soon I picked up their trail headed along the ridge. Suddenly their tracks turned abruptly to one side as if something had frightened them.

There were no fences on this open, rolling prairie, and the trail led into an open wheat field, where the cattle had stopped to graze for a while. Then, their tracks scattered out in all directions, again looking like something had scared them.

I wasn't long in finding out what had happened, for on the far side of the wheat field I unexpectedly came across four cow hides bearing my brand. My first thought was that the Brules Sioux were responsible, but as I thought about it, I remembered that when an

Indian killed an animal, he usually took the hide along with him to use for making his tepees and clothing. When I discovered the entrails of my butchered cattle lying nearby, I knew then for certain that the culprits were white men, since Indians were fond of a cow's intestines and would not have discarded them.[7]

Examining the surrounding ground carefully in search of tracks, I found the imprints of wagon wheels about one hundred yards from where the hides and entrails lay. Since it was evident that this wagon had been used to carry away the quartered carcasses, I followed its tracks, which led to a small cluster of ranches.

Noticing a buckboard wagon standing beside one of the farm houses, I rode over and looked inside of it. There were fresh blood stains and pieces of bone in the bed, which convinced me that this was the wagon used to transport the butchered cattle. Dismounting, I walked over to the farm house and knocked. A woman opened the door.

"Is your husband at home?" I asked.

"No," she answered, looking at me curiously.

"Could you tell me who last used that wagon standing over there in front of your place?"

"A neighbor of ours by the name of Shanklin borrowed it a day or so ago," she said, beginning to look scared. "Why do you ask?"

"I'm lookin' for some cattle rustlers who shot and dressed out four of my cows. Where does this Shanklin live?"

"I'm not sure," she replied evasively, apparently very much alarmed.

Seeing that I could get no more information from the frightened woman, I walked back to my horse and followed the wagon tracks down the road to find out what other houses the buckboard might have stopped at.[8]

I had not gone far when I noticed two men walking toward me. When they saw me, they turned off the road and started to run. I set spur to my horse and overtook them.

"Slow down there," I said. "I'd like to talk to yuh."

"What's on your mind, cowboy?" one of the men asked belligerently.

"What's your name?" I inquired.

The man hesitated, then answered, "My name is Shanklin. Why do you want to know?"

"Mr. Shanklin, you've been killing some of my beef."[9] As I spoke, I pulled a small derringer out of my pocket. I had left my big six-shooter back at camp.

"Don't shoot," Shanklin said, instantly getting over his antagonistic attitude. "Yes, I helped shoot your cattle, but I'm willing to pay for it."

"I'll pay my share, too," the other man said.

"Who else was in this with you?"

Shanklin named half a dozen men but refused to tell me where they lived. However, he and his companion pointed out their own farm houses and reiterated that they would reimburse me for their part in the rustling.

I rode on and finally came to another ranch house where the tracks indicated that the wagon had also stopped. The door happened to be open; so after tying my horse, I walked inside without knocking. A group of men were sitting around a table, eating dinner. They looked up in amazement as I entered.

"I imagine that those fresh steaks you're eatin' are off one of my cows," I said.

"So those were your strays?" one of the men said nervously when he had recovered from his surprise. "We're sorry for what we've done, and we'll give you some of our cattle to help make up your loss."

"I'll be back after them," I said, "just as soon as I find the rest of your associates."

The wagon tracks led to two more farm houses. At the first of these I caught a man and his wife salting down some beef in a washtub.

"It looks like I'm furnishing meat for the whole damned community around here," I said to the astonished culprits.

They sheepishly admitted their guilt and, like the others, agreed to repay me for the damage they had done.

At the second house two hostile looking men confronted me with long needle rifles.

"My name is Shores," I greeted, "and I understand that you

helped kill some of my cattle. Do you want to make some kind of a settlement?"[10]

One of the men was a great big fellow with red hair and whiskers. He introduced himself as Reed and said, "I'm a lawyer, and if you want to get a settlement out of me, it will have to be through a court of law."

"I can't wait around that long," I said, riding away. Both men were ready for a fight, and realizing that my little derringer was no match for their rifles, I decided that it was not the right time to start anything.

I rode back to my camp along the Missouri and got my big .45 caliber Sharps rifle, which would help even up the odds. On my return trip, I stopped for the night at another neighboring community. While there, I learned from a chance acquaintance—a former cavalry man in the Civil War—that the big, red-headed lawyer named Reed was the ringleader of the rustlers who had killed and dressed out my strays. I was told that the culprits all shot at once into the bunch so that if the owner showed up he would be unable to pin the blame on any one person.

"I wouldn't go over there now," my casual friend advised, "since Reed and his group intend to hang you if you ever come back."[11]

"Well, I don't want to disappoint them," I said. "I'll look them up tomorrow."

The next day as I approached the cluster of farms where my beeves had been killed and butchered, I saw a man out plowing. As soon as he espied me riding up, he abandoned his team and plow and headed for his house on a dead run.

I galloped between the man and his house and jumped off, jerking my Sharps rifle from its scabbard. It was nearly dark, and in the dusk it looked as if the fleeing farmer was carrying a big six-shooter in his hand.

"Don't shoot! Don't shoot!" he screamed, dropping the object in his hand, which proved to be a large monkey wrench.

I walked up to the frightened stranger and said, "Apparently you're another one of the cattle thieves."

"I know I done wrong, but I'll make it up to you if you give me a chance and don't kill me."

I visited with the man for a while, and he told me that he and his neighbors had killed seven of my cattle, leaving eight survivors. I found these many miles farther south on the Elkhorn River. As I drove them back, I picked up six additional steers, which the various rustlers contributed as a payment for my losses. Only the ringleader—Reed—refused to make a settlement.

After returning the fourteen recovered head to my main herd, I rode back to Reed's ranch—twenty miles away—determined to even up the score. When I arrived, it was late at night and raining hard. It was so dark that I couldn't see a thing except when there were flashes of lightning.

Reed had one yoke of work oxen, which I had seen staked out in front of his house. My intention was to shoot these oxen in retaliation for what he had done to my cattle, but the two oxen were not there. I saw a milk cow grazing in the vicinity, but since I had been told that it belonged to Reed's sister-in-law, I did not bother it. I looked around for Reed's oxen until morning but without success. Having other more pressing matters to attend to, I finally returned to camp without getting retribution. I later found out that Reed had taken the oxen away from his ranch that night to get a load of timber the next day.[12]

After my herd had taken on a good fill, I sold some of my cattle to the post butchers at Fort Randall, South Dakota. I then drifted the rest of them down the Missouri River to the Santee Sioux Agency—thirty-five miles above Yankton.

The Indian agent there bought six steers from me, which had been broken to work. He paid me in government vouchers, but when I went to cash them at a bank in Yankton, I found that the discount was so great that I took the vouchers back to the agent.

At that time it was customary for the government to appoint Quakers as agents for Indian reservations. This agent was no exception. When I told him about the big discount on the vouchers, he said, "Then I suggest that thee sell the cows to me again at a price high enough to offset the discount."[13]

So, I raised my price accordingly, and the deal was completed. The steers or oxen hadn't been worked for some time, and they were hard to handle. The Indians couldn't do anything with them and complained to the agent about the purchase.

The agent told me that he wanted his money back on the grounds that I had misrepresented the steers as being broke to work.

"They are good work oxen," I said. "Your Indians just don't know how to manage them."

I had a lot of experience handling oxen as a bullwhacker, and with the help of a long switch and a liberal vocabulary, I yoked them up and drove them around as if they were veterans to the harness. After this demonstration, the Indians and the agent had no more to say.

We continued on down the Missouri to Sioux City, where I sold the rest of the herd to a shipper. I also sold all my horses except three or four. My two employees and I hitched two of these to our chuck wagon and started the long journey home to western Kansas.[14]

I remained in the Saline River country of Kansas for the next seven years, buying and selling cattle. In January, 1877, I married and moved to Hays City, although I kept my cattle interests on the Saline.

Three years later in March, 1880, my wife, Agnes, and I sold our ranch and came to Colorado with the intention of settling near Durango in the southwestern part of the state. However, at Fort Garland in Colorado I was told that the Ute Indians were causing trouble in that area. So, Agnes and I changed our plans and decided to try our luck in the booming, year-old mining town of Gunnison, about a hundred miles north of Durango.[15]

At Fort Garland I bought a freighting outfit, composed of two wagons drawn by an eight mule team and a six mule team, for the purpose of hauling supplies to the mushrooming silver camps around Gunnison. Then we headed for the new El Dorado, where my career was to take a strange and unexpected turn.[16]

FOOTNOTES

[1]C. W. Shores, "Killing My Beef Cattle in 1872," original manuscript, Denver, Colo., Jan. 6, 1928, pp. 1-2. In possession of Western History Dept. of Denver Public Library.

[2]*Ibid.,* pp. 5-6.

[3]*Ibid.,* pp. 2-3.

[4]*Ibid.*, p. 4.

[5]*Ibid.*, pp. 6-7.

[6]*Ibid.*, p. 7.

[7]*Ibid.*, p. 8.

[8]*Ibid.*, p. 9.

[9]*Ibid.*

[10]*Ibid.*, p. 10.

[11]*Ibid.*

[12]*Ibid.*, p. 11.

[13]C. W. Shores, "My Political Career," original manuscript, Denver, Colo., Mar. 28, 1929, p. 1. In possession of Western History Dept. of Denver Public Library.

[14]*Ibid.*, p. 2. Also see "Killing My Beef Cattle in 1872," *op. cit.*, p. 13.

[15]C. W. Shores, "Autobiography of C. W. Shores," original manuscript, Denver, Colo., Jan. 17, 1928, pp. 49-50. In possession of Western History Dept. of Denver Public Library.

[16]Shores, "My Political Career," *op. cit.*, p. 5.

Chapter XIII

My wife and I arrived in Gunnison, Colorado, on May 1, 1880, driving our two freight wagons. We put up a tent in a clearing close to the Gunnison River a half mile from town. Many other camps were located on the same flat, which were the temporary abodes of prospectors who had been swarming into the region ever since the discovery of silver a year previously in 1879.

The newly-born town of Gunnison was growing like a weed, and it consisted largely of tents and canvas-covered buildings. Hundreds of people were arriving daily, and the community had all the appearances of soon becoming a metropolis because of its location as a supply center for the surrounding mining camps, such as Tin Cup, Irwin, and Ohio City.[1]

A short time after my arrival on this active scene, a tall thin man rode into Gunnison on a small black horse, leading three pack burros. He put up a tent next to my camp, and although I was willing to meet him half way, he kept to himself and showed none of the camaraderie typical of western men. Consequently, I, like his other neighbors, left the sullen newcomer strictly alone. Therefore, one Sunday morning I was surprised to see him walk over to my tent and speak to me.

"Do you know how to pack burros?" he asked. There was a nervous air about him as if he had something on his mind.

"Yes," I replied, "I've packed a lot of them."[2]

"Then, I wonder if you'd help me pack mine. It's all sort of new to me."

While I didn't owe the aloof stranger much consideration, I helped him break camp and pack his two burros. He had recently sold the third burro for thirty-five or forty dollars.

As we worked, he told me that this was his first attempt at prospecting, and he was pretty green at it. He said that he was going on up to Rock Creek near Irwin—a booming mining camp thirty-five miles north of Gunnison—to try out his luck there.

His friendly manner was forced, and he seemed jumpy and on edge. When a stray boy unexpectedly walked into the tent where we were working, he lost his temper and raved at the frightened child like a madman.

The stranger not only acted oddly, but I made other observations which did not add up. He had enough guns, provisions, and camping equipment to take care of two or three men. I at first attributed this surplus of equipment to his inexperience, but as I was folding some blankets, I noticed some blood stains on several of them.

"Where did all this old blood come from?" I asked.

"What blood?" he exclaimed, startled.

I pointed out the dark, tell-tale stains on the blankets. My companion was evidently disturbed at my discovery, but with an effort he controlled his alarm and said, "I killed a deer the other day, and the blood must've come off the meat."

After this lame explanation, he crawled back into his shell and didn't say anything more than was absolutely necessary. When he did speak, he was ill-tempered and abrupt.

When the burros were finally packed, he mounted his black pony and started north in the direction of Irwin. However, after he had gone three or four hundred yards and thought he was out of my sight, he turned east and rode up Tomichi Creek, where the present highway is. This was not the way to Irwin, where he told me that he was going, which aroused my suspicions all the more that he had murdered his partner and made off with his equipment. I had knocked around on the frontier long enough to know that such occurrences were not uncommon. Although I voiced these deductions to several of my neighbors, I did not feel that I had seen enough evidence of foul play to take any action.

The next morning while I was loading my wagons at a warehouse to take some freight up to a mining camp called Gothic—some thirty miles north of Gunnison—a man by the name of Cox came running over to me.

"You were right about that funny duck who pulled out yesterday," Cox said breathlessly. "He did kill his partners."[3]

"How do you know?" I asked.

"Marshal Reasoner from Irwin rode in this morning, lookin' for a man by the name of Breckenridge, who answers to this fellow's description. Breckenridge is wanted for the murder of two brothers named Edgley, who he killed over on Indian Creek—seven or eight miles from Irwin. According to the marshal, the brothers had let Breckenridge come into their camp when he told them that he was alone and new at prospecting. Reasoner found one brother lying in his blankets shot through the head, while the other one was killed some distance from camp. The marshal figures that the killer murdered one brother while they were out prospecting and then returned to shoot the other who was lying in camp sick.

"You know," Cox concluded, "this fellow Breckenridge asked me to go prospectin' with him just the other day, and I almost took him up on it."[4]

Feeling a personal interest in this manhunt, I suddenly decided to postpone my trip to Gothic.

"Let's get a warrant and go after this fellow," I said. "I never liked him."

"Marshal Reasoner has already organized a posse," Cox said, "but we can overtake them. They only have about an hour's start on us."

We followed the tracks of the posse up Tomichi Creek as far as the village of Parlin (at that time called "Parlins Station")—twelve miles distant. Here the posse had turned up Quartz Creek passing through the new silver mining camp of Ohio City—then just a town of tents.

Cox and I followed along at a lope and finally overtook Marshal Reasoner and the posse just south of Pitkin—another mushrooming mining town about seven miles north of Ohio City. Shortly after we joined the group, we ran on to Breckenridge, still riding the black pony and leading the two burros, which he had stolen from the brothers he had killed.

We galloped up to the surprised prospector, and Marshal Reasoner clapped a pair of handcuffs on him.

"I thought you told me that you were headed for Rock Creek," I said to the prisoner.[5]

"I guess you can understand now why I didn't," he answered, breaking down and beginning to sob.

"Brace up and try acting like a man," Reasoner said, disgusted at Breckenridge's lack of self-control.

As we rode back through Ohio City on the return trip to Gunnison, a mob of miners gathered around us. Somehow word had got around that the posse had captured Alfred Packer—the notorious man-eater who six years before had killed and eaten his five companions near Lake San Cristobal. Packer had been taken into custody but escaped from the Saguache jail and was still at large.

"Give us Alfred Packer," the leader of the mob demanded. "He's not gonna get a chance to escape again because we're gonna string him up here and now."

"We don't have Packer," the Irwin marshal replied. "Now, clear the way so that we can ride through."

Breckenridge was terrified, and cringed forward in his saddle. "Don't turn me over to those miners," he pleaded. "They'll hang me for sure."

"If it ain't Packer, who have you got?" another miner asked, puffing violently on a short clay pipe.

"A prospector who murdered his two partners up near Irwin," Reasoner said. "Now, please get out of the way."

With difficulty we pushed our way through the angry mob, who were still halfway inclined to hang our prisoner—even though he wasn't the man-eater.

At Parlin, which consisted of a saloon, post office, restaurant, and stage station, the posse stopped for a drink of whiskey, leaving Sam Howe, who was the Gunnison night marshal, and me in charge of Breckenridge for a few minutes.

"Yuh know, Sam," I said aside to Howe with a laugh, "if we put a rope around Breckenridge's neck and threw it over a tree branch, we could get a full confession out of him in short order."

"I agree," Sam said. "He's so scared now that it wouldn't take much to break him down."

When the rest of the posse began filing out of the saloon, I suggested to Marshal Reasoner that now would be a good time to scare a confession out of Breckenridge.

"It won't be necessary," Reasoner said. "We've got plenty of evidence against him. He's bound to hang, anyway."

The marshal got on his horse and rode over to the cowering prisoner. "Well, lets get movin', you murderin', yellow-bellied rat. I should've turned you over to the mob back in Ohio City and saved myself all this trouble of escortin' you to jail."

"Take it easy, Reasoner," I said. "The poor devil has troubles enough without you abusin' him."[6]

"Are you standin' up for the bastard?" Reasoner asked in surprise. "You know as well as I do that he killed the two brothers who befriended him. A snake like that ain't worth no consideration."

"I know he's guilty," I said, "but there's no use bullying him. Leave him alone."

On the way back to Gunnison I found myself riding beside the prisoner. It was nearly daybreak, and everyone was tired and sleepy. As we rode along in silence, Breckenridge said quietly, "I want to thank you for the way you stood up for me."

When I did not reply, he continued in a low voice that only I could hear, "I should never have come West. I had a good job in Philadelphia working on a newspaper called 'The Morning Star.' I was well off but wanted to be better; so here I am with my neck in a noose."

I thought that he was stringing me along, but events later proved that this time he was telling the truth.

It was daylight when we finally reached Gunnison. Breckenridge was turned over to the city marshal, who put him in jail.

A few days later Breckenridge's mother arrived from Philadelphia. She was accompanied by an influential newspaper man from Denver by the name of Zeigfus, who was a friend of the family. Unlike the prisoner, they were good mixers and pretty smooth opertators. It was not long before they had won the sympathy and good will of many prominent Gunnison people, including the city marshal and the county sheriff.

A grand jury was called to conduct a preliminary investigation to determine if there was sufficient evidence of guilt to recommend a trial. Because of the influence of Zeigfus and Mrs. Breckenridge, no witnesses familiar with the murder were asked to testify before the grand jury. Marshal Reasoner of Irwin, for example, who had discovered the dead bodies of the two brothers, was not even subpoenaed. I, who had noticed the blood stains on Breckenridge's blankets, was not asked to testify either, although I only lived a half-mile from the courthouse and was easily accessible.

After the hearing was completed, the grand jury found no bill of indictment against the defendant, and Breckenridge was released. He was provided with a body guard of two gunmen to see that he got out of the county safely, for there were many of us who believed that there had been a serious miscarriage of justice.

To make the farce complete, many years later Breckenridge wrote an article for a national magazine telling how near he came to being hanged in Gunnison County for a crime that he didn't commit.[7]

This was a sample of how justice was meted out in Gunnison County during its early boom years. All kinds of crimes were taking place, and very little was being done about it. Not only were very few outlaws captured, but those few who were caught usually broke jail or failed to be convicted.[8]

I felt that the sheriff—as the leading peace officer of the county—was primarily responsible for this woeful lack of law enforcement. So, in the fall of 1883, I said to my friend Tom Maloney, Gunnison County Treasurer, "Tom, a lot of people have been askin' me to run for sheriff, and I think I'll make the race. It's about time that a little law and order was brought to Gunnison County."[9]

I was duly nominated and elected, becoming the third sheriff of Gunnison County.[10] I held the office for a total of eight years. My career as a lawman had begun.

Gunnison's Main Street about 1883 when Doc Shores first ran for sheriff. Note town well on corner. *Photo courtesy of Denver Public Library Western Collection.*

FOOTNOTES

[1]C. W. Shores, "My Political Career," original manuscript, Denver, Colo., Mar. 28, 1929, p. 5. In possession of Western History Dept. of Denver Public Library.

[2]*Ibid.*

[3]*Ibid.,* p. 6.

[4]*Ibid.,* p. 7.

[5]*Ibid.*

[6]*Ibid.,* p. 8.

[7]*Ibid.,* p. 9.

[8]*Ibid.,* p. 4.

[9]*Ibid.,* p. 3. The present boundaries of Gunnison County were established in February, 1883. When Gunnison County was first formed in 1877, it included the present counties of Delta, Montrose, Mesa and Gunnison.

[10]George Yule was the first sheriff, serving from 1880-'81; J. H. Bowman was the second, serving from 1882-'83; and C. W. Shores was the third, serving from 1884-1892.

Part II

THE OUTLAW TRAIL

Chapter I

On the crisp fall morning of November 3, 1887, Jeff Gwynn, train master for the Denver and Rio Grande Railroad at Gunnison, Colorado,[1] hurried into my office.

"Take a gander at this, Doc," he greeted with ill-suppressed excitement, handing me a telegram.

The brief message brought me up with a start. While I don't recall the exact words, the gist of the communication was that the Salt Lake passenger train on the Denver and Rio Grande Railroad had been held up and robbed near Grand Junction early that morning at about two o'clock. The express company was offering a reward of $3000, which was being supplemented by an additional $1000 by the federal government.[2]

While the holdup had occurred in Mesa County, which was out of my jurisdiction as sheriff of Gunnison County, it did come within my authority as a deputy United States marshal. I had been appointed to that federal office shortly after being elected sheriff. Not long after the train master had departed, I received a wire from United States Marshal Hill, my superior in Denver, alerting me of the robbery and asking me to do everything possible to help apprehend the culprits.[3]

As information continued to sift in throughout the day, I was able to establish a fairly detailed picture of the dramatic holdup.

The train had left Grand Junction at about 1:30 A.M. on its way to Delta. As it slowly rounded a sharp curve at Unaweep Switch, about five miles east of Grand Junction, the headlights of the engine suddenly fell on a pile of rocks and ties lying across the tracks. Ed Malloy, the engineer, threw on the brakes and brought the train to a jolting stop.

When he did so, a number of masked men[4] appeared out of the darkness on each side of the engine. One of them scrambled up into the cab and pointing his six-shooter at the surprised engineer and fireman ordered them to get out. After the trainmen had climbed down on to the ground, the bandit kept them covered with his gun while his companions walked over to the mail car and began pounding on the locked door.

"Open up," one of the them shouted.

The clamor awakened H. W. Grubb, the mail clerk, who assumed that the train had arrived at the Delta station. Hastily he grabbed the Delta mail pouch and threw open the door. The cold night air began blowing into the warm car.

Grubb stared in amazement at the three masked men standing before him outside the open door. One of them held a rifle while the other two carried revolvers. All of their guns were pointed toward him. In the background he could see the engineer and fireman standing on a pile of ties with their hands held in the air. In front of them facing the mail car was a fourth bandit who kept the two trainmen covered with his six-shooter while allowing him to see how his comrades were faring.

"Put up your hands and get out of the car," one of the men carrying a six-shooter ordered.

The dazed mail clerk dropped the pouch and jumped to the ground.

"Is anyone else inside the mail car?" the same man asked. He seemed to be the leader of the group.

"No," Grubb answered. "I was all alone."

"Then get back inside and stand up against the wall with your face toward it."

He crawled back in, followed by the three robbers. As he stood at the far end of the car with his hands in the air, the road agents went through the various mail pouches, setting aside all of the registered letters and packages.[5]

"Gentlemen," the mail clerk said apologetically, "it's gettin' awful cold in here and I've been coming down with the grippe. Would you mind if I got my coat?"

"Go ahead and put it on," one of the bandits said pleasantly. "But no tricks because I'm keeping you covered."[6]

A few minutes later the group moved out of the car, taking the clerk with them. He was told to take his place beside the fireman and engineer.[7]

The three outlaws then proceeded over to the express and baggage car. Once more they hammered on the locked door and called to the express and baggage master to open up. Dick Williams, who was in charge of this car, was more alert than the sleeping mail clerk. He was awake when the train made its untimely jarring stop and soon surmised what was taking place.

When the banging started at the door, he knew that it was a hold-up and refused to unlock the door. It was only after the robbers threatened to blow up the car with dynamite that Williams finally opened the door.

"Get out of the car," one of the armed men said.

After Williams had complied, he was asked if anyone else was inside. Upon replying in the negative, he was told to re-enter and open the safes. There were two safes in the express and baggage car —a messenger's safe, containing about $150, which Williams had access to, and a much larger safe, containing several thousand dollars, which could only be opened by station agents along the route.[8]

At the point of a gun Williams worked the combination to the smaller safe, at the same time explaining that he was not allowed to know the combination to the other.

However, after ransacking the open safe and pocketing the small amount of money therein, the man who appeared to be the leader of the bunch turned to Williams and said, "I'm giving you just three minutes to open the big safe."[9]

As he spoke, he pulled out a watch. "I mean business," he continued, aiming his six-shooter at the baggage master. "If that safe ain't opened in three minutes, I'm going to blow your head off."

"Can't you understand that I don't know how to open it," Williams pleaded. "We messengers are not allowed to have the combination to the through safe. It is known only to the agents at the more important depots."

"Quit stalling," the man holding the watch snapped. "Your time is running out."

"If you let me get my coat, I'll show you a letter from the general manager of the express company proving that I am not authorized to know the combination."

"All right, get the letter, but I'm not stoppin' the time."

Williams hurried over to his coat and went desperately through the pockets. "The letter don't seem to be here," he said finally, quaking in his shoes. "I must've mislaid it, but I swear to God I'm tellin' you the truth."

"You only have thirty seconds left."

It suddenly became so still in the express car that all could hear the outlaw's watch ticking away the remaining seconds. Unable to think of a final plea for his life, Williams stood there paralyzed with fright, expecting at any moment the shot which would end his life.

"Time's up!" the leader said, pocketing his watch.

"Shall I let him have it?" one of the other robbers asked, menacingly raising his revolver.

"No, let him go. I believe he's tellin' the truth."

The outlaws then took a three-pound express package and a few worthless envelopes marked C.O.D. and jumped out of the car. Putting Williams with the other prisoners on the pile of ties, the robbers made one more excursion through the mail car. They ransacked everything in sight, littering the floor with letters and papers.[10]

In the meantime, the four railroad men were growing more and more uncomfortable standing there in the cold November night with their tired arms held high over their heads.

"My arms are getting too tired to hold up much longer," the fireman finally said. "May I lower them for a moment?"

"Lock your fingers together and place your hands on the top of your head," the guard said obligingly. "That will help. The rest of you may do the same."[11]

When the robbers came out of the mail car, they considered going through the coach and pullman car to rob the passengers. However, they finally decided against it, and warning their prisoners not to follow, they disappeared into the night.

In spite of all the planning and daring that went into the spectacular train robbery, the total take did not exceed $150 in cash and a few comparatively worthless registered packages and letters. One of the ironies of the robbery was that the holdup men neglected to go through the pockets of their prisoners. If they had done so, they would have found $119 in the pocketbook of the fireman.[12]

The holdup delayed the train for about thirty-five minutes. The conductor awakened the passengers and calmly informed them that the train was being held up. He tried to reassure them by saying that the robbers were only after express and mail matter. But in spite of this assurance the passengers were very much excited and frantically set about trying to hide their money and valuables.

A young Scotchman in the Pullman was so frightened at the information that he grabbed some woman's clothing to disguise himself. The conductor quieted him down and returned the garments to their proper owner.

Late the next afternoon I caught the train for Grand Junction to participate in the manhunt. Not only had my superior—United States Marshal Hill of Denver—asked me to do so, but the local officers of the railroad at Gunnison had all personally urged me to join in the search.

"We've seen you in action, Doc," one of them had said, "and it's going to take a bloodhound like you to catch up with those train robbers."

An added inducement was the $4000 reward money. A sheriff's income needed supplementing in those days by such means, and the reward was unusually large for that time. So, I made arrangements with Undersheriff Sam Harper to look after my duties in Gunnison and set out for the scene of the holdup. I was accompanied by my brother-in-law, M. L. Allison, who was visiting my wife and me on a vacation from his duties as registrar in the land office at Grand Junction. While he had no experience as a manhunter, he went along to keep me company and help out in any way that he could.

He had hunted game considerably and was a good reliable companion to have along in case of an emergency.

When the train stopped at Kannah Creek about ten miles from Unaweep Switch where the crime had occurred, we got out of the coach and climbed up into the engine cab with the engineer and fireman. They were the same two men who had been on duty when the train was held up, this being their first trip back from Denver after the robbery.

It was late at night when the train approached Unaweep Switch. Ed Malloy, the engineer, appeared tense and jumpy as if he expected a repetition of his last run through that area. He refused to slow down as he neared the scene of the crime, and when we went sailing by, the fireman, Fred Sellinger, yelled, "Pull her up! There's the switch!"[13]

However, Malloy kept his hand pressed on the throttle until he was well past the danger point. Then he finally applied the brakes and let Allison and me off. By this time it was one or two o'clock in the morning; so we walked back to the switch and built a little fire, waiting for daylight.

As soon as it was light enough to see, we started our investigation. I looked around for some evidence of where the robbers might have hidden while waiting for the train. At such a time a holdup man is under a nervous tension, and if he ever uses tobacco, he does so then, often leaving matches, cigarette butts, or tobacco juice scattered on the ground. Several times I have even found train robbers' pipes lying where they had put them when the train pulled up. Such clues often proved important in tracing the guilty men.[14]

In this instance, however, any such evidence had been largely obliterated by the tracks of the posse who had already examined the area. Before leaving Gunnison I had received word that Sheriff Bradish of Mesa County had organized a posse shortly after the holdup and was in search of the outlaws.

In sizing up the terrain I noticed that the railroad ran close to the north bank of the Gunnison River all the way to Delta. Therefore, in order to avoid fording the river, which was deep and difficult to cross in most places, the outlaws in making their getaway would have had to either head northward or go parallel with the stream along the railroad tracks. To the north the ground was very rocky and cut by many gulches and canyons.[15]

In an effort to pick up the tracks of the fugitives, Allison and I walked several miles down the railroad toward Grand Junction and then made a big circle to the north, reaching the railroad again a number of miles above Unaweep Switch. The farther away we got from the scene of the holdup, the less the ground was cluttered up by the horse tracks of the posse. At the extremity of our circle we lost them entirely, which gave us a better opportunity to pick up the trail of the train robbers. However, the only interesting track we discovered was that of a medium-sized mule. It led up-country to the top of a hill where a good view could be obtained of the surrounding country and then turned downhill toward the river, as if the mule's rider was some sheepherder or cowboy out looking for stray stock. If the rider had been one of the holdup men, the tracks, in all probability, would have led straight out of the area instead of winding about.

Upon again reaching the railroad we were fortunate enough to run across a section crew. It was about nine or ten o'clock and we were tired and hungry. One of the crew had shot a deer that morning, and he gave us some pieces of liver, which we fried over a fire on an old shovel blade for breakfast.

During the rest of the day Allison and I continued to make even wider and wider circles north of the railroad, but we did not find any tracks which could have possibly been made by the road agents. By nightfall I was convinced that the robbers had not gone north after the holdup. Neither could we find any evidence of their having gone any distance up or down the railroad track. The only other route which they could have taken was southward across the Gunnison, and we decided to have a look on the other side of the river in the morning.

That evening we flagged down a freight train and rode it into Grand Junction, where we spent the night at the Brunswick Hotel. There was a lot of talk going on in town about the holdup, and I learned that Sheriff Bradish's posse had disbanded after a two-day search in which they had found no trace of the train robbers.

Early the next morning Allison and I rented two broken-down

saddle horses from a stable, and crossing the Gunnison on the ferry just below town, we rode slowly up the south side of the river, looking for tracks. We searched all that day without finding a track which could possibly have been made by the train robbers. When it became too dark to look further, we swam our unwilling horses across the Gunnison, climbing ashore on the opposite bank near Unaweep Switch, where the holdup had occurred.

"I'm beginning to think that our train robbers had wings," Allison commented as we were returning to Grand Junction. "They must've flown away from the scene of the crime."

"Don't let it get you down," I said. "Tracking down outlaws is the most tedious, heart-breaking work in the world. And even after you finally pick up a trail or a lead, ninety percent of them take you to a dead end."

After turning our horses over to the stable boy, we walked over to the Brunswick Hotel, arriving there about midnight. When the clerk handed us our key, he said that a man by the name of James Duckworth left word to be called as soon as I returned.[16]

"Go ahead and call him," I said. "I'll talk to him here in the lobby."

"If you don't mind," Allison remarked, "I think I'll turn in. I'm dog tired."

"Go ahead," I said, handing him the key to our room. "I'll be up in a minute."

While waiting for Duckworth, I glanced at the hotel register lying open on the desk. My attention was caught by a signature written in a flourishing hand which read, "Ed S. Keith, Detective of the Denver and Rio Grande Railroad, Denver, Colo."

Apparently he had been sent over by the railroad to investigate the train robbery. My first impression was that the man was a little pompous and indiscreet to unnecessarily display on the register his profession and his reason for being in Grand Junction.

Not far below Keith's registration was that of the man who wanted to see me. He had signed the register simply as "James Duckworth, Denver, Colo." He was probably some sort of an investigator also, but did not propose to advertise it.

Duckworth did not keep me waiting long. He was a tall, dis-

Grand Junction as it looked in November, 1887, at time of Grand Junction train robbery. Scene is looking southwest from 556 Main Street. *Photo courtesy of Library, State Historical Society of Colorado.*

tinguished looking man who introduced himself as a special agent for the Denver and Rio Grande Express Company and showed me his credentials.

After we were seated in the dimly gas-lighted lobby, he asked, "Have you ever met Mr. Kramer, general manager of the D. and R. G. Express Company?"

"No, but I've heard of him often."

"Well, he's heard a good deal about you, too, Mr. Shores, in tracking down criminals. He was pleased to learn from the train master in Gunnison that you had decided to take part in this man-hunt. While the robbers didn't get away with much, he wants to make an example of them, and he's counting on you more than anyone else to do the job. He sent me over to help you out in any way I can and to sort of keep him posted on how you are making out. I can assure you, however, that everything you tell me will be kept strictly confidential between Mr. Kramer and myself."[17]

I liked the stranger's appearance and was naturally flattered at what he said. "There's not much to report as yet," I said. "For the past two days we've been trying to pick up the train robbers' trail, but so far all that we have discovered is where they didn't go. But they must've left a trail somewhere, and by the process of elimination we should run across it pretty soon now."

Renting two fresh horses the next morning, Allison and I again crossed at the ferry and trotted up the river to where we had discontinued the search on the previous night. Upon resuming the hunt, we pulled our horses to a walk and moved slowly along with our heads down looking for tracks. While we assumed that the outlaws had made their getaway on horseback, we did not rule out the possibility that they were travelling on foot.

We had gone less than a mile beyond Unaweep Switch when I noticed the fresh footprints of a man leading out from the river. There was a comparatively shallow riffle at this place in the river through which he had obviously waded from the opposite bank. He had walked out on the gravel and wash boulders for some distance and then passed under some large cottonwood trees before going up on to the bank of the stream. Through this area where it was muddy the imprints were deep and blotched. Examining them more closely, it was apparent that one man had walked along behind another, carefully stepping in his companion's tracks to make it look to the casual observer as if only one person had come out on the bank. We followed the footprints for about half a mile away from the Gunnison before they separated and proceeded side by side. The steps were far apart and pointed as straight as a die for the rough, broken country south of the river.

"Well, Allison," I commented finally. "Those tracks have all the appearances of being made by two of our train robbers."[18]

"Maybe so, Doc, but I'm inclined to think that they were made by a couple of hunters."

"Not likely," I disagreed. "You see, a hunter's footprints would be closer together and more meandering as he wandered about looking for game. These are far apart and heading out of here in a beeline, showing that whoever made them had a definite destination and were in a big hurry to get there. Besides, why would hunters go out of their way to step in each others' tracks back there near the river in an apparent effort to conceal the number in their party?"

"Then, where are the tracks of the other robbers?" Allison asked, still disbelieving. "More than two men were involved in the holdup!"

"It looks like the group split up after the robbery to make it harder to trail them," I replied.

The tracks led in a southwesterly direction in a more or less parallel course with Bangs Canyon, which lay a quarter of a mile beyond. We followed the trail of the two men until late afternoon and then retraced our steps back to the river. By this time it was nearly dark, and Allison, who was not accustomed to outdoor work, was exhausted.

"You wait here," I told him. "I've got a hunch the tracks of the other train robbers are not far from here."

While Allison lay down for a needed rest, I continued on up the river. As my horse slowly picked his way through the rocks and gravel, I kept watching the shoreline of the stream for additional tracks. My assumption now was that in order to hide their trail the bandits had crossed the river at different places with the intention of meeting each other at some prearranged rendezvous. After crossing Bangs Canyon, which leads southwestward from the river about a mile above Unaweep Switch, I progressed only a short distance—perhaps a half-mile—when I found the fresh footprints of two more men, who had forded the river and struck out for the broken country in the same deliberate, hurried manner of their associates on the opposite side of the canyon.

It was getting too dark to follow the tracks; so I rode back to where my brother-in-law was impatiently awaiting my return. When I told him that I had probably picked up the trail of two more of the train robbers, he merely shook his head skeptically, still believing that they were the footprints of hunters.

Jim Duckworth was waiting up for us when we arrived at the hotel after midnight. I told him about the suspicious tracks we had run across that afternoon on both sides of Bangs Canyon.

"They were about two days old," I said, "and the men who made them were travelling fast and as straight as an arrow for the rough, open country to the southwest. I feel sure that they are the footprints of the train robbers."

"So they were walking?" Duckworth commented in surprise. "I had supposed they made their getaway on horseback."

"That would be much faster, but unless they had some horses hidden out somewhere, they are on foot."

"Discovering those tracks is our first break in the case," Duckworth remarked enthusiastically. "Sheriff Bradish disbanded his posse today after finding no trace of the bandits, and although Detective Keith has been interrogating everyone who might possibly know anything about the robbery, he hasn't got anywhere either."

"If anyone asks," I said, "just tell him that I've run up against a blank wall also."

"I surely will. Keith, the railroad detective, was asking me today if you were having any luck. I, of course, told him that so far as I knew you weren't."

The following day Allison and I again obtained second-rate saddle horses and took a shortcut to the place where we had left off trailing the two men on the lower side of Bangs Canyon. Their tracks led southwestwardly for a number of miles and then turned into the canyon. We dismounted and led our horses down the precipitous, rocky slope. The canyon was composed of a red sandstone formation, and the farther we went the rockier it became.

We had not gone far when we discovered the tracks of the other two outlaws where they came down the opposite side of the canyon to join their comrades. The trail of the four men then continued westward up the ravine for a short distance to a shelving rock. The markings here showed that the group had huddled up under this jutting rock for the night—probably the first night after the hold-up.[19]

Satisfied now that we were on the right trail, we turned back to Grand Junction, again arriving at our hotel late at night. The faithful Duckworth, however, was there awaiting us. I reported to him that we had struck the trail of all four train robbers about fourteen miles from the river in Bangs Canyon. He was very much pleased to learn of this and felt that with a little luck we would soon overtake the fugitives.

In our hurry to get started the next morning, Allison forgot his customary plug of tobacco and the cartridges to his Winchester. Fortunately, he did remember to load the little British Bull Dog pistol, which he carried in a holster at his hip.

I was armed with a Winchester rifle of a different caliber and a long-barrelled Colt six-shooter, which guns I always carried when making dangerous trips of this kind.

Upon riding down into Bangs Canyon that day, we dismounted and proceeded on foot, leaving our horses to graze with dropped bridle reins. Like most western horses they would not wander far with dragging reins. In many places the outlaws' trail led over solid rock, making their tracks almost impossible to find. We scrambled along, picking our way around huge boulders as large as haystacks. About the only tell-tale markings I could discover were occasional scratches made by boot heels of the bandits on the reddish colored stone formation. Also, scattered here and there along the way were leaves out of an old comic almanac, which one or more of the fugitives had made use of for various purposes.

At another place I saw lying ahead of us on a rock a plug of tobacco and a wooden-handled pocket knife with the small blade open. Apparently each robber had cut himself a quid, leaving the knife and plug on the rock for his companions to do likewise. In so doing they had neglected to pick them up.[20]

Examining the knife I noticed that both blades were filed off square at the ends so that they could be used as screw drivers for dismantling and cleaning guns of different sizes. I pocketed the knife and picked up the plug of tobacco.

When I showed it to Allison, who was coming along some distance behind me, he shouted, "For God's sake, give that to me!" I handed it to him, and he bit off a chew. From then on he was much more agreeable and entered more enthusiastically into the hunt.

As a registrar in the land office at Grand Junction, he was not accustomed to climbing around the hills, and toward the end of the day he fell farther and farther behind. In concentrating on the difficult trail we were following, I forgot about him until it was growing dark and time to turn back. He was nowhere in sight; so suddenly fearful that he might be lost or in trouble, I threw caution to the winds and yelled several times to attract his attention. The shouts echoed and re-echoed up and down the canyon.

As I tensely awaited an answer in the ensuing portentous stillness, Allison unexpectedly came scrambling into view holding in readiness his small British pistol. He was panting hard from exertion, and his face was very red.

"Where are they?" he called softly to me. "Where are they?"

"Where are who?" I asked. "I don't know what you're talking about."

"The train robbers!" he exclaimed breathlessly. "Didn't you hear them yelling?"

"That was me yelling for you," I said. "I thought you were lost."

"Well, you really gave me a scare." He holstered his pistol and sat down on a convenient rock to recover his wind.

I joined him and said, "We've trailed those fellows for at least twenty miles up this canyon, and after going this far I don't believe they're going to hole up and stop until they reach the Dolores River."

"That would be a good country to hide out in," Allison observed. "It's about as far off the beaten trail as a man can get."

"If that's where they're headin' for," I said, "they should be about there by now. The quickest way to head 'em off is to ship in a couple of good saddle horses from Gunnison. We could unload them at Whitewater and ride up the wagon road through Unaweep Canyon to the Dolores River. It shouldn't be hard to pick up their trail again in that isolated area if they're hidin' out there."

Darkness overtook us before we got back to our horses, which we had left behind us in Bangs Canyon. There was no moon, and we could not see more than a foot or two around us. As we picked our precarious way down the rocky draw, I missed my footing on a big boulder and fell ten or fifteen feet into a water hole. The water broke my fall; so fortunately I wasn't hurt seriously, but I landed on my holstered six-shooter, which bruised my hip. The stock of my rifle was bent as a result of the accident, but the gun was not disabled.

I climbed out of the water hole and continued more carefully. The farther down the canyon we crawled, the more open it became and the easier it was to travel. Occasionally we stopped to listen for the sound of our horses, but it was only after an interminable length of time that we finally heard the welcome sound of their grazing not far from where we had left them early that morning.

My horse had stepped on his bridle reins during the day and broken them off at the bit. After improvising substitute reins out of an old lariat rope, which was tied to my saddle, we mounted and let our horses pick their way down the pitch black, rocky draw. They found their way better than we did, and before long we rode out of the big canyon and approached the Gunnison. It was very late; so to save time we forded our horses across the deep stream, the cold water coming up above the saddle skirts and giving us a good sousing.

It was only an hour or two before daylight when at last we walked into the Brunswick Hotel. As was his habit, the tireless Duckworth was on hand to get the latest information. After listening to our plans, he said that he would like to accompany us on our search into the Dolores River country.

The next day I caught the train for Gunnison and made arrangements to freight three of my best saddle horses to Whitewater. When they arrived, Duckworth, Allison and I started up the road through Unaweep Canyon, which ran parallel to Bangs Canyon, where we had left the trail of the four train robbers.

After a ten or eleven-hour ride, we finally reached the Dolores River at the present site of Gateway. There was a cowcamp near here, and although it was late at night, Tom Denning, owner of the camp, invited us in.[21] He knew that uninhabited, mountainous country like a book, and the next morning at breakfast we persuaded him to go along with us and act as our guide. It was a slack time of year for him and the reward money was appealing.

After breakfast we started south along the Dolores in search of some sign of the outlaws. We had not gone far when we met several placer miners working along the river. I asked them if they had seen anything of four men travelling on foot.

"A couple of days ago," one of them answered, "I was prospecting over in Sinbad Valley about twelve miles southwest of here near the Utah line when I ran across some fresh tracks of a group of men on foot. I particularly noticed them because it's very unusual to see human footprints in so isolated an area."

"I'll wager those are the tracks of the men we're after," I said. "Thanks for the information."

Crossing the river our cowboy guide led us in a southwesterly direction toward the Utah border. The region was rough and rocky, and the only trails then in existence were those made by the Ute Indians before their removal from western Colorado only six years before. We were lucky indeed to have a man with us who was familiar with that wild country. Late that afternoon I shot a small buck which we dressed out and tied behind our saddles.

It was nearly dark when the old Indian trail we were following began its precipitous descent into Sinbad Valley. Judging from their trails, Indians were great believers in the old proverb that the shortest distance between two points is a straight line, even when it meant going directly over a cliff instead of around it. This trail was no exception, and it led straight down the sheer slope with a minimum of zigzags through a forest of pinons and cedars.

A number of times our horses slipped and fell on the rocky, perpendicular Ute highway. The going was so slow that we had negotiated only a small portion of our descent when darkness enveloped the mountains. To add to our discomfort, a hard rain began falling from the overcast sky.

It was eleven o'clock before we rode out into the open valley below. The downpour showed no sign of stopping, and we were soaked to our skins. We peered around for a light from some kind of habitation which might be in the desolate area. Seeing none, we fired a few shots into the air, hoping that if anyone was in the valley they would answer them and give us shelter. Receiving no response, we removed our saddles and hobbled the horses. Since there was no dry wood in the timberless valley, we couldn't build a fire. So, making the best of an unpleasant situation, we bunched up together and put our saddle blankets over us. In this manner we spent the remainder of a cold, disagreeable night.

When it grew light enough to see around us, we noticed in the distance what appeared to be a dwelling, partially hidden in the brush at the mouth of a small gulch. It was still raining and any type of shelter looked good. Catching and saddling our horses, we rode over to it. As we approached, we saw that it was a dugout, extending back into the bank and covered with logs and dirt. The front was closed in by upright posts and a makeshift door. It was unlocked, and as we dismounted and walked up to enter, I suddenly espied an animal stretched out on the roof rolling his eyes at us. Startled, I reached for my Colt six-shooter, but before drawing it, I noticed that one of his legs was caught in a big steel trap.

"Look up above you on the roof," I said to my companions.

They glanced up and instinctively stepped back from the door.

"What it it?" Duckworth asked.

"It's a lynx caught in a trap."

"Let's shoot him," Allison said, pulling out his pistol.

"I think we've shot enough around here," I said. "Our shots last night already have probably scared away the fellow who lives here."

As I spoke, I picked up a long pole and walked over to the snarling beast. I hit him across the back, killing him.

The one-room dugout had just recently been occupied. There was a distillery inside which had been used so recently that a little moonshine whiskey was still dripping from it. Nearby was a five-gallon oil can two-thirds full of bootleg liquor. Although it was a poor class of whiskey, we were all glad to take a drink of it to warm ourselves after our all-night sojourn in the rain.

The shelter was full of supplies, and it was evident that the bootlegger had only been gone a short time, without doubt frightened away by our SOS shots of the previous night. In one corner of the room was a pile of dry wood, which we immediately took advantage of to build a fire in the rusty but still serviceable cook stove. We were also fortunate enough to find a plentiful supply of flour, lard, and coffee.

While Allison and Duckworth unsaddled and hobbled the horses, I fixed a pot of coffee, made biscuits and fried some of the deer meat which we were carrying on our saddles. We washed all this down with several more drinks of moonshine and, thus reinforced, our spirits rose from the nadir of despair to the zenith of well being.

The drizzle had turned to snow by the time we finished breakfast; so we decided to remain in our refuge until the storm was over. This proved to be a wise move, for the wet, heavy snowfall continued unabated for three days and nights. We remained comfortable in the bootlegger's hideout, using his grub and whiskey to supplement our diet of venison. Each day we expected our unknown host to appear, but he never showed up during our extended stay.

On the fourth day the storm finally broke, and the sun shone from a clear sky on the frozen, snow-covered landscape. Fate, in this instance, had been on the side of the fugitives. The untimely storm had effectively covered their trail and materially lessened whatever chances we might have had to find them.

Before leaving the dugout, I wrote a note to our absent host thanking him for the use of his place during the storm. I concluded the message by saying,

> We invite you to come and call on us if you ever come over into our respective parts of the country, and we'll try to return the compliment.
>
> Best regards,
> Doc Shores—sheriff of
> Gunnison County

M. L. Allison—recorder in the land office at Grand Junction
Jim Duckworth—agent for the Rio Grande Express Co., Denver.[22]

To help offset our appropriation of his supplies, we hung up what was left of the deer meat where our benefactor would find it upon his return.

Years later I found out that the name of the bootlegger was Kirk Puckett. Although there was no road into Sinbad Valley at that time, he had carried a plow and parts of a wagon in there by pack horse. He cleared and plowed up a little field, where he raised corn to make moonshine whiskey for the cowboys around Moab and the LaSal Mountains who rode in to buy it.

The severe storm heralded in an early winter, and we found out later that it completely changed the plans of the four men we were following. They had, as we had guessed, planned originally to hide out for a while in Sinbad Valley until the manhunt had let up somewhat. However, the snow and freezing weather drove them back out of the mountains the way they had come to a lower and more hospitable elevation.

We, on the other hand, rode south to the Paradox Valley, hoping once more to pick up their trail in the fresh snow. Near the present village of Paradox we stopped at a ranch house and inquired of some cowboys if they had seen any fresh tracks of men on foot. They replied that although they had ridden extensively since the storm they had seen no sign of anyone on foot. This convinced us that the train robbers were not in that part of the country. So, we decided to return to Grand Junction.

We were told that ten or twelve feet of snow had fallen on the high range between the Dolores River and Unaweep Canyon, which made it impossible to go back the way we had come. Consequently, we continued on south, reaching the Dolores River near the present site of Bedrock. Turning down the Dolores, we rode to its junction with the San Miguel and then followed the San Miguel to the present town of Uravan. A good deal of placer mining was going on here at that time. Near the site of Uravan was a place called Blake's Ranch, where we stayed for a day and two nights to weather out another snowstorm. After the storm we made our way up the San Miguel to the town of Placerville.[23]

Shortly after we left the dugout in Sinbad Valley, Jim Duckworth, who was not used to roughing it in such inclement weather, became sick. Although he did not complain and tried to do his part, Allison and I tried to save him in every way we could. We gave him the most comfortable horse to ride and insisted that he remain mounted at those times when we got off to lead our horses up the steeper hillsides. In camp we refused to let him help with the cooking and chores so that he could save his waning strength.[24] However, in spite of everything we could do, he continued to grow worse.

From Placerville Allison and Tom Denning took the horses and rode across the Horsefly Range to Montrose, while Duckworth and I took the stage to Dallas, where my sick companion boarded the train for Denver to recuperate after his ordeal.[25] Dallas, an extinct town, was three miles north of present Ridgway.

I met Allison and Denning at Montrose, and we rode on to Grand Junction by way of Delta. While in Delta we stumbled on some pertinent information. We learned that shortly before the train robbery four strangers had come into Delta on foot, leading a black pack horse. They set up camp on the outskirts of town along the Gunnison River and remained there for several days constructing a boat.

Such an occupation naturally attracted attention, and a good many townspeople stopped by to observe the activity. They exchanged remarks with the newcomers and overheard bits of conversations that the strangers had passed among themselves. I questioned a number of these townspeople and finally pieced together the following story.

Apparently the four men had worked for a short while at Carbondale on the Midland Railroad, which was being built through there at the time. Here they had joined forces. Quitting their jobs, they came down Crystal River, crossed over McClure Pass, and proceeded down the Muddy to its junction with Coal Creek, where the North Fork River originates. They then followed the North Fork past the newly born towns of Paonia and Hotchkiss to the Gunnison. They continued down this stream to Delta, where they build their boat.

From my talks with the Delta residents, I learned that two of the strangers were brothers who called themselves Jack and Bob Smith. Their companions went by the names of Ed Rhodes and Bob Wallace. The Smiths were described as big men with dark hair. Ed Rhodes was a medium sized blonde, while Bob Wallace was small and wiry with red hair and mustache. Bob Smith appeared to be the leader of the group.[26] One Delta resident informed me that he recalled Bob Smith saying that he lived on Limestone Creek near Cawker City, Kansas.[27]

While there was no direct evidence connecting these men with the train robbery, they left Delta in their boat, filled with guns and supplies, only a day or so before the holdup occurred, which made them definite suspects.

Reinforced with all this interesting information, my two companions and I rode on to Grand Junction, where we put up our horses at a stable. While I had expected Tom Denning to return to his cowcamp on the Dolores, it both pleased and surprised me when at the last minute he said that he had become so interested in the manhunt that he wanted to continue on for a while longer in hopes of getting part of the $4000 reward money.

After arriving in Grand Junction we took a couple of days off getting rested and reorganized for a new campaign. During this interval I went to Denver to see Mr. Kramer, the general manager of the Denver and Rio Grande Express Company, to bring him up-to-date on my investigation.

While there I dropped in at a branch office of the famous Pinkerton Detective Agency, which was also working on the case for the railroad. I introduced myself to the superintendent, Charlie Eames, and told him that from information I had received two of the suspects in the robbery were Bob and Jack Smith who lived near Cawker City on Limestone Creek in central Kansas. Mr. Eames said that he would make inquiry down there and let me know what he found out.

Returning to Grand Junction Allison, Denning, and I resumed the hunt. We surmised that the fugitives had been driven back out of the mountains by the storm and cold weather. However, we had no idea where to begin looking for them.

"If those four men who left Delta in a boat pulled off this train robbery," Denning observed, "they must have hidden their boat somewhere along the river. Let's take a look for it."

This seemed like a good suggestion; so the next day we rode up to the scene of the robbery at Unaweep Switch. Here I swam my horse across the river and rode down one side of the stream while my two companions rode down the other side, all of us keeping our eyes peeled for any sign of a boat. It was not until evening that I finally saw it hidden in the brush just a short distance below the junction of the Grand (now called the Colorado) and the Gunnison Rivers.

In examining the camp ground, we found several leaves from the same comic almanac which we had noticed along the trail of the train robbers in Bangs Canyon. The fugitives had used these pages to wipe off their razors after shaving. From the smeared pieces of paper we could tell the color of their whiskers. The discarded almanac leaves definitely linked the four men who had camped here with those we had trailed up Bangs Canyon toward the Dolores River.

"I wonder why they banked their boat so far from the scene of the holdup?" Allison commented.

"Apparently they wanted to go into town for some supplies," I answered.

"It must've been important," Denning observed, "to risk being noticed in a strange place just before the robbery."

"Maybe that's why they took the time to shave," Allison added. "They may have figured that a several weeks' growth of whiskers would make them even more conspicuous."

These casual, off-hand deductions proved to be closer to the truth than we suspected. After the case was solved, we found out that the loaded boat had run into an eddy and capsized near Whitewater. Although the occupants managed to right the boat and salvage their roll of blankets as it floated downstream, they lost all of their Winchesters and shotguns which sank to the bottom of the river. They were carrying their six-shooters, or they too would have been lost.

Because of this loss, they did not stop at Unaweep Switch as they had at first intended but continued on down the Gunnison to its junction with the Grand. Landing their boat on the south side of the river opposite the town of Grand Junction, they shaved and spruced up somewhat before going into town to purchase a couple of rifles. The next day they walked up the railroad tracks to Unaweep Switch—three miles distant—where they held up the train.[28]

That evening when we returned to the Brunswick Hotel, the clerk handed me a letter from Jim Duckworth, the special investigator who had accompanied us on our unsuccessful trip into the Paradox Valley. He wrote that Ed Keith, who had recently registered at the Brunswich as "Detective of the Denver and Rio Grande Railroad," had arrived in Denver claiming he had reliable information that the train robbers were camped away up on Grand River near a post office called Ravens Beak. The letter went on to say that Mr. Kramer, manager of the express company, wanted me to go up there and investigate this report.[29]

So, that night Allison, Denning, and I set out on horseback for Ravens Beak, leading a pack horse which carried our blankets and other supplies. It was very cold, and a solid crust of snow held the horses as they jogged along. Toward midnight we came to a deserted cabin near the present town of Palisade. We staked out our horses and spent the remainder of the night in this cabin. There was no fireplace or stove in the cabin; so we were unable to build a fire. The shack felt like an ice box, and we passed a most uncomfortable night trying to sleep on some old bunks which had been left there. The deep snow and howling wind made camping outside even more formidable. We all awakened the next morning with colds.

At daybreak we broke off some dry cedar branches and built a fire on the crusted snow. After cooking breakfast and thawing out a little we caught our horses and continued the journey. Upon arriving at Ravens Beak we made inquiries concerning the outlaws, but were told that no newcomers had been seen in the region. Although suspecting it would be a wild goose chase, we spent another day riding around the area, but there was no sign of anyone having camped there. Apparently the railroad detective's report was without foundation.

We paid a big price for his mistake. During our investigation

Tom Denning's cold, which he had caught in the frigid cabin, grew rapidly worse. By the time we were ready to return he had a high fever and was too sick to ride horseback. So, I hired one of the local ranchers to take him to Grand Junction in a wagon. As soon as he arrived, he was placed in a hospital with pneumonia. I learned that my friend Jim Duckworth was likewise very sick with pneumonia resulting from our ill-starred trip through the Sinbad and Paradox Valleys in search of the outlaws. Denning finally recovered but Duckworth died—a tragic fatality of the manhunt.

After returning from our wild goose chase at Ravens Beak, I had to continue the frustrating search alone. Denning was critically sick, and Allison had to get back to his duties in the land office. I took a few days to recuperate from the cold and exposure suffered in this latest ordeal. Then, trying not to let the repeated setbacks discourage me too much, I once more set out to pick up the lost trail of the elusive train robbers.

Still confident that the unusually cold weather had forced the fugitives back out of the hills, I saddled my horse with the intention of looking around the valley for possible tracks. Crossing the Gunnison at the ferry I rode over to where I had discovered the boat. To my surprise it was gone. Apparently the outlaws had returned to recover it and proceed down the river. It did not take me long to find where the boat had been dragged over the ice and snow in the unnavigable portion of the stream. The tracks of the men who pulled the craft were about a week old.

I rode down the Grand as far as Cisco, Utah, where I was told that four men had been seen coming down the river in a boat. Later they came into town and caught a freight train going west. The next morning I rode westward into the town of Green River where I again inquired about any strangers being seen in the area. I was informed that four men had arrived there a day or two before on a freight train. They had camped outside of town for a while and then departed. They were last seen heading north along the road toward Price River.

While in Green River I received a telegram from the Pinkerton Detective Agency asking me to come to Denver at once.[30] With the trail of the train robbers growing warm, I didn't want to interrupt the hunt at this crucial time to go to Denver. However, the Pinkerton Agency apparently had picked up some vital information that I could not afford to ignore. So I sent word to my undersheriff in Gunnison and to Allison, my brother-in-law in Grand Junction, telling them that I had good reason to believe the train robbers were probably in the vicinity of Price River, about twenty miles north of the town of Green River, Utah. I asked them to come immediately and pick up the trail before it grew cold while I went to Denver to see what the Pinkerton Agency wanted of me.

When I arrived at the Agency, I was greeted by Charlie Eames, manager of the branch office, who told me that after talking with me he had written the city marshal of Cawker City about the Smith brothers.

"Two days ago," Eames continued, "I received a telegram from him stating that Jack Smith was at home and his brother Bob was due to arrive in a few days. If you want to check on this report, Charlie Seringo, one of our operatives, will be glad to accompany you."[31]

That evening Seringo and I caught the Kansas-Pacific train for Cawker City. Like so many other promising leads in the case, this report also proved to be a dud. The city marshall had sent the wire solely on the basis of what someone had told him. Later upon checking the story, the well-meaning but inefficient marshal found that the parents of the Smith brothers had not heard from them in a long time and had no idea where they were. The marshal apologized for all of the wasted time and trouble that his impulsive action had caused us.

Seringo and I took the disappointing news in stride since we had been in the game long enough to know that it was all part of the often dull, heart-breaking routine in solving a difficult criminal case. I caught the next train back to Denver, but Seringo remained a day or so longer to visit the Smith ranch. He planned to represent himself as a book salesman and talk with the family, hoping to pick up some information concerning the whereabouts of the Smith brothers.

In Denver I reported the failure of the mission to Mr. Kramer, manager of the D. & R. G. Express Company, and to Mr. Eames of the Pinkerton Detective Agency. Then I boarded the train for Gunnison, anxious to find out how my undersheriff and brother-in-law had fared in following up my lead.

My wife met me at the station with the good news that they had captured three of the train robbers near a station called Woodside on Price River.

I left on the next train for Utah. At Thompson's Springs (now called Thompson) I got off my train in time to catch the one going in the opposite direction on which the peace officers and prisoners were returning. I found them in the smoking car. In addition to Undersheriff Sam Harper of Gunnison and M. L. Allison of Grand Junction was Sheriff Bradish of Mesa County, who Harper and Allison had asked to accompany them on their dangerous assignment. Sitting between them were the three prisoners who were introduced to me as Ed Rhodes and the Smith brothers—Jack and Bob. Jack had a big bandage on his face.

"Well, you fellows have sure been causin' me a lot of grief, trackin' you all over the country," I said to the three handcuffed men.[32]

"You're the damnedest bloodhound I ever seen," Ed Rhodes said with a wry smile, "but the last couple of months ain't been no harder on you than on us. We've been living outdoors in this damned weather freezin' and starvin' like wild animals."

"That's right," Jack Smith agreed. "In a way I'm glad you finally caught up with us. I ain't been warm or had a square meal since the robbery."

"You look like things haven't been going so well with you," I said. "What happened to your face?"

"Ed here accidentally shot me with his shotgun while we were hiding out in Bangs Canyon."

"He was hurt so bad," Bob Smith said, "that I walked clear back to the river intending to go on into Grand Junction to get a doctor. But when I seen the big posse down in the valley looking for us, I lost my nerve and turned back. I expected to find Jack dead, but when I got back he was sitting up smoking a cigarette. Ed had washed out the wound and bandaged it up after a fashion. Without the help of a doctor it's a wonder he made it."[33]

"Oh, I'm too tough to die," Jack said with a laugh.

The train robbers seemed to be in a jovial mood, and we all visited and compared notes like old buddies rather than as lawmen and prisoners.

"What happened to your partner—Bob Wallace?" I asked finally.

"Bob caught a freight train for Price when we were camped at Green River," Rhodes said. "He wanted to get a job in the coal mines."

"Where does he live?" I asked.

"I don't know," Rhodes answered. "He didn't talk much about himself. Could you make me a cigarette?"

"He wrote once in a while to a girl in Paola, Kansas," Bob Smith volunteered as I rolled Ed Rhodes a cigarette. "He said that she was his sister."

"Did he ever tell you her name?"

"Boyle—Maggie Boyle, I think."

"Then, his name was Boyle, not Wallace?"

"I don't know," Smith said. "We always knowed him as Bob Wallace. Maybe this Maggie Boyle ain't his sister, like he claimed, but his girl friend."

"Could be," I said, "but, whatever she is, she might be able to help us out. I think I'll look her up."

In Gunnison the three prisoners were given a preliminary examination before the U. S. commissioner. Then, I took them to Denver where they were placed in jail pending their trial before a federal court.

After delivering the prisoners, I caught a train for Paola, Kansas. Upon arriving I handed the postmaster a letter to identify myself. It was written by the post office inspector in Denver and read:

> To the Post Masters Serving in the U.S.
> By Authority of the Post Master General
> Sir:
>
> This will introduce you to C. W. Shores, an officer of the United States Government, a man of character and ability, who may need the aid and information which is in your possession regarding work he has in hand or in view. I

> would be very much gratified to have you aid him in every conceivable way possible in the duties of his office.
>
> Very truly yours,
> W. W. Patterson
> Inspector in Charge.[34]

After reading the letter the postmaster peered curiously up at me as if I were some sort of a celebrity.

"I'm glad to know you, Mr. Shores. My name is Sheritan."

After shaking hands and visiting for a while I asked him if he knew of a lady in this part of the country by the name of Maggie Boyle.

He shook his head. "Can't place the name, but maybe my assistant would know her. She's lived here longer than I have."

He called the lady assistant over and introduced her to me. "The officer here wants to know if there is anyone in the community by the name of Maggie Boyle."

"I don't know a Maggie Boyle, but there's a Lizzie Boyle who teaches school out in the Baker district about two or three miles from here. I can find out more about her if you want me to. Has she done something wrong?"

"No, I just want to get some information from her. I would appreciate it if you would find out more about her. But don't tell anyone about me. If I'm going to succeed, my identity and mission must be kept secret."

A day or so later the assistant postmistress told me that Lizzie Boyle's parents lived on a farm about twenty-five miles south of Paola. She also said that Lizzie usually went down there on Saturday mornings to spend the weekends.

The Boyle ranch was some distance away from the railroad, and it was a complicated process to get there.

"You'll have to change trains at Garnet," the postmistress said. "Then, there will be a several hours wait before the next train comes along. You get off this train at a sidetrack about three or four miles from the Boyle place. You'll have to walk the rest of the way."

I stayed at the Paola Hotel until Saturday morning. I wanted Lizzie to visit her parents and impart the latest information about her brother before I made my appearance. It was the middle of January, and the weather was very cold. The hotel was inadequately heated, and my wait-over proved to be most uncomfortable.

When Saturday morning finally dragged around, I checked out of the hotel and went down to the station. When the train pulled in, a young lady climbed aboard ahead of me. Thinking it might be Lizzie Boyle I took a seat directly behind her, hoping that I might overhear her talking to someone. However, she spoke to no one. After travelling fifteen or twenty miles she got off at some station, where she was met by a middle-aged man in a buckboard wagon. I concluded then that she was not Lizzie Boyle.

I continued on to Garnet, where I waited for several hours in a hotel lobby until it was time for the next train to arrive. I got off this train at the designated sidetrack and proceeded to the nearest farm house, which was occupied by a preacher who the Paola postmistress said would give me lodging.

I told the preacher that I was working for a livestock commission firm at Kansas City and was contacting cattle feeders in the area to ascertain how many fed steers and heifers would be shipped to market. I said that my firm intended to send out weekly postal card quotations to the men I contacted in order to get some of their business.[35]

The preacher gave me the names of his neighbors who were feeding cattle, including the Boyle family. He told me where the Boyles lived and commented that they had come to the area just a few years before from Pawnee Rock, Nebraska.

"Are they pretty good neighbors?" I asked casually.

"Yes. They are well liked around here and seem to be very nice people. One of their daughters teaches in a country school near Paola, and one of their sons is a doctor at Lewisburg. They usually come down and visit their parents on the weekends."

"Are there any other children?"

"There's a boy and girl still in school and an older son out west. I don't know much about him, but I understand he is the black sheep of the family."

"What's his name?"

"Bob, I believe."

From this discussion I was sure that Bob Wallace's real name was Bob Boyle. I changed the subject, believing that it might arouse the preacher's suspicions if I appeared to be too interested in the Boyle family.

The next morning I walked through a snowstorm to the Boyle residence—three or four miles from the minister's house. I knocked on the door, and it was answered by the attractive young woman I had seen on the train.

"Hello," I greeted, removing my white sombrero, "I knew your brother Bob when he was working at Carbondale, Colorado, and he told me to look you folks up if I ever came through here."

"Come in," she said pleasantly. Then she turned and called out, "Mother, here is a man who knows Bob."

A small, kindly looking woman came hurrying into the living room. "So, you are a friend of Robert," she said, grasping my hand. "Sit down and make yourself at home. I am Robert's mother."

"Bob has spoken of you often," I said, disliking my role as an imposter. "My name is Wells, and I'm connected with the Producers Commission Company at the Kansas City Stockyards. I met Bob in Carbondale a few months ago while I was drumming up some business over there for my firm."

"Robert is not in Carbondale now," Mrs. Boyle said. "He's in Utah."[36]

"I thought perhaps he might have left, since I wrote him a letter from Kansas City some time ago, and it came back uncalled for."

"How did you and Bob happen to become such good friends?" Lizzie asked.

"Well," I lied, "we were both interested in mining. We planned on getting together and doing a little prospecting together next spring. Bob is a good assayer, and I'm familiar with the Colorado mining country."[37]

As we visited, other members of the family came drifting into the room to see me. They were Mr. Boyle, the doctor, and a younger son about fourteen.

After introducing me to the three newcomers, Mrs. Boyle said, "Which one of them do you think looks the most like Robert?"

Lizzie glanced at the young boy, which gave me my clue. "This lad here resembles Bob quite a good deal," I ventured cautiously, "but, of course, Bob is a lot older."[38]

"That's right," Mrs. Boyle said. "There's fifteen years difference in their ages."

"Mr. Wells hasn't seen Belle yet," Lizzie said. "She resembles Bob even more."

She called to Belle who was preparing breakfast. A shy, red-haired girl entered, wearing a mother hubbard dress.

"This is Mr. Wells," Lizzie said. "He knew your brother Bob out in Colorado."

"Yes, she does bear quite a resemblance to Bob—especially that red hair," I said, shaking the girl's hand.

"Won't you have breakfast with us?" Mr. Boyle asked.

"Thanks, but I've already eaten over at the preacher's house where I spent the night."

"Then, if you'll excuse us, we'll go on ahead," Mrs. Boyle said. "We're a little late getting started this morning."

"Here are some recent letters from Bob," Lizzie said, "which you might enjoy while you're waiting for us."

She handed me several letters, and then all of the family except the young boy went into the dining room.

The family album lay on a nearby table; so I walked over and picked it up. I fingered through it hoping to find a picture of the wayward son.

"Are there any pictures of Bob in here?" I asked the boy finally.

"No. He wouldn't ever have any taken."

Responding to his mother's call, the boy disappeared into the dining room. As soon as he was gone, I proceeded to read the letters which Lizzie had given me. The gist of them was that Bob said he had been herding horses for some outfit near Carbondale, Colorado, until he got into a fight with the foreman. As a result of this altercation, he lost his job and had come to Price, Utah, where he procured a job working on a big irrigation canal for a contractor named Mulholland. While his excuse for leaving Colorado was undoubtedly fabricated, the account of his present whereabouts and job was probably correct. I jotted down in my notebook the name of the contractor in Price whom he was working for.[39]

I had finished reading the messages by the time the family completed breakfast and returned to the parlor. Although I had obtained all the information that I could get from them, I remained a while longer to carry out my assumed role as a livestock commission agent.

While we were discussing the cattle market, the boy came running in. As he was doing his chores, he had found a mare lying down sick in the stable. Mr. Boyle, the doctor, and I put on our coats and accompanied the youth to the corral. On our way the doctor stepped back beside me to ask, "Didn't Bob have a little trouble of some kind over in Carbondale?"

"You mean with his foreman?" I asked, recalling the letter.

"No, something a lot worse. Reading between the lines of Bob's occasional letters, I have a hunch he got into some kind of a jam. It wouldn't be the first time."

How right the doctor was, I thought, but I couldn't very well tell him about the train robbery; so I lied, "Well, it is true that he was indicted for running some kind of a gambling joint, but it didn't amount to much and will probably soon blow over. I don't think it's important enough to worry your mother and father about."

"All right, I won't say anything about it to them. Bob has a wild streak in him which has caused them enough trouble."

After treating the mare and getting her on her feet, we returned to the house. I told the doctor that I had better be on my way to interrogate some of the other cattle feeders.

"Mr. Wells is leaving," he called to the women, who were working in the kitchen.

"Wait a moment," Mrs. Boyle said as she and her two daughters appeared. "Let's all line up here against the wall so that Mr. Wells can tell Robert just how we looked when he sees him next spring to go prospecting."

The family then proceeded to take their places according to age—Mr. Boyle first, then Mrs. Boyle, followed by the doctor, Lizzie, Belle, and finally the boy. I glanced up and down the tapering line as if to imprint a lasting picture of them on my mind, suddenly wishing that I was in some other kind of a profession. To deceive such a friendly and fine family went against my grain. However, I played out my unwanted role to the bitter end.

"I'll tell Bob exactly how you all look," I said. I thought of walking down the line and shaking hands with each one in turn as I bid them goodby, but I lacked the gall to play my part quite that far.[40]

"Whenever you write to Bob, tell him I called," I said in parting.

"Liz and I will write him today," Mrs. Boyle said. "Goodby."

It was still snowing hard as I made my way toward the sidetrack to catch the train. When I got out of sight of the Boyle house, I stopped under a sheltering tree and wrote down in my notebook some pertinent facts that I had just learned about Bob Boyle, alias Bob Wallace. Then, I continued on to the sidetrack where I caught a train going north into Osowattomie. From here I made the fastest connections I could to Price, Utah, going by way of Kansas City, Denver, Gunnison, and Grand Junction. In Denver I stopped off long enough to see Mr. Kramer and read to him the memorandum from my notebook concerning the latest dope on Bob Wallace. He rolled his big brown eyes around as he listened and acted as if he thought my whole account was a fairy tale.

Between trains in Gunnison I went home to see my family for a moment and make a change in my wearing apparel. I left Gunnison wearing a white, broad-brimmed sombrero and an old canvas, blanket-lined overcoat. This coat had a long pocket on the right side in which was sewn a leather scabbard, where I could carry my .45 caliber six-shooter without its being seen.[41]

Among the several people who boarded the train with me was an old prospector by the name of Brown. He carried a roll of blankets and was on his way to Salt Lake City to do some prospecting. He was a well-known, respected citizen of the Gunnison area, and I had put him on a number of juries. In returning from a trip in the mountains he often brought me a mess of trout, and I reciprocated by giving him a good many drinks of whiskey.

During the course of the journey I confided in this old, trusted friend about the purpose of my trip. I told him that I was going to Price, Utah, to apprehend the fourth train robber, who had not as yet been caught.

"I don't have a warrant or extradition papers," I explained, "so

I'm going to have to kidnap this outlaw, in a way, in order to bring him back into Colorado. I may need a substantial citizen like you as an eye witness in case I get in a jam. So, why don't you get off at Price with me?"

"I'd be glad to help you out, Doc," Brown said. "You can count on me."

When the train was pulling into Price, I said, "Take your roll of blankets and go into the waiting room. Stay there until I call for you. If anyone gets curious, tell him that you want to get a mule train out of there to Duschene, Utah, but don't say anything more."[42]

After leaving Brown I looked up Mr. Mulholland—the contractor who Robert Boyle wrote that he was working for.

After introducing myself, I said, "Do you happen to have a young man working for you who calls himself Bob Wallace?"

"Why, yes," Mulholland answered. "He started working for me just a week or so ago."

"His real name is Bob Boyle, and he's wanted for helping to hold up a train near Grand Junction, Colorado, last November."

"I'll be damned," the contractor exclaimed. "He seemed like a nice fellow. He's a good worker too."

Our conversation was interrupted by a tall, clean-cut man who entered the office. He exchanged a few words with Mulholland concerning a ditch they were constructing and then departed.

After he had gone, the contractor turned to me and said, "That man is Conroy. He works a lot with Wallace—I mean Boyle—on the drill."

"What sort of a fellow is he?"

"I can vouch for Conroy. He's worked with my firm for a long time."

"Then, could I talk with him for a minute?"

Mulholland stepped to the door and called Conroy back.

"This is Sheriff Shores of Gunnison, Colorado," he said. "He wants to ask you some questions about Bob Wallace."

"What's Bob done? Robbed a bank?" Conroy asked jokingly.

"You're not far from the truth," I said. "He's going under an assumed name, and he took part in robbing a train over in western Colorado last November 3rd."[43]

Conroy's handsome face grew serious. "You're mistaken, Sheriff," he said. "Bob is no crook. You're after the wrong man."

"It could be," I said, "but I'm afraid not. Where is he now?"

"He's workin' on a ditch two or three miles from here."

"Is he alone?"

"No, there are three other men working with him. But you'll know Wallace by his big red mustache. One of his fellow-workers has a red mustache also, but he has a big scar on his face."

"I may not have time to look for scars," I said, "so I would appreciate it if you'd go along with me to identify Wallace."

"No, Bob is a friend of mine, and I don't want to get mixed up in this thing."

"Well, suit yourself. I have a partner over at the station, and we'll go over now and make the arrest if you'll tell me how to get there."

After pointing out where the outlaw was working, he said, "You'd better be prepared for trouble. Bob usually carries a six-shooter."

At the station I gave Brown the small pistol and holster that I was wearing at my belt. Then I opened my suitcase and procured a Colt six-gun which I placed in the scabbard of my overcoat pocket.

After checking Brown's roll of blankets and my valise with the baggage clerk, we started out on foot toward the canyon where Conroy said that Bob Wallace was working. We walked uphill over very rough ground for a couple of miles until we came to a divide. As we started down the other side into the canyon, someone called to us from behind. Looking around we saw Mr. Mulholland approaching.

"I decided to go along with you," he panted.

"I'm glad you did," I said. "It is the proper thing for you to do."[44]

The three of us continued on until in the distance we could see four men working. They were teamed off in pairs, one man holding a drill while his partner was striking it with a sledge hammer.

"This is as far as I'm going," Mulholland said when we got about a hundred yards from the workers. "Bob Wallace is the man farthest away striking the drill."

The contractor, fearing gunplay, walked back up the hill out of shooting range, where he stopped to watch the proceedings.

The four men paid no attention to Brown and me as we walked

up, apparently believing that we were merely a couple of fellows looking for a job. We passed by the first team of drillers, and as we neared the next two, I put a hand in my overcoat pocket and grasped the cold wooden handle of my long six-shooter.

Both men were red headed and had red mustaches, but the larger man, who was holding the drill, had a scar on his face. He was carrying a revolver, but the small, wiry man swinging the sledge hammer with strong accurate strokes was unarmed. The man using the hammer was Bob Boyle alias Bob Wallace, the train robber.

Neither Boyle nor his partner paused in their work to glance at us as we approached. When I was about even with the big man holding the drill, I jerked out my gun and leveled it at Boyle.

"Drop that hammer and put up your hands, Boyle!" I ordered.

The startled outlaw complied instantly, but his companion made a motion toward the revolver he was carrying. I covered him immediately, causing his wandering hand to pause in mid-air.

"Get his gun," I said to Brown. As the old prospector pulled it out of the scabbard, the other two drillers hurried over.

"What's the matter?" one of them asked.

"I'm arresting this man for train robbery," I answered, holding my gun in readiness. "Don't come any closer."

While I held the four men at bay, I reached in my pocket with my left hand for a pair of handcuffs.

"Put these on Boyle," I said, handing them to my assistant. As Brown fastened them on, I noticed that Boyle was wearing a lady's wrist watch.

"This looks like one of the articles taken at the time of the robbery," I commented, unfastening the watch and putting it in my pocket.

"That's my watch," one of Boyle's companions said belligerently, trying to cover for him. "I loaned it to Bob."

Boyle took the arrest more complacently than did his fellow workers.

"I know whose watch it is and where he got it," I said.[45]

"Have you got a warrant for this man?" another one of the men asked.

Ignoring the question, I turned to Boyle. "We might as well start back up the trail to Price. You take the lead."

When we reached Price, I bought Brown a pint of whiskey and gave him ten dollars for helping me make the arrest. Before leaving me to catch his train, he said, "As soon as I get to Salt Lake City, Doc, I'm going to the *Salt Lake Tribune* and tell them how you arrested a train robber at Price."

"Don't forget to tell them the part you played in it," I said.[46]

The train going east to Grand Junction and Denver was not scheduled to arrive until about midnight; so my prisoner and I had a lot of time to kill. I hunted up the constable and told him that I was a deputy U. S. marshal from Colorado and that I had arrested my prisoner for robbing a mail train. I bought the officer a drink and some cigars in order to get on good terms with him since, after all, I didn't have a warrant or extradition papers, and he could have made trouble for me if he had wanted to check into the matter.

Boyle and I had dinner together in a little Chinese restaurant. I removed his handcuffs so that he could eat. He ate hurriedly and finished before I did.

Wiping his mouth, he said casually, "I believe I'll go over and stand by the stove over there until you finish. I'm cold."

"I don't think you'd better do that," I objected. "You might try to get away, and then I would have to kill you."[47]

When I completed my dinner, I again handcuffed the prisoner and we left the restaurant.

"Do you have some things that you want to take with you?" I asked. "You probably won't be comin' back here for a long time."

"I've got a trunkload of stuff over at the section house where I room."

We walked over to the section house and he packed his belongings. We then carried his trunk down to the baggage department and checked it through to Gunnison.

Boyle and I spent the remainder of the afternoon and evening at the depot waiting for our train. My handcuffed prisoner and I created a good deal of attention and comment as we sat there on a deserted bench.

Several men attempted to engage one or the other of us in conversation to find out what was going on, but I always made a practice of never visiting with strangers while a prisoner was in my custody.

Several of Boyle's fellow workers came into the depot late that afternoon after work. They tried to visit with him, but my uncommunicative presence discouraged any lengthy conversation.

"Can we give Bob a drink of whiskey?" one of them asked me.

"No," I said.

"Can we give him a bottle?" inquired another.

"I don't care if you give him a barrel," I answered, "but I don't want him to drink now."[48]

Discouraged, Boyle's friends finally left. That night about eight o'clock a company of Negro cavalry came into town to catch a train for the Uintah Indian Reservation in northeastern Utah, where they were escorting the Utes' monthly allotment from the federal government. The soldiers eyed the handcuffed man curiously. A sergeant was in command of the company, and when he walked by, I got up to speak to him.

"I'm glad to see you, sergeant," I explained. "I'm a deputy U. S. marshal, and my prisoner here helped hold up and rob a mail train. I'm taking him back to Gunnison for arraignment, but we've got a long wait before our train arrives, and there are a lot of tough characters around this town who might cause trouble. I may need your help."[49]

I then handed the soldier a few dollars and told him to buy his boys some drinks or cigars.

"Thanks," he said, "our train is late also. We'll stick around and give you a hand in case you need it."

Everything went smoothly until I noticed a man dragging Boyle's trunk out of the baggage room, which we had checked through to Gunnison that afternoon. Taking my prisoner with me, I walked over to the stranger and told him that the trunk belonged to Boyle.

"I have some things in it," he replied angrily.

"What has he got in there?" I asked Boyle.

"Nothing but a razor."

I opened the trunk and told the man to get out his razor. When he had done so, I closed it again and said, "Now drag it back into the baggage room where you found it."

"Like hell I will."

"All right then, I'll have to put you under arrest for stealing another man's property."

Growling to himself, the newcomer pulled the trunk back into the baggage room and departed.

The remainder of the long evening passed without incident, but I breathed a sigh of relief when the train at last arrived and my prisoner and I had boarded it for Gunnison.

When we reached Gunnison, Boyle went before a U. S. commissioner, waived extradition, and, like his three associates, was taken to Denver to stand trial before a federal court. All four were found guilty and sent to the federal penitentiary at Laramie, Wyoming, to serve their sentences. Ed Rhodes and Bob Boyle received five-year terms, and the Smith brothers ten.

After the train robbers were convicted, I was paid the $4000 reward—$3000 from the Denver and Rio Grande Express Company and $1000 from the federal government.[50]

About twenty years later I met Jack Smith on the main street of Grand Junction. In spite of the long lapse of time since our last meeting, we instantly recognized each other. The scar on his face, which he had received in Bangs Canyon, was still noticeable.

"What are you doing around here?" I asked, shaking his hand.

"I'm married now, and my family and I are living at Whitewater." I recalled that Whitewater was only a few miles from where he had held up the train.

"I'm glad to learn that you've settled down, Jack. What happened to your three buddies after they got out of prison?"

"Well, my brother Bob is up in Alaska, and the last I heard from Bob Boyle he's up there also. They're both doing fine and have turned out to be pretty good citizens. After Ed Rhodes served his time, he got a job working in a mine near Boulder, Colorado. One day he got in an argument with another miner by the name of Jim Riches, who shot and killed him. Incidentally, I hear about you now and then. I understand that you are still a lawman."[51]

"In a way. I'm now a special investigator for the Denver and Rio Grande Railroad. My headquarters is in Denver, but I come over to Grand Junction once in a while to see my brother."

"I know your brother," Smith said. "The other day I was in his store and bought a fifty-dollar harrow. He has my note for it."

That night I asked my brother if he had sold a harrow to Jack Smith on credit.

"That's right, but who is that fellow, anyway? He said he was a good friend of yours and had done some business with you at one time. So, on that basis I let him sign for the harrow. I was too busy to ask him just what business he had with you." My brother looked at me questioningly.[52]

I hesitated a moment, then replied, "Oh, he and I covered a lot of ground doing some legal work for the Denver and Rio Grande Railroad."

FOOTNOTES

[1]C. W. Shores, "Train Robberies—Express Robberies on Rio Grande Railroad," original manuscript, Denver, Colo., April 19, 1929, p. 1. In possession of Western History Dept. of Denver Public Library.

[2]C. W. Shores, "The First Train Robbery on the Denver and Rio Grande Railroad in 1887," original manuscript, Denver, Colo., Jan. 10, 1928, see page 1 and page 39. In possession of Western History Dept. of Denver Public Library.

[3]*Rocky Mountain News,* Denver, Colo., Nov. 5, 1887, p. 3.

[4]While it was at first thought that six men participated in the hold-up, later events showed that there were only four.

[5]*Rocky Mountain News,* Denver, Colo., Nov. 4, 1887, p. 6.

[6]Shores, "The First Train Robbery, etc.," *op. cit.,* p. 35.

[7]*Rocky Mountain News, op. cit.*

[8]Shores, "The First Train Robbery, etc.," *op. cit.,* p. 36. Also see *Rocky Mountain News, op. cit.*

[9]*Ibid.*

[10]*Rocky Mountain News, op. cit.,* p. 6.

[11]Shores, "The First Train Robbery, etc.," *op. cit.,* p. 35.

[12]*Rocky Mountain News, op. cit.*

[13]C. W. Shores, "The First Train Robbery, etc.," *op. cit.,* p. 2.

[14]C. W. Shores, "Following The Trail of Criminals," original manuscript, Denver, Colo., Mar. 25, 1927, p. 4. In possession of Western History Dept. of Denver Public Library.

[15]C. W. Shores, "The First Train Robbery, etc.," *op. cit.,* p. 2.

[16]*Ibid.,* p. 4.

[17]*Ibid.*

[18]*Ibid.,* p. 5.

[19]*Ibid.,* p. 6 (and note to page 6).
[20]*Ibid.,* p. 8.
[21]*Ibid.,* p. 11.
[22]*Ibid.,* p. 13a.
[23]*Ibid.,* p. 13.
[24]*Ibid.,* p. 14.
[25]In his memoirs Doc said that he and Duckworth caught the stage for Telluride. However, there was no railroad in Telluride in 1887, so he apparently meant Dallas, where there was a railroad. It was not until 1890 that Otto Mears started construction of his Rio Grande Southern Railroad which ran from Ridgway to Durango via Telluride.
[26]*Ibid.,* pp. 14-15.
[27]*Ibid.,* p. 20.
[28]*Ibid.,* p. 15.
[29]*Ibid.,* p. 16.
[30]*Ibid.,* p. 20.
[31]*Ibid.,* p. 21.
[32]*Ibid.,* p. 22.
[33]*Ibid.,* p. 23.
[34]*Ibid.,* p. 24.
[35]*Ibid.,* p. 25.
[36]*Ibid.,* p. 26.
[37]*Ibid.,* p. 27.
[38]*Ibid.,* p. 26.
[39]*Ibid.,* pp. 27 and 29.
[40]*Ibid.,* p. 28.
[41]*Ibid.,* p. 29.
[42]*Ibid.,* p. 30.
[43]*Ibid.,* pp. 30-31.
[44]*Ibid.,* p. 31.
[45]*Ibid.,* p. 32.
[46]*Ibid.*
[47]*Ibid.,* p. 33.
[48]*Ibid.,* p. 33.
[49]*Ibid.,* p. 34.
[50]*Ibid.,* p. 39.
[51]*Ibid.,* p. 38.
[52]*Ibid.,* p. 37.

Chapter II

As I look back upon my long life, I am surprised to find how many of my past acquaintances have become blurred by the mists of time. However, there are a few who, for some reason or other, stand out over the years in sharp profile, never to be forgotten. One of these was Jim Clark.

I first met Jim during the winter of 1890[1] when he was city marshal of Telluride, Colorado. I was deputy United States marshal and sheriff of Gunnison County at the time and was on my way to Montrose to investigate a counterfeiting charge against three suspects.

About 1:30 P.M. the narrow gauge train I was on stopped at Cimarron—an eating station midway between Gunnison and Montrose. Since I had already eaten in Gunnison before boarding the train, I remained on the train while most of the other passengers got off to have lunch.

While the train was standing there, two men entered the car I was sitting in. Each was wearing a six-shooter and a belt of cartridges, which were visible under their coats. One of them was a large, efficient-looking, brown-eyed man with a dark mustache. He was followed by a smaller man with a long black beard. They glanced at all of us in the coach and then continued on into the next car. From their looks and actions I judged that they were peace officers looking for some criminal.

After about a thirty-minute wait the train pulled out of Cimarron and went on to Montrose, where I got off. I completed my investigation and returned to Gunnison the next day, arriving there about three or four o'clock in the afternoon.

Upon reaching my office I was told that two men were awaiting my return and wanted me to get in touch with them immediately. They proved to be the lawmen who had walked through the train at Cimarron on the previous day. The big man with the dark mustache introduced himself as Jim Clark, the city marshal of Telluride, while the smaller man, who was acting as Clark's deputy, said that his name was Gillespie. Clark told me that they were on the trail of a horse thief, who had stolen a valuable gelding from a rancher near Telluride. The city marshal knew the identity of the fugitive and described him to me. The thief had recently been working as a cowpuncher for a rancher at Cimarron by the name of McClintock. After quitting his job he had wandered up in the Telluride country and stolen the horse. When last seen he was headed in the direction of Gunnison.

Jim Clark, Telluride's marshal, was sort of a legendary figure, and I had long looked forward to meeting him. I had heard so much about him that although this was our first meeting I felt that I was intimately acquainted with him. Our district attorney, Mr. H. M. Hogg (pronounced "Hoig"), told me that Clark was the greatest fighting man that he had ever met—not only with a gun but with his fists.[2] He was a man who never drank, and he had no use for women. "Old John Barleycorn will beat them every time" was a favorite expression of his when speaking of the fate of men addicted to alcohol.[3]

From Mr. Hogg and other reliable authorities I had learned that Jim Clark was born about forty-nine years previously in Clay County, Missouri. His real name was Jim Cummings, but his father died while Jim was very young and his mother later married a man by the name of Clark.[4]

When seventeen years old Jim Clark started out on his life of crime. He and another boy stole a mule from Jim's stepfather. They ran away from home, riding this mule down to San Antonio, Texas. Here the two boys sold the mule, and with the money thus

Jim Clark—Telluride Marshal from 1887-1895. From a line drawing in *Rocky Mountain News,* August 8, 1895. *Photo courtesy of Library, State Historical Society of Colorado.*

obtained they bought some cowboy clothes, high top boots, and a pair of good six-shooters. They then held up a stockman just outside of the city and robbed him of $1400. Upon returning home Jim's stepfather wouldn't have anything more to do with him, but his mother welcomed him back and hid the stolen money in a dresser drawer so that his stepfather wouldn't find it.

Around this time William Quantrell came from Ohio to teach school in Jackson County, Missouri, where the Clark family then lived. Quantrell boarded a good deal with Jim's mother and stepfather while he was a teacher. As a result, Jim became intimately acquainted with him.

During the school year of 1855, Quantrell received a letter from his brother asking him to accompany him to California. William accepted, and while on their way the brothers were attacked by a company of General Jim Lane's Jayhawkers. At that time there were a lot of border skirmishes between the people of Kansas, which was a free state, and the people of Missouri, which was a slave state. The Kansans or Jayhawkers made frequent raids into Missouri to steal slaves and set them free, and the Missourians or Border Ruffians —as they were called—retaliated by raiding back. The Quantrell brothers were innocent victims of this feuding.

William Quantrell's brother was killed by Lane's Jayhawkers, and William was badly wounded and left for dead by the Kansans. He never got over this injustice and became a fanatic in his desire for revenge against General Lane's men and the people of Kansas.

After being rescued by an old Indian and nursed back to health, William Quantrell returned to Jackson County and completed his year of teaching. Then, he went to Leavenworth, Kansas, and enlisted in Lane's Jayhawkers. He became a first-class soldier, and in 1858—three years before the Civil War—was promoted to a first lieutenant.

During his enlistment with Lane's regiment both as an enlisted man and an officer, he methodically proceeded to bushwhack sentries and other fellow soldiers whenever the opportunity offered. In this undercover manner Quantrell killed nearly every man who had anything to do with the ill-advised attack upon him and his brother before he was suspected of being the mysterious traitor. Before charges could be brought against him he deserted the Jayhawkers and went south into Missouri, where he fought openly against the Kansans. He organized a band of guerillas of about 350 men and continued his fanatical struggle all through the Civil War.[5]

Jim Clark was one of the first to enlist in Quantrell's notorious guerillas on the side of the Confederacy. He was twenty years old at the time—big, strong, and fearless. He became one of Quantrell's most trusted officers and was in the thick of the fighting. He learned the use of a gun and practiced continuously, becoming noted as a dead shot. Among his associates were other young men destined to become well-known outlaws and gunmen. These included the James brothers and the Youngers.

Many were the stories told about Jim Clark's feats during the war. On one occasion he was riding along a side road in southwestern Missouri when he unexpectedly came upon four northern cavalymen, who were out looking for members of Quantrell's guerilla band. Clark, who was always armed like an arsenal, placed his bridle reins between his teeth, and grabbing both revolvers he charged the surprised Yankees at top speed, shooting like a madman. When the smoke cleared, four dead federal cavalrymen were lying outstretched on the ground.[6]

Such experiences were commonplace to Jim Clark and so hardened him that to his last day he was not affected at all by the violent taking of human life.

Although William Quantrell himself died in battle during the Civil War, many of his followers, including Jim Clark, Jesse James, and the Youngers, kept on robbing banks and holding up stages and trains even after the war was over.[7]

When the outlaw gang finally dispersed, Clark drifted into Leadville, which was a booming silver mining camp. He got a job as a miner, always doing heavy physical work, which kept him in top condition. Once the world's champion heavyweight prize fighter visited Leadville. He offered one hundred dollars to any man who could box with him in an exhibition ring and stay on his feet for five minutes. Clark, who was as big as the champion and just as tough, accepted the challenge. Not being as skilled a boxer, Jim took a beating, but he managed to slug it out with the world's champion for five minutes without once being knocked down.[8] So Jim won the money, but as he once told me, it was the hardest hundred bucks that he ever earned.

Leadville was a lively mining camp during the late 70's and early 80's, and the stage coaches were coming into town each day loaded down with passengers. Holdups were common occurrences, and it is likely that Jim Clark participated in some of them.

One time a bandit by the name of Luke Short borrowed Clark's double-barreled shotgun. Accompanied by another man, he went down below town to the head of California Gulch, where the two highwaymen held up an incoming stage and robbed the passengers. When Luke Short returned the shotgun the next night, Clark was not in his cabin. So, Short left the gun standing in a corner with a roll of bills sticking out of the muzzle. Wrapped around the bills was a note which said, "This will buy some cartridges for your gun."[9]

Clark came to Telluride in 1887.[10] He got a job helping to dig a pipe line into town. This was a strenuous job because the only way of digging a pipe line in those days was with a pick and shovel.

Telluride was wide open and full of badmen who had the authorities buffaloed. They would often get drunk and shoot up the town, but the city marshal, who was afraid of them, did not interfere.

Clark soon sized up the situation, and one day when a bunch of gunmen were terrorizing the town, he walked into the mayor's office and said, "If you give me a special appointment as deputy city marshal, I'll go out and arrest them fellers for you. It's about time that we had a little peace and quiet in this man's town."

"They're pretty tough," the mayor answered, "but you look big enough to give them a run for their money. Go ahead and see what you can do. I'll stand back of you."

By evening the jail was full of bewildered prisoners, and for the first time in its comparatively short history the town was strangely quiet. Telluride had taken on the aspects of a peaceful, law-abiding community.

Although quick as lightning on the draw and probably the best shot in Colorado, Clark did not find it necessary to use his guns that day. When any boisterous gunman started to draw on Clark, he knocked him down with his fists and took his gun away from him.

The mayor and the city council were so impressed by Clark's efficient work that they immediately made him city marshal, which job he still held when I first met him.[11]

I had been told that while Clark rigorously kept the peace in Telluride and wouldn't stand for any disorderliness whatsoever, he continued his life of lawlessness outside of the city limits by disguising himself and participating in various holdups. It was also rumored that he often tipped off his outlaw cohorts when big gold or silver shipments were going out on the stage from Telluride to the nearest railhead at Dallas, three miles below present Ridgway,[12] and Clark would receive his cuts from the holdups.[13]

After hearing so much about this legendary Telluride marshall, I had wanted to meet him for a long time and find out what the real Jim Clark was like. This was my opportunity.

Clark and I spent most of the night combing the town of Gunnison for the horse thief he was after. During the course of the hunt, Clark said, "It's a real privilege to work with you, Doc. Ever since you captured those Grand Junction train robbers, I've wanted to meet you. I've heard a lot about your ability to track down outlaws."

"Maybe that comes from knowin' 'em so well," I said with a laugh. "In my younger years I was pretty wild and used to run around with the Wild Bunch some."

The "Wild Bunch" I referred to was what in those years they commonly called Butch Cassidy and his gang who operated primarily in southern Wyoming and Utah. I made this false remark in order to make Clark think that he and I were of the same breed of cat—part lawman and part outlaw. In this way I hoped to win his confidence and get him to talking about his extra-curricular activities. I wanted to find out sooner or later if all the rumors that I had heard about Jim Clark's criminal career were true.

The next morning after breakfast Clark came to my office to continue the manhunt. While we were visiting preparatory to taking off, someone from West Gunnison sent word to me that he had just seen a man who answered the horse thief's description.

My horse was already saddled and tied to a hitching post outside my quarters, which consisted of an office and apartment over the jail.

Main Street of Gunnison as it looked when Doc Shores was sheriff of Gunnison County. *Photo courtesy of Library, State Historical Society of Colorado.*

I rode over to West Town a half-mile away at a full gallop, where I looked up the informer.

"He went into that little outhouse over there in the alley," the man said. "I ain't seen him come out yet."

I rode over to the outhouse and dismounted. I knocked on the door and ordered, "Open up!"

When there was no response, I said, "Open the door or I'll kick it in."

"You'd better not try it," a deep voice answered threateningly. "What's the big idea, anyway?"

"I'm Sheriff Shores, and I'm arresting you for stealing a horse over in the Telluride country. Now, come on out."

"Go to hell! I'll come out when I'm good and ready."

I drew my six-shooter and kicked open the door. The man inside threw up his hands to show me that he had no gun. Once more I ordered him to come out, and again he refused.

I grabbed him by the collar of his coat with my left hand and pulled him out, keeping my revolver pointed at him all the time. Clark came running up as I was dragging my reluctant prisoner out into the open.[14]

"I've got to hand it to you, Doc," Clark said. "This is one horse thief that you really caught with his pants down."

On our way to the jail I asked the prisoner what he had done with the stolen horse, and he said that he had sold it a couple of days ago to a rancher near Gunnison.

I wrote a note to this rancher telling him that the horse was stolen and to turn it over to the bearer of the note, who was Gillespie, Clark's deputy. Gillespie intended to ride the animal back to Telluride—a distance of about 120 miles, where he would return it to its rightful owner.

Before locking up the horse thief, I went through his pockets and took everything away from him. I was surprised to find that he had no gun, but he informed me that he pawned it off the day before to get some spending money. Apparently during the several days he had been in Gunnison, he drank and gambled away all of the cash he had received for the stolen horse.

The most interesting item that I found on the horse thief was a number of love letters from a woman by the name of Mrs. McClintock. The prisoner had apparently been carrying on quite an affair with this woman during the several weeks he had lived with the couple, working for her husband on a cattle ranch near Cimarron. She mentioned in several of the letters that her husband and a few of the neighbors had been rustling cattle and killing them for beef.

I showed some of these incriminating letters to Jim Clark, who had intended to catch the train that evening and return home with the prisoner.

After Clark had finished reading them, I said, "Why don't you leave your man here for a couple of days and go down with me to Cimarron to check on the cattle rustling which this Mrs. McClintock refers to."

"I'd be glad to, Doc," he said. "You helped me out, and maybe now I can return the favor. By the way, I want to show you something."

He unbottoned his shirt and pulled out a roll of bills from a secret pocket sewed in the waist of his underwear.

"This was my cut out of the Telluride bank robbery," he said confidentially, removing a hundred dollar bill and replacing the roll. "Let's get this bill changed, and I'll buy you a box of cigars."[15]

I was pleased to have him take me into his confidence, but his statement that he was an accomplice of the Telluride bank robbers sort of took me by surprise. While it was generally believed that he was involved in stage holdups outside of Telluride, he was given credit for keeping out of all types of lawlessness within the city limits.

I was familiar with the bank robbery that he referred to. It had occurred the previous summer on June 24, 1889. About noon on that day three horsemen, generally believed to be Tom McCarty, Butch Cassidy, and Matt Warner, rode up in front of the San Miguel Bank. One of the outlaws remained mounted and held his companions' horses, while the other two entered the bank and held up C. L. Hyde, the assistant cashier. Grabbing all of the money in sight and ransacking the safe, they backed out, jumped on the waiting horses and galloped west on Main Street, shooting their six-shooters into the air.[16]

"Well, Jim," I said, "I sure didn't suspect that you had anything to do with that holdup. How did you happen to get involved?"

"The fellers who held up the bank were friends of mine. They told me their plans and said that if I made a point of being out of town at the time of the robbery they would give me a fair share of the take. They agreed to hide it under a big log along the trail on which they planned to make their getaway. They were true to their word and left me this roll of bills amounting to about $2200."[17]

Clark and I walked over to Sam Gill's bank where the hundred dollar bill was changed. Then Clark went into a cigar store and bought a large box of cigars which he handed to me. "This is just a little half-baked way of thankin' you for findin' the horse thief," he said.

While it was against my usual practice to accept gifts for merely doing my duty, I didn't want to risk offending this celebrated character whom I was anxious to get acquainted with; so I thanked him for his generosity and put the box on my office desk.

Later that morning we caught the train for Cimarron to investigate the cattle stealing which we had learned about in the horse thief's love letters. When we arrived about 1:30 P.M., we made inquiry about one of the accomplices that Mrs. McClintock had accused of participating in the thefts. We were told that this man lived twelve miles from town up Cimarron Creek. So, Clark and I borrowed a couple of saddle horses and rode up to this fellow's ranch. We found him working on an irrigation ditch. His horse was tied nearby.

As Clark and I approached, I pulled out an old writ of some kind from my coat pocket and said, "I'm Doc Shores, deputy U. S. marshal, and I have a warrant here for your arrest for cattle rustling."

I didn't have a warrant, but my bluff worked, and he got on his horse and accompanied Clark and me back to Cimarron, where we all caught the return train for Gunnison. While en route Clark went into the men's lounge to smoke a cigar, giving me an opportunity to talk with the prisoner privately.

"You're a pretty young fellow to be getting mixed up with a bunch of cattle rustlers," I said, soft-soaping him a little to get a confession. "You are in serious trouble, and I have the goods on you in some letters written by Mrs. McClintock. But because of your youth and since you have undoubtedly been led astray by your older associates, I'll give you a break and do the best I can for you if you will make a written confession and turn state's evidence against the others."

He agreed to do so, and as soon as we arrived in Gunnison, we obtained a lawyer who typed up a complete confession telling all about the rustling and who had participated in it. The prisoner signed this statement in front of witnesses, and we turned him loose saying that we would be calling on him later to testify in court.[18] I paid his fare back to Cimarron.

These cattle rustlers were brought to trial and convicted on the basis of this young man's written confession and testimony. True to my promise, I helped him get a suspended sentence for turning state's evidence. Before concluding this case, however, one interesting incident occurred which gave me further insight into Jim Clark's character.

In one of her letters Mrs. McClintock said that when butchering the stolen beeves, her husband made a practice of cutting the revealing brands out of the hides and using the skins for rawhide, which at that time was utilized for many purposes without being tanned.

When asked about this matter, our horse thief claimed that he had seen McClintock bury a bunch of these removed brands under a flat rock beneath a cedar tree some four or five hundred yards from his house. He said that if we took him there he would show us where these brands were hidden.

I didn't believe this story but Clark had more confidence in the prisoner's statement and wanted to give him a chance. I voiced my opinion that he was lying and only wanted to get in some isolated spot where he could make a run for it. "Besides," I said, "we've got enough evidence to convict McClintock and the others with their accomplice's signed confession."

"I know," Clark said, "but this extra evidence of buried brands might come in handy. I think this guy is tellin' the truth, but if he's double-crossin' us, I'll kill him."

Being familiar with Jim Clark's background, I realized that he was not bluffing. I sort of felt sorry for the horse thief who apparently did not know as yet the kind of law officer he was dealing with.

We took the horse thief to Cimarron and, putting handcuffs on him, told him to ride on ahead and take us to where the brands were buried. He led us up a long slope on the cedar-covered hillside. When about a quarter of a mile from McClintock's house he got off his horse and looked under a few flat rocks as if searching for the brands. However, they weren't there, and he mounted and rode on again.

It was obvious to me that he was merely putting on a show and waiting for an opportunity to make a sudden break and get away. He was handicapped by the handcuffs, which he hadn't counted on, and he had seen enough of Clark by this time to know that the Telluride marshal would shoot him down in cold blood if he tried to escape.[19]

Several times he dismounted and peered under various flat rocks, which abounded in the region, in pitiful attempts to prolong the deception, but he knew he had got himself into a jam and that his time was fast running out.

After spending several hours leading us around through the cedars, he finally said, "I can't seem to remember just where McClintock buried those brands. This damned country all looks so much alike."

"You're a liar," Clark said, dismounting and walking over to the frightened thief. "You never saw McClintock or anybody else bury any brands out here. I think I'll plug you for making such a fool out of me and wasting so much of my time."

Clark's face was drawn by a tense, controlled ferocity which left no doubt that he meant what he said. I hoped the time would never come that I would have to cross swords with such a merciless opponent.

The outlaw started to cry. "Please don't shoot me," he pleaded. "I admit that I lied about the brands, but I didn't know it would make so damned much difference to you. Don't kill me and I'll turn state's evidence against McClintock and a lot of other cattle rustlers around here."

"A liar's testimony won't do no good," Clark said, drawing his revolver, "but I can assure you of one thing. You've told your last lie."

The rustler stood there paralyzed—a completely broken man. I had no sympathy for him. He was obviously a coward as well as a liar. However, I couldn't just stand there and let a defenseless, handcuffed man be shot down like a dog.

"There's no use in killin' the poor devil," I said to Clark, coming to the rescue. "While he's not worth a damn, he's unarmed and our prisoner, and if you kill him, I'll have to testify that you shot him down without any real justification."

Clark hesitated a moment, and then, without saying a word, put his six-shooter back into its holster. The three of us returned to Cimarron on our borrowed horses. The next day Clark and his prisoner caught the train for Ridgway, where they boarded the stage coach for Telluride.

This was the beginning of a friendship between Jim Clark and me that I came to value very highly. In spite of his serious faults, Clark had many admirable qualities which I learned to appreciate as I got to know him.

During the next few years I often visited Telluride in line of duty as sheriff and deputy U. S. marshal. Each time I was there I looked up Clark, who lived in an old cabin down along a little creek in the willows on the outskirts of town.

Each evening he patrolled the town, and whenever I was there, he insisted upon my accompanying him. He kept strtict order in Telluride, and if there was any noisy demonstration anywhere, he soon put a stop to it.

One evening as we were walking along the Row, or Red Light District, the madam of a sporting house came outside, leading a little dog which trotted along beside her.

"Marshal," she said, walking up to us, "my dog here is getting to be very old, and I would appreciate it if you would take him out of town sometime soon and kill him for me."

Clark immediately jerked out his six-shooter and shot the dog between the shoulders, killing him instantly. The woman screamed, and it looked for a moment as if she was going to faint.

Clark sheathed his gun and walked right along as if nothing had happened. "Damn those women," he said in disgust. "I don't even like to talk to them."[20]

I noticed that he always cut short his conversations with sporting women, and as the above incident indicated, he seemed unduly prejudiced against them. I always suspected that some tough woman had once made trouble for him to cause this deep and undying hatred for prostitutes.

Another night when I was walking with Clark through a large gambling house, a gigantic Austrian, said to be the largest man in Telluride, stepped up to me and demanded that I have a drink with him. I refused, but he kept insisting.

"Leave him alone!" Clark said.

We then continued our tour of the building, and on our way back out the Austrian grabbed me by the arm and started pulling me toward the bar.

Clark stepped up in front of him and said, "I thought I told you to leave this man alone."

The big miner, who towered above us both, let loose of my arm and swung a sledge-hammer blow at the marshal. Clark ducked and reciprocated with a left hook to the man's jaw. The Austrian fell like a slaughtered bull with blood running from his nose and mouth. This took the fight and arrogance all out of him, and Clark and I walked outside without any further interference.[21]

I learned later that the Austrian had once before tangled with Clark, and in spite of his smaller size Clark had beaten up the big man unmercifully. Except when his courage was enhanced by a great deal of liquor, the giant from that time on gave the marshal a wide berth.[22]

On his patrols of the town it was customary for Clark to drop around at the homes of needy elderly people for a few minutes to say hello and see how they were getting along. They appreciated his frequent visits as well as his various contributions to their welfare, such as helping them out with their chores or making repairs on their rickety old shacks.

Telluride as it looked when Jim Clark was the town marshal. *Photo courtesy of Library, State Historical Society of Colorado.*

When money was badly needed by any destitute family in Telluride for food or medical care, Clark often made generous donations, telling the recipients, in order to save their self-respect, that he was lending them the money which they could repay him whenever they struck it rich. Of course, he did not expect to ever get the money back, but it didn't matter to him because such gifts were more often than not proceeds which he had obtained from some robbery or stage coach holdup. He was in certain respects a modern Robin Hood who robbed from the rich and gave to the poor.

Another paradox in Clark's character was his fondness for children, and the youngsters of Telluride readily responded to his warm friendliness for them. They idolized the big colorful city marshal who could lick any man in town. While making his rounds Clark often stopped and visited with his young admirers, who flocked around him in much the same way as a group of present-day youngsters would gather around some cowboy movie star.

One afternoon when I was with him, he saw a small boy struggling up a steep hill toward his mother's cabin, carrying two big camp kettles full of water.

Clark hastened over to the boy and said, "Can I give you a hand?"

Pleased at this attention from so illustrious a celebrity, the boy handed Clark one of the kettles, and together they walked up the hill to the dilapidated cabin where the boy's widowed mother took in laundry to support her family.

That was the last kettle of water the boy ever had to carry up the hill, for before the day ended, Clark bought an old gentle workhorse for his young friend and fixed an empty whiskey barrel in such a way that the horse could be hitched to it. The bung hole of the barrel could be opened and filled with water down at the creek and then pulled by the horse up to the washerwoman's shack. Clark kept the old horse provided with plenty of hay and grain.[23]

This unexpected quality of kindliness in the man's makeup was further seen one day when we were riding down the San Miguel River to look at some placer mining claims. Whenever Clark rode out in the hills, it was customary for him to practice shooting with his six-shooter. One of his stunts was to shoot under his horse's

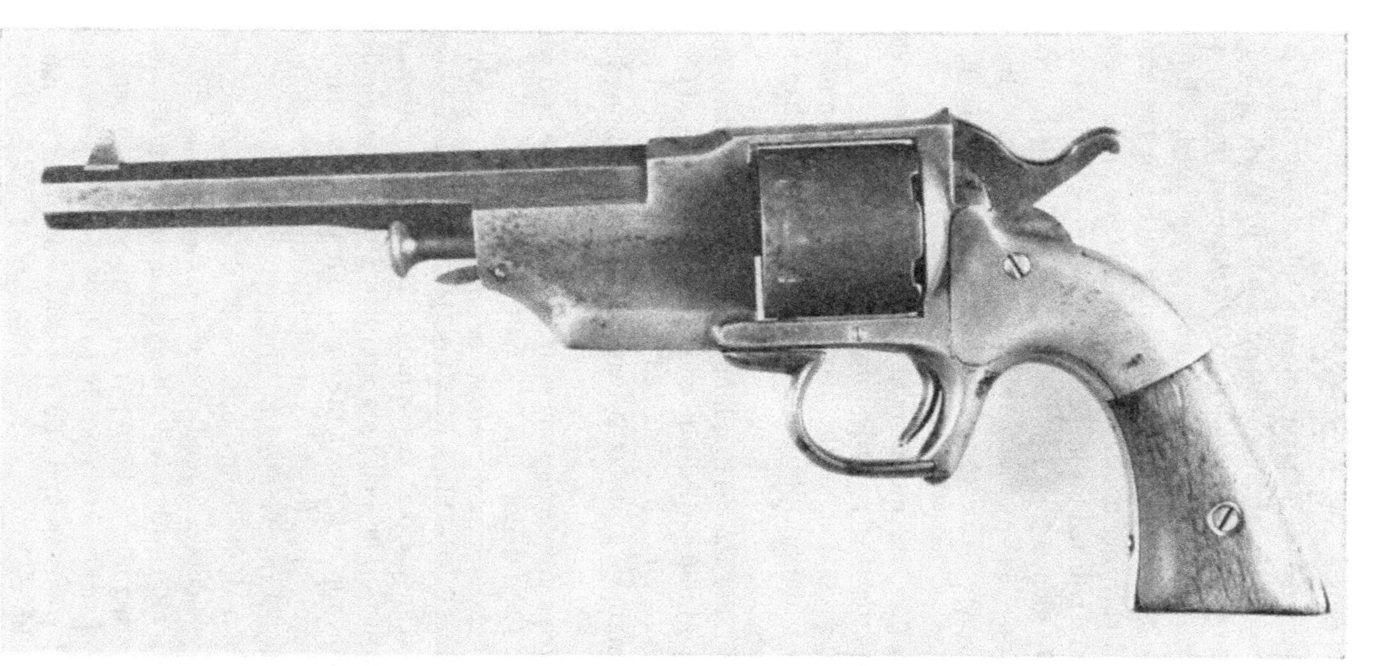

.38 caliber six-shooter used by Jim Clark when he was marshal of Telluride. This gun was found on him when he was shot from ambush on Telluride's Main Street August 7, 1895. Wording on revolver reads:

"Allen and Wheelock (maker), Worcester, Ms., U. S., Allen's Patent Sept. 7, 1858."

Photo Courtesy of Frank Wilson of Telluride and Bob Wright Wilson of Cortez.

neck at chance targets while travelling at a full gallop. On this day he took a fast shot at a robin sitting in a nearby tree.

I don't believe that he intended to hit the bird since it was a difficult shot while his horse was running at top speed. However, he winged the robin which went fluttering away on the ground, making a loud chirping noise. Clark immediately straightened up in the saddle and whirled his horse around to where he had seen the victim fall. He spent a long time looking around for it in order to see if he couldn't do something to fix the injured wing. But the robin was nowhere to be found, and he eventually gave up the search.

"You know, Doc," he commented, "that was a crazy thing to do—shooting such a defenseless little thing as a robin."[24]

He was so depressed about the matter that my mouth must have fallen open in astonishment, thinking of all the men he had killed without a qualm.

One night while I was visiting him, he pried loose a board on the floor of his cabin and pulled out several faro dealing boxes which he intended to repair. He explained that he had two or three associates who ran brace games of faro at some of the gambling houses in Telluride.[25]

"It sort of helps supplement my salary as marshal," he said with a knowing smile, "and so does this."

He then lifted out a gum overcoat or slicker with a belt around it, a cap, and a set of false black whiskers. He put the disguise on for my benefit, and in the dark he would be hard to recognize as the Telluride marshal. The belt held the slicker tight around his big frame and made him look like a thin man. He pulled the cap down low over his eyes, and the false whiskers, which were long and scraggly, concealed the contours of his face.

"What do you think of my business suit?" he laughed. "This is what I wear whenever I hold up some miner coming into town from the stamp mills with a lot of high grade ore to throw away in a saloon or sporting house. I can put the money to much better use. It always sort of tickles me, though, to have these fellers who I've accommodated come around the next day to report to me that they've been robbed."[26]

It might be wondered why I chose to maintain a friendship with a man of such strange contrasts. In spite of certain criminal tendencies which shocked me, I liked and admired him in many ways. He was a man of strong character, great courage, and a fanatical loyalty to his friends. He had a self-made set of standards which he lived up to; so he was not without principle. He was a capable peace officer and probably did more than any other man to bring law and order to Telluride.

In those days there was often just a thin line between a lawman and an outlaw. Wyatt Earp, for example, was a highwayman even while he was marshal of Tombstone. Wild Bill Hickock was a natural killer and often shot men down for minor offenses without giving them a fair draw. Yet these lawmen and their like, of which I knew many, played a major role in the winning of the West. Their good deeds outshone their bad. So it was with Jim Clark.

Clark's friendship proved valuable to me in tracking down a lot of criminals. As a peace officer, I soon learned that if one is going to be successful in his work he must have friends on both sides of the law. Even today more crimes are solved through eye-witnesses and informers than from all the scientific laboratory tests known to man. While Clark was not a stool pigeon, he was acquainted with every outlaw in the region, and through the underworld grapevine usually knew who was involved in most major holdups and robberies in Western Colorado. He gave me many fruitful leads concerning crimes in which he and his friends did not participate.

One time Clark saved my life. In 1894 as special investigator for the Rio Grande Southern Railroad, I arrested a man by the name of Bill Schafer for holding up the railroad station at Mancos in Montezuma County. Strangely enough, Schafer was working for the sheriff of La Plata County, whose headquarters were in Durango, at the time of his arrest. He was popular with the people of southwestern Colorado and northwestern New Mexico, especially with the bad element among whom he was a ringleader.

The trial was held at Cortez, the county seat. Armed outlaws from all over that region rode in to help Schafer out in any way they could. Most of them set up their camps at the head of MacElmo Canyon, located a few miles from town.[27]

Montezuma County was then in such a state of lawlessness that anything could happen at the trial of this well-liked bandit. Grim-faced gunmen attended the trial, armed to the teeth. Since I was the main witness for the state, it was widely rumored that my life wasn't worth a dime.

Jim Clark heard about the danger I was in and came down from Telluride with another man named Marmaduke, who had served with Clark during the Civil War in Quantrell's guerillas. They got off the train at Dolores, which was then the end of the line. Hiring a couple of saddle horses, they rode on into Cortez, arriving there in the middle of the night.

They didn't know where I was staying, but the next morning they located me in the courtroom. Everyone turned to look at these two formidable looking newcomers as they entered. Each had a couple of six-shooters at his belt and a Winchester rifle in his hand. There were many other armed men in the audience, and it meant a lot to me to see at least two who were on my side.

Jim Clark was well-known, and word soon got around that he and his companion had come down to protect me and prevent gun-play. Their presence had a healthy effect on the threatening crowd and dampened the ardor of the gunmen who intended to cause trouble.

Judge Gabbard, who was presiding, told me to have my friends continue bringing their rifles into the courtroom each day to help maintain order. Clark and Marmaduke were on the job during the entire trail. One or both of them also made a point of accompanying me wherever I went, pretending that they had just happened along, although it was obvious that they were acting as my body-guard. Clark had apparently been tipped off through the under-world grapevine that the defendant's outlaw friends were out to get me before I could testify. I appreciated Clark's constant attention, although I felt as if I could take care of myself. It was not until much later that I learned that my friend's vigilance had disrupted an assassination plot against me. If he had not been there, I would probably have been killed. But the plotters were afraid to tangle with the deadly guns of my famous escort.

As it was, nothing happened and I gave my testimony, which was the deciding factor in Bill Schafer being convicted and sentenced to fourteen years at hard labor in the state penitentiary.[28]

Clark and Marmaduke helped me and the Montezuma County sheriff conduct the prisoner to Canon City. It was a good thing since a lot of hostile desperados watched us leave Cortez on horseback with the popular bandit. We expected trouble and were ready to shoot it out with the ruffians if necessary. Some of the prisoner's mounted friends followed us for a ways, but they didn't quite have the nerve to attack us.

Upon reaching Dolores we put our horses in a stable and went over to the hotel to await the train. While we were sitting there in the lobby, a half-drunk cowboy walked in. He took a long look at our prisoner sitting there on a couch with a pair of shackles on his legs. Then he came over to us and said, "Is it necessary to have irons on a man like Bill Schafer?"[29]

Since I was in charge, everyone looked at me. When I didn't say anything, the drunk continued in his belligerent tone of voice, "Well, what have you got to say about it? This man is a friend of mine."

I knew that it wouldn't do any good to argue with the newcomer; so I merely said, "Quit howling, you coyote, or I'll put irons on you too."

That quieted him down for the time being, and he turned abruptly around and stomped out of the hotel in righteous indignation.

Shortly thereafter I was summoned to the telegraph office to answer a wire from Denver. As I stepped out of the hotel, I threw a cartridge into my Winchester. I was glad that I did so since my assailant came out of a saloon on the other side of the street with a six-shooter in his hand. Apparently a few extra drinks had enhanced his courage.

Jim Clark saw what was happening and came running up behind me. "Watch out, Doc," he warned, "that feller is out gunning for you."

Clark raised his six-shooter to shoot the troublemaker, but before he could fire, the sheriff of Montezuma County bolted out of the hotel door, yelling, "Don't shoot! Don't kill him!"

"Why not?" Clark said, hesitating. "He's going to kill Shores."

"Shores can take care of himself."[30]

Clark holstered his gun, and the two of us continued over to the telegraph office while the sheriff returned to the hotel to help Marmaduke guard the prisoner. I wrote my message, and we started back. The drunken cowboy crossed the street and followed us. Clark and I turned around to face my antagonist and backed up to the hotel so that he wouldn't have an opportunity of shooting us in the back.

When we arrived, I said to the sheriff, "Why don't you arrest that man?"

"I can't," the sheriff replied. "He's a deputy of mine."[31]

The train pulled in about this time, and we escorted the prisoner over to the depot. The cantankerous cowboy deputy followed us, hurling insult after insult.

Clark accepted it as long as he could. Then, he quietly removed his coat and said, "If I can't shoot the bastard, I'll knock hell out of him."

Our pugnacious friend was a small man, and I knew that a few blows from a powerful street fighter like Clark would probably be fatal. So, I grabbed Clark by the arm and said, "Let him go. If you kill the son of a gun, we'll have to come back and testify before a coroner's jury and go through a lot of other red tape. As for me, I've had enough of this country for a while. Take it easy, and we'll soon be out of here for good."

Clark's threatening attitude put a stop to the drunk's abusive language, but, to play it safe, we stood on the rear platform of the train as it pulled out of the station, holding our rifles in readiness in case the troublemaker got up enough nerve to take a pot shot at any of us. If he had so much as raised his gun, we would have gladly let him have it. However, he wasn't quite that drunk; and it was with a sigh of relief that I left southwestern Colorado where I had spent so many long months tracking down, arresting and convicting the Mancos station robber.

I will always feel that I would not have got out of that country alive if it hadn't been for Jim Clark.

In his last few years as city marshal, Clark worked on a day shift while another man served as night marshal under him. The night marshal's name was MacDuff,[32] and he proved to be nearly as capable a peace officer as Clark. One reason that Clark had been kept on so long in spite of all the unsavory rumors about his extra-curricular activities as a holdup man and an accomplice of outlaws was because no one tough enough could be found to take his place. Consequently, when the town council finally ran across a man who could do the job, they let Clark go and promoted MacDuff to the position of city marshal.

Clark did not like this maneuver and became quarrelsome with the town council and the peace officers. District Judge Gabbert and County Clerk Charlie Watson, who were both friends of Clark, wrote me that Jim was in serious trouble and asked me to come immediately to Telluride.

When I arrived, they gave me a detailed account of all the difficulties Clark was causing the city authorities. He had assaulted the new night marshal, known as "Sore-eyed Dave," and had threatened the various members of the city council, stating that he was in the market to kill them for fifteen cents apiece or two for a quarter.[33]

"If Jim doesn't leave Telluride soon," Judge Gabbert said, "somebody is going to get hurt. You have more influence on him, Doc, than any man alive; so I suggest that you have a talk with him and persuade him to get out of town."

"I'll have a talk with him," I said, "but I doubt if it will do any good."

That evening I walked down to Clark's cabin. He was home and seemed very glad to see me. I spent the night with him, and we had a long talk about old times. I never mentioned the purpose of my visit until the next morning.

During breakfast I broached the subject. "Jim," I said "I understand that you've been having a little trouble with the city fathers."

"Oh, it don't matter," he answered evasively. "They're no good."

"Jim, you've sort of got the lawmen of Telluride over a barrel. They won't try to arrest you or have it out with you openly because they know you're too much for them. Their only alternative is to shoot you in the back or resign, and we both know they won't resign. If I were in your place, I'd get out of this man's town before I get bushwhacked."[34]

Telluride's Main Street as it looked on August 6, 1895, when Jim Clark was assassinated in front of the Colombo Saloon. *Photo courtesy of Walker Art Studio.*

While I imparted my good advice, he gazed off in the willows. When I finished, he remarked, "Do you think I'm afraid of them?"

"No, Jim, but you should be. Your life is in real danger."

"That no-good bunch ain't gonna run me out of town, Doc, but I would like to get another job as city marshal somewhere. I like the work, and I'm only fifty-four. Would you give me a letter of recommendation?"

"I sure will, Jim. You've got a lot of good working years left in you, and I'd like to see you get a job some place a long way from here."

That was the last time I saw Jim Clark alive. Upon arriving home I composed a letter of recommendation for my friend in which I said that I considered him one of the greatest peace officers that I had ever known.

A day or so after I sent this letter, I received a telegram from Charlie Watson dated August 7, 1895. It read:

> Jim Clark killed last night.
> Come if you can.[35]

When I got off the train at Telluride the next evening, I was met there at the depot by Judge Gabbert and Charlie Watson. They told me what had happened.

About midnight on August 6th, Jim was walking down Main Street toward his cabin with a man known as Mexican Sam. As they passed the Colombo Saloon, a shot rang out in the night. Clark grabbed his chest with both hands, exclaiming, "I'm shot. Go for a doctor."[36]

He then turned halfway around and walked out into the middle of the street, peering at the roofs of the lower buildings in that block as if looking for his assassin. Unable to locate him, he returned to the sidewalk and fell in front of Agee's Barber Shop.

By this time a large crowd had assembled, gathering around the fallen man. A doctor was sent for, and Clark was carried to a cabin. An examination of the wound showed that the bullet, which had come from a large caliber rifle—probably a Winchester—had entered Clark's body six inches above the right breast. It passed downward through one of his lungs and came out beneath his right

Jim Clark's grave in Lone Tree Cemetery at Telluride. Clark, famed Telluride marshal, was shot from ambush on August 6, 1895, while passing the Colombo Saloon on Main Street.

shoulder blade. The injury might not have been fatal if the slug hadn't severed an artery. As it was, Clark bled to death within fifty minutes. Oddly enough, my recent letter of recommendation was found in one of his pockets, covered with blood.

Although Jim had served in the Civil War on the side of the Confederacy, he was shown the same recognition as a Union soldier and buried in the Grand Army Plot of the Telluride Cemetery beside the men he had fought against. A marble slab, set in a concrete base, was erected at the head of his grave. Under his name were engraved the letters C.S.A., meaning "Confederate States of America."[37]

About everyone in town attended the funeral, including not only the shady element and the many children and needy people whom he had befriended, but also the most respected citizens of the community, showing their mutual respect for a man, who in spite of his paradoxical character, had done so much to bring law and order to Telluride.

That night after Clark was buried, I went down to his cabin. Tearing up a plank in the floor, I took out his slicker, cap, and false whiskers and burned them. It was the last favor that I could bestow on a loyal friend who, like most of us, had a lot of good in him as well as a lot of bad.

FOOTNOTES

[1]In his memoirs Doc Shores sets the date of their first meeting as during the winter of 1886-1887. However, in the same manuscript he states that at the time Jim Clark had a wad of bills concealed in a secret pocket of his underwear, which Clark said was his cut from the Telluride bank robbery. Since this robbery occurred on June 24, 1889, their first meeting probably took place during the winter of 1889-1890.

[2]C. W. Shores, "The Story of Jim Clark, a City Marshal Who Stood in with Criminals," original manuscript, Denver, Colo., Jan. 7, 1928, pp. 3-4. In possession of Western History Dept. of Denver Public Library.

[3]*Rocky Mountain News,* Aug. 8, 1895, p. 1.

[4]Shores, *op. cit.,* pp. 19-20.

[5]*Denver Republican,* Mar. 5, 1899.

[6]*Rocky Mountain News, op. cit.*

[7]Shores, *op. cit.*, p. 20.

[8]*Ibid.*, p. 14.

[9]*Ibid.*, p. 20.

[10]*Rocky Mountain News, op. cit.*

[11]Shores, *op. cit.*, pp. 13-14.

[12]It was not until 1890 that Otto Mears started to build the Rio Grande Southern Railroad which ran from Ridgway to Durango via Telluride, Ophir, Rico, Dolores, and Mancos.

[13]Shores, *op. cit.*, p. 5.

[14]*Ibid.*, pp. 6-7.

[15]Shores, *op. cit.*, "The Story of Jim Clark, etc.," pp. 7-8.

[16]C. W. Shores, "Story of the David Moffatt Bank Robbery," original manuscript, Denver, Colo., April 30, 1929, p. 16. In possession of Western History Dept. of Denver Public Library. Also see *Telluride Journal*, Jan. 14, 1938.

[17]*Ibid.*, p. 15.

[18]*Ibid.*, p. 9.

[19]*Ibid.*, p. 12.

[20]*Ibid.*, p. 16.

[21]*Ibid.*, p. 18.

[22]*Ibid.*

[23]*Ibid.*, p. 16.

[24]*Ibid.*, p. 17.

[25]*Ibid.*, p. 15.

[26]*Ibid.*, pp. 18-19.

[27]C. W. Shores, "The Holdup and Robbery of Mancos Station and Rico Station on the Rio Grande Southern Railroad," original manuscript, Denver, Colo., Dec. 29, 1927, pp. 18-19. In possession of Western History Dept. of Denver Public Library.

[28]*Ibid.*, p. 21.

[29]*Ibid.*, p. 22.

[30]*Ibid.*, p. 23.

[31]*Ibid.*

[32]Shores, *op. cit.*, "The Story of Jim Clark, etc.," p. 21. In another manuscript by Shores entitled, "Story of the David Moffat Bank Robbery," *op. cit.*, p. 22, Shores refers to this night marshal as "McIntosh."

[33]Shores, *op. cit.*, "Story of the David Moffat Bank Robbery," p. 23.

[34]Shores, *op. cit.*, "The Story of Jim Clark, etc.," p. 22.

[35]*Ibid.*, p. 24.

[36]*Rocky Mountain News*, Aug. 8, 1895, p. 1.

[37]Shores, *op. cit.*, "The Story of Jim Clark, etc.," p. 25.

Chapter III

After moving to Western Colorado I rarely again crossed paths with any of my old acquaintances that I had been associated with back in those former years when I was a riverman, bullwhacker, and trail driver. Therefore, on February 8, 1884, I read with unusual interest an account about our neighboring town of Montrose being shot up on the previous day by a lame cowboy named Jack Watson. I had known a lame cowboy by that name eleven years before when I was punching cows down on the Saline River near Hays City, Kansas, and my natural presumption was that the wanted man was none other than my old friend.

Jack Watson was a man that one did not easily forget, and although I only saw him twice, I clearly remembered him. I first met him when he rode up to my winter cow-camp on the Saline River in 1874. He was a well-built, muscular fellow with black hair and the pale blue eyes of a natural killer. In spite of a thick, bristling growth of whiskers which covered his face, he was good looking in a rough sort of way. He looked like a man who could take care of himself in any emergency.

He dismounted in front of my camp and walked over to where I was shoeing a horse. I noticed that he walked with a pronounced limp as if one leg was several inches shorter than the other. I learned later that his lameness was caused by a bullet wound through his instep which he had received while serving in the rebel army during the Civil War.[1]

After introducing himself Watson told me that he was following the trail of a Texas drover named Juvinal, who had allowed fourteen head of branded stray horses to mix with his remuda while driving a big herd of steers through the Texas Panhandle. Instead of cutting the stray horses back out as he should have done, Juvinal had taken them along with him on his journey north to the railhead in Kansas. When the horses were missed, Watson had been hired by the various owners to retrieve the stolen animals. This type of work was right along Watson's line since he had once been a Texas ranger.

I was acquainted with Juvinal, who was wintering his herd a few miles below me on the Saline near Salt Creek. I told Watson where the cattleman's camp was located, and after having dinner with me, he continued on his way.

About a week later he again came by on the return trip, driving the fourteen head of stolen horses ahead of him. He stopped to thank me for helping him out in his mission. He was in a friendly mood and seemed in no hurry to be on his way. So, once more I invited him to dinner, and we had a long visit before he departed.

During our conversation he told me about another horse thief that he had at one time tracked down for a group of Texas cattlemen. After trailing the rustler for nearly a week Watson finally overtook him one morning as the man was cooking breakfast over a camp fire. The rustled horses were grazing close by. Watson had been without food for the past two or three days in the isolated area; so he waited in hiding until the meal was fully prepared. Then he shot the horse thief from ambush and proceeded to eat his victim's breakfast. That was typical of the respect and treatment shown horse thieves and cattle rustlers in those early days.

Watson didn't tell me just how he recovered the fourteen head of stolen horses from Juvinal, but since I saw the cattle drover a week or so later, apparently the method used in this case was less drastic.

That was the last I saw or heard of Jack Watson until I received the dispatch telling of his wild escapade in the town of Montrose. According to the report which was sent to me as sheriff of the adjoining county, the itinerant Watson was arrested and put in jail for drunkenness on the day prior to the shooting. Before locking him up the city marshal had removed his personal belongings, including eighty-five dollars in cash.

The next morning Watson was taken before the police magistrate, who fined him eighty-five dollars. This was the entire amount of money he had in his possession before being placed in jail and seemed like an exorbitant penalty for just being intoxicated.

At least Watson thought so, for upon being released he immediately obtained his horse, saddle, and six-shooter from a livery stable and went in search of the marshal and magistrate. Finding them on Main Street, he shot the peace officer in the arm and the magistrate through the side, narrowly missing his stomach.

"Don't think I was tryin' to kill yuh," Watson yelled. "I'm just tryin' to get my money's worth out of that fine you charged me."

He then galloped up the street, firing his remaining cartridges into the air before the startled citizenry. When he got outside of town, he pulled up his horse and reloaded. Then he came pounding back, firing his gun and yelling like a drunken Indian.[2]

The district judge happened to be in Montrose at the time, and he tried to exhort the frightened residents to arrest the berserk cowboy. However, while a few of the townspeople returned Watson's fire, no one attempted to follow him as he thundered out of town toward the surrounding hills.

The Montrose city council offered a six-hundred dollar reward for Watson's capture, but there were no immediate volunteers. Everyone seemed to be a little afraid of the hard-riding, fast-shooting stranger, and although he had created quite a commotion, no one was seriously hurt and there was a certain amount of justification for his rampage.

Several weeks after the disturbance I was up in the Surface Creek country near present Cedaredge on an investigation. I was working under an assumed identity with the family I was investigating; so I didn't want to be recognized by anybody up there who might know me. Consequently, as I rode back toward Delta on a rented horse through the cold, murky weather, I kept the collar of my slicker turned up and my wide-brimmed hat pulled down low over my

Montrose Main Street as it looked in 1884 when Jack Watson shot up the town. Town well located near hitching post beside Robinson Grocery Store. Picture taken from the corner of Cascade Avenue and Main Street, looking northwest down Main Street. *Photo courtesy of Tom J. Reeves.*

eyes. In spite of these precautions I was recognized by a horseman who came galloping up behind me.

"Hello, Doc," he greeted, reining in his horse and jogging along beside me on the wagon road. "What are you doin' away up here in this country? I'll wager you're on somebody's trail."

"That's right," I said frankly. "I've been checking a report about an escaped convict from the Missouri penitentiary. He's supposed to be living up here with his uncle, but I've been representing myself as a cattleman looking for a ranch; so I'd appreciate it if you don't mention about seeing me."[3]

"I sure won't, Doc," he said confidentially, "and now let me tell you something. There's another wanted man up here on the mesa."

"This place seems to be getting quite a hideout for outlaws," I commented. "Who is he?"

"Do you remember the fellow called Jack Watson who shot the police magistrate and city marshal some time ago in Montrose?"

"Very well," I remarked with growing interest.

"Well, he's camped up here in a tent a few miles back. You might've noticed it as you passed."

"Yes, I do remember seeing a little tent standing off in the cedars by a stream," I said. "But how do you know it's Watson's camp?"

"I rode by yesterday to get a look at the newcomer. He has a game leg and in other ways answers to Watson's description in the wanted posters. He also has a flesh wound in his arm where one of the Montrose residents shot him when he was running his horse up and down Main Street."

"Thanks for the information," I said. "I'll report the matter to the Montrose officials when I go through there this afternoon."

When I rode into Delta, I turned my rented horse over to the livery stable and caught the train for Montrose. I got off there to see the county sheriff, a powerfully built man by the name of Johnson. Unfortunately, his courage did not measure up to his size, and, as a result, law enforcement was so lax in the area that soon afterward a vigilance committee was organized in Montrose to restore order.[4]

After exchanging a few pleasantries with Sheriff Johnson, I got to the purpose of my visit.

"I've been told on pretty good authority that Jack Watson is hiding out on Surface Creek Mesa," I said.

"Is that so?" Johnson responded unenthusiastically.

"I know where he's supposed to be camped," I continued. "I'll take you there and help make the arrest if you want me to."

I didn't look forward to the unpleasant task of participating in the capture of my old acquaintance, but as a peace officer I felt that it was my duty to notify the Montrose County Sheriff of Watson's whereabouts and offer to help in the dangerous mission of arresting him.

"We still have time to ride up there tonight," I said. "We could stake out our horses in the timber a mile or so from his tent, and then walk over there and nab him when he steps out in the morning."[5]

"Such a long time has gone by since Watson made the disturbance," Johnson said with a surprising lack of interest, "that people don't care any more. I think we'd better just forget about him."

"What about the six-hundred-dollar reward?" I asked. "Don't that interest you?"

"Now, that all the excitement has died down," the sheriff replied, "I'm satisfied that the town wouldn't pay up the offered reward even if we did bring him in."

"Well," I said, "if you want to let him go, it's all right with me. He shot up your town, not mine."

There were others, however, who felt differently than Johnson about the reward money. A notorious horse thief by the name of Howard lived on Surface Creek Mesa a mile or so from Jack Watson's camp, and he was always in the market for an easy dollar. When he learned through the local grapevine that there was a bounty of six hundred dollars on one of his neighbors, he ran true to form.

In carrying out his objective he again proved the old adage that there is no honor among thieves. He extended an invitation to the wanted man to have Sunday dinner with him and his wife. Another guest at the dinner was Howard's accomplice—a muscular young ranch hand with whom Howard had agreed to split the reward.

Since there were only three chairs in Howard's small one-room cabin, the bed was used for additional seating space on this occasion, and, as planned, the guest of honor was asked to sit on it.

"It's the most comfortable seat in the whole house," Howard laughed as the unsuspecting Watson took his designated place at the table.

The chicken dinner progressed pleasantly. One might have suspected that the talking advanced too smoothly—that the Howards were a shade too attentive and cordial to the man on the bed.

When the group were nearly finished eating, Howard said, "Let me pour you another cup of coffee, Jack, so that you can wash everything down."

He picked up the coffee pot from the stove and walked over to where Watson was sitting on the bunk. Howard quietly filled the nearly empty tin cup, and then setting the pot down on the table, he suddenly pounced on his surprised guest, pushing him over on the bed.

At the same time Howard's bulky associate also leaped on top of the wanted man, and before Watson realized what was going on, he was disarmed and his wrists were securely bound together with rawhide thongs.

"What's the big idea?" Watson asked when his assailants allowed him to get up.

"We're takin' you to Montrose for that reward money," Howard explained. "Now get outside and climb on your horse. We want to get started." He had lost all semblance of his former friendliness.

Watson limped toward the open door holding his bound hands in front of him. Before stepping outside in the cold afternoon sunshine, he turned toward Mrs. Howard.

"Many thanks for the fine dinner," he said with a smile. "Your hospitality is overwhelming."

Howard and the young ranch hand rode on each side of the prisoner as the group made their way to Montrose about thirty-five miles away. The bounty hunters were heavily armed and gave Watson no chance to make a run for it.

Upon arriving in Montrose Watson was turned over to the city marshal. In due time the two conspirators received the full reward, contrary to Sheriff Johnson's prediction.

Jack Watson was sentenced to serve a few months in jail. After he was released, I did not hear of him again until the next winter around Christmas time.

In celebration of the holiday season a group of miners at the silver mining town of Crystal (now a ghost town), fifty miles north of Gunnison, got drunk and had a free-for-all fight. During the course of the fray, one of the miners pulled out a knife after he had been knocked down and slashed open his opponent's stomach.

Since the disturbance had taken place in Gunnison County, I was duly notified about it. While free-for-all fights were too common around frontier towns to be of much importance, the use of a knife or gun gave cause for investigation. So, I sent my deputy up to Crystal to arrest the man who had done the knifing.

When the prisoner was brought into my office for questioning, I saw that he had taken quite a beating himself. His eyes were mere slits in his bruised and swollen bewhiskered face.

"You look as if you were in worse shape than the man you stabbed," I commented.

"Yes, I got the worst end of the deal all right. I always seem to after a few drinks."

There was something about the man's voice and appearance that seemed vaguely familiar.

"What's your name?" I asked.

"Don't you remember me, Doc? I'm Jack Watson."

Startled, I again looked at the battered face. This time I recognized the former Texas ranger who had ridden up to my cow camp on the Saline River in search of a horse thief.

"Why, you old son of a gun," I said, getting to my feet and extending my hand in greeting. "Your face is so beaten up that I didn't know you."

"I can well understand," he said dryly. "When I looked in the mirror this morning, I didn't recognize myself either."

"I've been getting reports about you from time to time," I said, "so I knew that you had been in this part of the country."

"I don't guess that the reports have been very flattering," Watson remarked with a wry smile.

"I admit that you've sort of surprised me, Jack," I replied. "For an old Texas ranger you seem to be getting into more than your share of trouble. Just what is the matter, anyway?"

"My only alibi is that I'm hittin' the bottle too hard and too often, and whiskey and trouble seem to stick pretty close together."

"In that case, Jack, the solution to your troubles is easy. Just quit drinking."

"You might as well ask me to stop breathing," Watson said. "Whiskey to me is like women are to some men. They can't live with them, and they can't live without them."

"You've got a point there," I laughed, "but when you come right down to it, heavy drinking is not the real sickness but only a symptom. In my experience, people who drink a lot are merely trying to escape from something. I don't know what you're trying to get away from, Jack, but whatever it is, I believe it would help you a lot to get back on the outlaw trail. That's where you belong, and I need another good deputy. Will you take the job?"

Watson looked up to meet my gaze. "You mean," he said as if he had misunderstood me, "that after all the jams I've been getting in and drinking so heavy, you still want me to be your deputy?"

"That's right, Jack. I think I've been around long enough to know a real peace officer when I see one."

My offer came so unexpectedly that Watson—as hardy as he was—had to pause a moment to get control of himself.

"Thanks, Doc," he said finally, again looking up at me. "Law enforcement work is my life, and it would mean a lot to me to get back into it again. But before I give you a definite answer, let's wait and see how I come out at my trial."

At the subsequent hearing before a grand jury Watson was acquitted. All of the witnesses, including the man who was stabbed, testified that Watson was no more to blame for what had occurred than any of the other participants, who were not brought to trial. The knife wound across the injured man's stomach was healed by this time, and no real harm was done.[6]

After he was cleared, Jack Watson accepted the job as deputy sheriff of Gunnison County. After he was sworn in, for a time there was a remarkable transformation in his character. He rose to his responsibilities, and his fine performance in the line of duty more than justified my faith in him.

An incident occurred on August 6, 1890, which illustrates my high regard for his work and ability. On that day I received a telegram from the coroner at Crystal, which read:

> Four men killed away up on the head of the Muddy. Please come at once and bring several of your best men.[7]

Watson happened to be in my office at the time; so I handed him the telegram. When he finished reading it, I said, "You are several of my best men, Jack. Let's get goin'."[8]

Within a short time we had rounded up the four surviving gunmen and brought them to Gunnison to stand trial. Two of them were arrested at Ouray, another at Aspen, and the fourth at Crested Butte. As usual, Watson was as good as three additional men in helping me run down the fugitives.

Of all the hard and dangerous assignments that I gave Watson, the most difficult one was when I sent him into Utah to clean out a large gang of cattle rustlers.

It all came about as the result of a visit from Preston Nutter, who was a big cattle operator near Price, Utah. Nutter had been one of the principal witnesses at the trial of Alfred Packer—the notorious Colorado man-eater—when Packer was in my custody at the Gunnison County jail. During the course of the famous trial Nutter and I had become close friends.

"Cattle rustlers have been causing me a lot of trouble on my range over on Nine-mile Creek," he said to me. "Do you know of anyone I could hire to go into that country and clear them out? I know it's a man-sized job, and I'll pay accordingly."

I thought for a while before answering. "I can't get away now," I said, "or I would like to give it a whirl myself. But I know of one man who can do as good or better job than I—if he'll take it. His name is Jack Watson, and he used to be a Texas ranger. He's worked with me a lot, and I've never known a better lawman."[9]

When I told Jack about the proposition, he agreed to take the job. I bought him a couple of cheap horses and gave him my .30-.30 Winchester carbine to take along with him.

Watson was a good horse shoer, and after due consideration we decided that he should circulate incognito among the cowboys and cattle ranchers on Nine-mile Creek in that capacity. By keeping alert and scouting around a little on the side, we felt that he could discover the identity of the rustlers.

I gave him the photograph of a good-looking girl and suggested that he represent this young woman as his fiancee and use her fictitious name when addressing his reports and letters to me. By putting my post office box number on the correspondence Watson could in this manner keep me informed from time to time on how he was progressing without anyone in the Price or Nine-mile area suspecting that he was writing to a lawman.[10]

After we had made our plans, I described to Watson the best route for him to take to Nine-mile Creek, which is located about thirty miles northeast of Price, Utah. I recommended that he follow the Denver and Rio Grande Railroad to Rifle and then turn north to Meeker. From Meeker I told him to go southwest through the Uintah Indian Reservation to his destination.

After receiving all of these instructions Watson packed a few blankets and a mess outfit on one of his ponies, and mounting the other he started out on his 300-mile journey.

Upon arriving in the outlaw country ten days later, he went into camp in an old abandoned cabin on Nine-mile Creek. Since the region was rough and mountainous, good horse shoers were in great demand, and it wasn't long before Watson had built up quite a clientele among the denizens of the area. From this vantage point he became widely acquainted, traveling from one ranch to another to shoe horses. He went out of his way to associate with the bad element, giving them the impression that he had drifted into that wild, inaccessible country to escape the law. Within a few months he had become acquainted with most of the cattle rustlers who infested the Nine-mile range.

Watson's appearance helped him in his assumed hole, because if anyone looked like a badman, he did. Many of the cattle thieves accepted him at face value, and he was asked to join up with them. In making his circuit from ranch to ranch he was useful to the rustlers in keeping them informed as to the whereabouts of the ranch owners and their employees. Watson played along with his unsavory associates for a while until he had enough evidence to put nearly all of them behind bars. He sent all of this information to me in his routine reports, and I marveled at my deputy's ingenuity in worming his way so quickly into the confidence of such rough and desperate men.

I continued to advise with and make suggestions to Watson in my answering letters; so from our correspondence I knew what his next step was going to be. I kept my fingers crossed and studied his reports carefully. Finally came the letter which informed me that the vital and dangerous move had been made.

Watson took the big gamble one afternoon while he was replacing the shoes on a string of horses for one of the lesser lights in the rustling ring. It was all a planned psychological act, designed to scare the outlaws out of the region.

"Yuh know," Watson confided to the rustler while taking a moment's rest, "if I was in your place, I'd get the hell out of this country just as soon as possible."

"Why?" the rustler asked in surprise. "What are you talkin' about?"

"Keep this under your hat," Watson continued, "but you're a good friend of mine and I want to give you a break. You see, I'm not what you think I am. I'm actually a United States marshal, and I was sent in here to collect all the evidence that I could against the cattle thieves in the Nine-mile country. I've worked with you fellows now for quite a while, and I've picked up enough evidence to put every one of you in the penitentiary."

Watson paused to roll a cigarette. His companion was too petrified with astonishment to say anything. He looked at Watson as if the horse shoer had gone out of his mind.

"Well," Watson went on, taking a puff on his smoke, "I've been sending this evidence in to headquarters, and all I'm waiting for now are reinforcements to crack down and make the arrests. Now, you're at heart a pretty decent sort of a guy. I've always liked you, and you don't belong with this bunch of crooks. So, I'm givin' you a chance to clear out of here while you still have a chance."[11]

As Watson and I had anticipated, this pre-arranged story made its way like wildfire through the undergound grapevine, sending a chill of terror up the spine of every cattler rustler on the creek.

Watson's bluff had the desired explosive effect on the badmen of the area. This was partly due to the high regard that my deputy had built up for himself among his outlaw acquaintances as a top gun fighter.

Watson had gone out of his way to display his talents along these lines and had shown interested parties the many bullet scars which he bore on his person as the result of countless gun fights. So, the outlaws felt that they were dealing with a man who was as tough and dangerous as they came.

As a result of all these maneuverings, one after another of the Nine-mile Creek rustlers began pulling up stakes and leaving the country in order to avoid the law's net, which they believed was rapidly closing in on them. Within a comparatively short time nearly all of them had migrated to more hospitable territory. And all of this had been accomplished without the firing of a single shot!

Before leaving, some of the more vindictive rustlers tried to ambush the man who had put the fear of God into them, but my wily deputy knew that he was on the spot and kept constantly on the alert.

When the cattle rustlers began moving out of the Nine-mile country, Preston Nutter—Jack Watson's employer—wrote me that he would like to meet the man who was responsible for their exodus. For obvious reasons Nutter didn't want anyone to suspect that he was paying Watson by the month to scare out the badmen; so he asked me to arrange for a secret rendezvous.

Accordingly, I wrote Watson to meet Nutter and me at the Price stock yards on a certain day about 8:30 at night.[12] Nutter and I made our appearance at the specified time, but Watson didn't show up. His camp on Nine-mile was thirty or thirty-five miles from town; so because of the long distance he had to travel on horseback, we waited at the stock yards for several hours, hoping that he would eventually appear.

When he didn't, Nutter finally asked, "What do you suppose is the matter?"[13]

"All I can think of," I replied, "is that he got drunk as soon as he hit town. He has a weakness for the bottle, and he's been on the water wagon for a long time."

"I hope you're wrong, Doc. A man in his position can't afford to get drunk. He's stirred up a hornet's nest around here among the badmen, and every gunman for miles around is waiting for a chance to kill him when he's off-guard."

The next morning we made some inquiries about our missing friend. We learned that a man answering to Jack Watson's description had ridden into Price a day or so before. He had then proceeded to patronize the various saloons and was soon dead drunk. He had remained in that condition until early that morning when he recovered sufficiently to obtain his horse and ride out of town. At least he had made an effort to keep his appointment with us.

When I returned home, I wrote Watson a letter roasting him good and plenty for not showing up at the scheduled time. In conclusion I asked him to meet us again two weeks hence at the same time and place.

In due time I received his answer. He apologized for missing us and assured me that he would not let it happen again.

When Nutter and I again arrived at the scheduled time to see our elusive associate, Watson once more failed to appear although we waited for him until far into the night.

"What do you suppose happened to him this time?" Nutter asked good-naturedly. "It's beginning to look as if Watson isn't very anxious to meet me."

"No, it isn't that. He probably got drunk again."

"Well, it's a good thing that he's a better hand at cleaning up outlaws than he is at keeping appointments," Nutter remarked with a laugh.

Early the next morning we walked over to the depot so that Nutter could catch his train back to Salt Lake City. As we approached, we saw a man lying on his back asleep in front of the station with his head propped up grotesquely against the wall.

When we got nearer, I saw that the reclining figure was that of

Jack Watson. I grabbed his shoulder and gave him a violent jerk to arouse him from his drunken stupor.

"What's the matter?" he cried, blinking his eyes.

"You're drunk again," I said, helping him to his feet.

"I was just takin' a nap, Doc," he said. "I swear I ain't had a drink in two months."[14]

"You can't fool anyone, Jack. You smell like a still. Now, take it easy and let me help you over to where those wagons are standing in that little clearing."

"I don't need no help," Watson said. "I can make it on my own."

"Well, then you go over and lay there in the shade until one o'clock," I ordered. "By that time you should be sobered up enough to meet Mr. Nutter. We'll see you then."

It was a hot day, and after all the whiskey that he had consumed, Watson must have been pretty well dehydrated and wanted a drink of water very badly. But, true to his promise, he remained there napping under one of the wagons all forenoon. At one o'clock Nutter and I walked up to him.

"We'll meet you down in the brush where no one will notice us," I said quietly as we passed by.

A few minutes later Watson joined us. He had apparently drunk no more whiskey, and although a little worse for wear he was sober enough to be in full possession of his faculties.

"Well, we finally got together," Nutter said, extending his hand to the gunman. "I've long looked forward to meeting you and congratulating you personally for getting rid of the cattle rustlers who used to infest this region. You've done a mighty fine job."

"I'm glad you're satisfied, Mr. Nutter," Watson replied, accepting the proffered hand.

"You bet I am," Nutter said enthusiastically. "The rustlers around here are now about as scarce as hen's teeth, but I'd like to have you stick around for a while longer so that they won't take a notion to come back."

"Things are getting pretty dull around here," Watson observed, "and now that my job is finished, I'd like to be goin' back to Gunnison."

"It's up to you, Jack," I interposed, "but it's a good chance to pick up some easy money. You will continue to draw your full salary from Mr. Nutter, even though there won't be much to do. It's a lot more than you can make in Gunnison as a deputy sheriff."

"I don't like havin' nothin' to do, but I'll stick it out for a while if I can move from Nine-mile down into Price where I can get a little recreation now and then to break the monotony."

"That'll be fine," Nutter agreed. "The longer you stay on my payroll, the better I'll like it."

"You'd better go easy on the recreation, Jack," I warned. "You've made a lot of enemies here who would like nothing better than to plug you when your back is turned. So, stay sober."

I probably should have known that under the circumstances Watson would never be able to follow this good advice. With little to do and living in town where liquor was easily obtainable, it was only natural that he should fall back into the old pattern. I made a fatal mistake in urging my deputy to continue on with his job.

I didn't realize the full extent of this mistake, however, until one day a railroad man whom I had once befriended came up to my office during his train's layover at the station.

"You'd better get your friend Jack Watson out of Price," he said. "I've been told on good authority that some gunmen have been hired to kill him. They're in Price now."

"Jack can take care of himself," I said. "I don't think there's much to worry about."

"Not if he could stay sober, Doc, but ever since he's been in Price he's been drinkin' like a fish."

"Well, that's different," I commented thoughtfully, feeling a chill of impending disaster. "I'll catch the next train for Price."

Upon arriving in Price I found my deputy in one of the saloons. I walked up behind him and laid my hand on his shoulder. He whirled around and gazed at me through bleary, bloodshot eyes.

"Why, hello, Doc," he greeted. "I wasn't expectin' to see you. Let me buy you a drink."

"Let's go outside, Jack, where we can talk in private."

He gulped his drink and followed me out the door. We seated ourselves on the board sidewalk in front of the bank.

"I want you to get out of here, Jack," I said, coming immediately to the point.

"The last time I saw you, Doc, you advised me to stay. What's caused you to change your mind?"

"You're hittin' the bottle too hard, Jack, and one of these days when you're drunk, someone is going to fill you full of holes. You need a change of scenery."

"All right," Watson laughed, "I'll leave when the month is up and I draw my last pay check from Nutter. I'd sort of like to take a little vacation and go down and see my brother in Amarillo."[15]

As we were visiting six hard-looking characters dressed in cowboy garb came walking up the sidewalk toward us.

"Those are some of the dirty bushwhackers who would like to shoot me in the back," Watson said, getting to his feet. Before I could stop him, he stepped out in front of the approaching cowboys.

"Take it easy, Jack," I said. "They're all armed."

"I understand that you jaspers are out to get me," Watson said to them. "Well, here I am and we might as well get it over with."

If Watson had been sober he would have realized that he didn't have a chance against these six hard-eyed gunmen. But the blazon courage of the man caught the group by surprise, momentarily saving his life. They stood there glaring at Watson, not sure of their next move.

Taking advantage of their hesitation, I stepped up beside my friend and grabbed him by the arm.

"Go on about your business," I said to the strangers. "I'll take care of him."

Fortunately Watson let me lead him away, and the cowboys continued on up the street.

"Now behave yourself while I'm here," I said, "or you're going to get us both killed."

A little later he accompanied me to the depot to catch my train. Before leaving, I shook his hand and said, "Now, please don't forget your promise, Jack, to get out of this town at the end of the month."

"Don't worry, Doc," he answered with a smile. "I'll be just as glad to get out of this hell-hole as you will to see me go. I'm already looking forward to that vacation in Amarillo."

But Jack Watson never took that vacation. A week after I said goodby to him at the station, I received word that he had been shot down and killed by a hired gunman named Ward.

According to the report, Ward had hidden himself behind a hay wagon which stood in front of a saloon that Watson was patronizing. When Watson staggered out on to the street, Ward began firing at him. Watson fell mortally wounded but managed to struggle to his hands and knees and began crawling back into the saloon to get his gun, which in a moment of drunken forgetfulness he had left behind. Before he could get inside, another burst of shots brought him down.[16]

Jack Watson was buried in the cemetery at Price, where he still lies. He never kept his promise to leave town at the end of the month.

Ward, the hired gunman, became quite a celebrity for shooting down the formidable lawman. But some of us knew that the real killer was not Ward but Old John Barleycorn.

FOOTNOTES

[1]C. W. Shores, "The Story of an Old Fighting Texas Ranger," original manuscript, Denver, Colo., Dec. 22, 1927, p. 2. In possession of Western History Dept. of Denver Public Library.

[2]*Ibid.,* p. 3.

[3]*Ibid.,* p. 7.

[4]*Ibid.,* pp. 8-9.

[5]*Ibid.,* p. 8.

[6]*Ibid.,* p. 9.

[7]C. W. Shores, "More about the Texas Ranger Jack Watson," original manuscript, Denver, Colo., Dec. 24, 1927, p. 1. In possession of Western History Dept. of Denver Public Library.

[8]*Ibid.* The full account of this gun fight may be found in the book *Sunset Slope* by Wilson Rockwell on pages 230-236.

[9]Shores, *op. cit.,* "More about the Texas Ranger, Jack Watson," p. 6.

[10]*Ibid.,* pp. 6-7.

[11]*Ibid.,* p. 7.

[12]*Ibid.*

[13]*Ibid.*

[14]*Ibid.,* p. 8.

[15]*Ibid.,* p. 9.

[16]*Ibid.*

Chapter IV

One day while I was on a business trip in Delta—about seventy-five miles west of Gunnison—I received a telegram from William Grant, superintendent of the Colorado Coal and Iron Company coal mine at Crested Butte in Gunnison County. The message was dated December 11, 1891, and read:

> Fans have been stopped by striking coal miners. Mines rapidly filling with gas. Explosion imminent which will blow up much of town as well as the mine. Your help needed immediately to protect life and property.[1]

I was familiar with the strike which had been going on for a week or more. The immediate cause of the trouble was a reduction of wages from seventy-five to sixty-five cents a ton, which went into effect on December 1st.

The mine, which was owned and operated by the Colorado Coal and Iron Company, bordered on the south side of the town and was the largest in the Crested Butte area. About 250 men were employed in this mine, most of whom were Austrians and Italians who had come over from the old country to make their stakes and then return.[2]

Shortly after the strike began, I had gone up to Crested Butte to talk with the participating miners. I told them that they were within their rights to organize and go on strike, but that they must keep their actions within the limits of law and order. I pointed out that if they started beating up men who wanted to work or endangered life or property in any way that I would have to interfere.

I was acquainted with many of these coal miners and considered them friends of mine. So, when they said that they would heed my advice and stay within the limits of the law, I considered the matter closed. Therefore, I was both surprised and disappointed to learn that they had allowed things to get out of hand.

After receiving the telegram I caught the next train back to Gunnison. While en route the road master came walking through my coach.

"I'm sure glad to see you, sheriff," he said, sitting down beside me to visit for a few minutes. "This strike up at Crested Butte has developed into a minor revolution."

He went on to tell me that the strikers were parading each night up and down Main Street to the music of an improvised band. A former officer in the Italian cavalry was in charge of the paraders and barked out orders to the demonstrators as if they were a company of soldiers.

"They've sent word down," the road master continued, "that if you come up there they'll cut off your head and carry it on a pole in front of their parades."[3]

"A most unusual welcome for an old friend," I commented with a smile. "In the excitement of the moment those miners probably think that if I go up there it will be to break the strike. Actually, my only interest in the matter is to get those fans going before that mine and town are blown to kingdom come."

This particular mine was notorious for being gassy, and seven or eight years before an explosion had occurred in it which killed fifty-nine men.[4]

I was met in Gunnison by my undersheriff and several mine officials, who were impatiently awaiting my return. They advised me to assemble a posse and get up to Crested Butte as quickly as possible. I immediately swore in twenty-four deputies, and we started up to Crested Butte on a special train provided by the Denver and Rio Grande Railroad. It consisted of two coaches and an engine, one of the coaches being occupied by me and my deputies and the other by a number of mine officials and a young Catholic priest. Just before leaving I told the Gunnison telegraph operator not to let anyone wire Crested Butte about our coming.

It was a twenty-eight mile ride from Gunnison to our destination, and the engineer, Alex Davidson, made it in record time. Crested Butte then had a population of about 1500 people, most of whom were coal miners. There were several mines near the town, which had been opened twelve years previously in 1879, and all of them were heavy producers of coking coal. Few women resided in this prosperous mining camp, most of the married men having left their wives and families in Europe where they intended to return. The few wives who did accompany their husbands kept boarding and rooming houses where most of the miners resided. Board and lodging were cheap, and the tenants were packed in the various habitations like sardines.

The miners at Crested Butte were great beer drinkers, and each evening they would gather in the various saloons where they visited and consumed great quantities of their favorite beverage until midnight or later. Frequently, a group would strike up a song of the fatherland, and others at nearby tables would gradually join in until thirty or forty men would be singing in drunken harmony. Whenever a refill was desired, someone would bang his beer mug on a table and the drinks were soon replenished by the bartender. They worked long hours from seven in the morning until six in the evening except on Sundays. Since nearly all of them were Catholics, they attended Mass each Sunday morning and spent the Sabbath afternoons visiting in the several boarding houses around a few kegs of beer.[5] They were a hard-working, hard-drinking, likeable group of people, and I prized their friendship very much.

It was about midnight when our special train pulled into the Crested Butte station. In order not to attract attention the headlights of the engine had been switched off several miles down the track, and no bell was rung or whistle blown when the train entered town. It was a cold quiet night, and about two feet of snow covered the ground.

The car containing the mine officials and the Catholic priest was disconnected at the depot, and the car containing me and the posse was then pushed up toward the mine entrance. As we moved slowly across the dump, we began passing by a long pile of coking coal, perhaps ten feet high.

It was then that we saw a crowd of men running toward us from the opposite side of the tracks. Before we realized what was happening, they began shooting at our lighted car and at the engine.

The engineer immediately applied his brakes and started to back up toward the depot, leaving our coach stranded in the line of fire. We wasted no time in extinguishing the lights and crouching down behind the windows. We had hardly got in position when John Tetard, the mayor of Crested Butte, suddenly appeared in the doorway. He was well in advance of the mob, and in our efforts to seek cover we had not seen him approach.

"You're sittin' ducks in here, Doc," he cried breathlessly above the uproar. "Get your men out of the car as quick as you can."

The charging strikers—about 150 strong—were only about a couple of hundred yards away and coming in fast.

"What about us getting behind the car?" I asked the mayor as my men poured out the door amid a hail of bullets, which crashed through the windows and ricocheted off the steel body of the coach.

"I think we can make it to the coal chute," Tetard yelled. "Let's run for it."[6]

I was amazed at this deadly onslaught. The strikers had apparently been forewarned of our coming. I found out later that the Gunnison telegraph operator—a strong union man—had been responsible for the reception. Contrary to my instructions, he had wired the Crested Butte operator that I was on my way up there with a big posse. Some of the Italian workers had jumped to the conclusion that we intended to break the strike and persuaded their fellow miners to procure all the guns available and ambush us when we arrived.[7]

The coal chute or tipple was about 200 yards away. It was connected with the mine entrance by a shed to protect the tracks from the deep snow which falls during the winter months at this altitude of nearly 9,000 feet above sea level. A wide stairway about fifty feet high led up to this rampart, which, if we could make it, would put us in an impregnable position—even against ten to one odds.[8]

We sprinted up the railroad tracks toward the stairway. The mob closed in on us, yelling like a huge pack of bloodhounds ready for the kill. As they ran, they shot at us with a wide assortment of guns, including rifles, pistols, and shotguns. In their haste and in the dark their bullets went wild, for the most part whistling over our heads.

We had no more than got past the long pile of coke when it became apparent to me that we would be overtaken before reaching the shelter of the coal chute.

"Get down behind the tracks," I yelled. "We've got to make our stand here." We all leaped down behind the protecting railroad grade, which served as a bulwark between us and the advancing miners.

"Don't shoot until I give the word," I ordered as we lay there in the snow panting for breath. My men were tense as they peered over the tracks at the bloodthirsty crowd. We were outnumbered nearly five to one, and, believe me, it is a terrifying experience to watch a frenzied mob come charging at you.

"Remember to aim low when you shoot," I shouted, "since we don't want to kill anybody if we can help it."[9]

The individual members of this half-crazed mob were fundamentally well-meaning, rational human beings, but as a group under the hypnotic influence of mass psychology, they were no longer men but destructive, predatory animals—cruel, violent, and beyond hope of reason. I hated to fire into them, but they had reached the stage of explosiveness where the only thing that could stop them was the basic instinct of fear—fear of being killed or hurt.

While the majority of the approaching strikers yelled taunts in their native tongues, a few called out to us in English.

"Shores," one of them cried, "you're a no-good, yellow-bellied strike breaker."

"Come out in the open, Sheriff," another shouted, "and fight like a man."

"You double-crossed us, Sheriff," still another voice shrieked, "and we're gonna work you over."[10]

Although most of my deputies were hand-picked and could be depended upon to remain steadfast under fire, a few were untried. Three of these suddenly broke under the pressure, and jumping to their feet fled like scared jackrabbits from the oncoming horde. One of them was so terrified that he ran head-on into a coal car standing on a sidetrack. Surprisingly enough, he had served in the Union Army where he had received a medal for outstanding courage above and beyond the call of duty. He took a great deal of pride in this medal, which he wore most of the time. But he didn't have much to be proud of that night.

"When are you gonna let us shoot?" another one of my deputies yelled, also on the brink of panic.

"You're gonna get us all killed here, Doc," a man by the name of Berryhill yelled.

"Pull yourselves together," I shouted, "and stay down low where they can't hit you."[11]

Nothing more was said as we crouched there peering over the railroad tracks with our Winchesters cocked and held in readiness. The strikers were bunched up more than they should have been and made an easy target. When the leaders were about twenty-five yards from the grade, I yelled, "All right, give 'em hell!"

Our rifles went off simultaneously in one gigantic blast. This broke the charge. Twenty-five or thirty of the strikers fell to the ground—some wounded and others stumbling over their fallen comrades. Those who could get to their feet started beating a hasty retreat toward town. Some shot back at us as they ran. The men in the rear, after a moment of surprised hesitation, followed suit, except for a few who hid behind trees and fences, exchanging shot for shot with us.

For a time the bullets flew thick and fast. One of my deputies got so excited that he pumped fourteen cartridges out of the magazine of his Winchester without firing a shot. I shot only about six times, aiming low so as not to seriously injure anyone.

When the shooting finally ceased, Mayor Tetard said, "I believe we can make it up to the coal chute now."

We hastened up the wide stairway, hoping that no hidden marksman would take a pot shot at us. We made it without mishap, and from our elevated platform in the shed that ran from the mine entrance to the chute, we could look down and see the confused activity going on in town.

Many of the strikers were still scurrying through the streets as if a pack of devils were at their heels. There was no more fight left in them. Women and children were carrying away some of the wounded or helping them limp to their respective residences. Quite a number still lay unattended in the blood-spattered snow. Many looked as if they were dead.

I glanced around to see if any of my posse had been hurt. Everybody seemed to be all right except for one man whose face was covered with blood.

"That fellow over there by the railing looks like he's been shot," I remarked to my undersheriff. "See what you can do for him."

"Oh, he's not as bad off as he looks," the undersheriff laughed. "He's the Civil War hero who panicked and ran into the coal car. He'll be all right."

"Are there any other casualties?"

"No, the rest of us are okay. We fared better than our attackers. It looks like twenty-five or thirty of them are layin' dead over there by the tracks."[12]

While it appeared then as if a lot of the strikers had been killed or critically wounded, I learned later that although thirty-six of them were hit, only one suffered serious injuries. However, for the next few days the town doctor, J. W. Rockefeller—no relation, incidentally, to the famous tycoon—was kept busy treating minor bullet wounds.[13] The deputies had apparently followed my orders and shot low, or the casualties would have been much greater.

The bitterly cold December night was accentuated at this high elevation, and we were without food or blankets. We didn't dare build a fire to warm ourselves for fear the light might expose us to some alert sharpshooter. None of us, including the mayor, thought it advisable to go into the aroused town to procure needed supplies. So, we all put in a very uncomfortable night, ever on guard against another surprise attack.

Early the next morning we heard the whistles blowing up at the Anthracite Mine, which was two or three miles away. This mine was not on strike, and its employees were nearly all American citizens of Irish descent. They made up the more law-abiding element of Crested Butte.[14]

With the coming of dawn we watched the little town gradually come to life, but in spite of all the activity going on below us, help was no nearer than before. For the time being at least we couldn't even safely venture down there to send a telegram to inform the outside world of our predicament. All that we could do was wait and hope for something to develop. We presented a haggard and grim little bunch of men as a result of our nightly ordeal.

Nothing of interest happened until late that morning when we saw four or five miners walk out of the Elk Mountain Hotel, where the strikers were evidently holding a meeting. They came directly up to the chute, occasionally gesturing to show they were unarmed and wanted to speak to us.

"Don't shoot," I said. "It looks like they want to hold a parley."

When they came within speaking distance near the foot of the stairway, one of them called out, "Where's Mayor Tetard?"

"Right here," the mayor answered, stepping forward.

"We have been appointed as a committee to inform you that the citizens and miners of Crested Butte have just passed a resolution asking you to resign."

"You can go back and tell your cohorts," the mayor replied, "that maybe they can beat me at the next election, but there will be no resignation."

"You'd better think it over," the spokesman said. "Everyone is pretty mad at the way you deserted us last night and went over to the enemy."

"Sheriff Shores and his deputies are not your enemies," the mayor commented. "They're just trying to do their duty, the same as I am."

"Maybe you call it that, but we don't," the spokesman continued belligerently. "Tell Shores to take his men and go back to Gunnison."

"The sheriff is here and can speak for himself," Tetard said.[15]

I walked up to the head of the stairway and said, "Do you gentlemen have something to say to me?"

"Sheriff," the spokesman responded, turning toward me, "the

miners and citizens of Crested Butte demand that you and your men get out of town."

I recognized the spokesman and addressed him by name. "Mike," I said, "when I was up here several days ago, I told you fellows that you had a perfect right to go on strike so long as you didn't violate the law and endanger life or property. By refusing to let the engineers keep the fans going, you did both, and that's why I'm here."

"Why didn't you come in the daytime like a man instead of sneaking up here at night?"

"My term as sheriff has nearly expired," I said, "but I want to make it clear once and for all that so long as I'm sheriff of this county I will go any place I please at any time I please."

"Then you intend to stay?"

"You can count on my staying here as long as lives and property are threatened."

"All right, Doc. Then you must take the responsibility of whatever happens. We are prepared to fight if we have to."

"After what happened to you last night," I replied, "I'd advise you not to."

After the committee had departed to make their report, one of the deputies called my attention to some abandoned guns lying in the snow below us. They had obviously been dropped there by some of our ambushers during their hasty retreat.

Several of us descended the stairs and retrieved the firearms. One of them was a new Marlin rifle which we found beside a small tree. I learned later that it had been dropped there by a portly Italian who was shooting at us from behind the trunk. However, he was so fat that sizeable portions of his anatomy protruded from his supposed place of concealment, and he was punctured by three bullets. He was the most critically wounded of the lot, but even he eventually recovered.

The monotony of the afternoon's vigil was again broken when two Italians walked up to our rampart to speak to us.

"We want to talk to Sheriff Shores," one of them called up.

"I'm at your service, gentlemen," I said.

"Have you seen a new Marlin rifle laying around here somewhere?"

"Is this it?" I asked, holding up the abandoned gun that I had found by the tree.

"Yes, that's my rifle. I loaned it last night to one of my friends, and he got shot up and lost it. Can I have it back?"

"No," I answered, "I'm keeping it as state's evidence. In the future be more careful who you lend your guns to."

Disappointed, the two miners walked away, gesticulating excitedly as they talked to one another.

The afternoon advanced without further incident. Finally, one of my deputies walked over to me and said quietly, "Some of the men are getting pretty restless, Doc. They're gonna balk at spending another night up here without food or blankets. Why don't I walk down to Gunnison and get help? We can't go on like this much longer."

"I appreciate your offer, Jack, but help should be arriving any time now," I said with a forced optimism I was far from feeling. "Let's wait a little longer."

About four o'clock a team pulling a sleigh appeared on Main Street. It was piled high in back with blankets and supplies, and my beleagured little force watched its progress through town with understandable interest.

"It looks like help is on its way," one of my men cried out.

"Don't get your hopes up too high," I advised. "Help will most likely come by rail instead of sleigh."

Guns were poked out of doors and windows as the sleigh jingled through town, but, fortunately, no shots were fired.

"Sure enough it's headin' this way," another hopeful deputy commented.

As the sleigh approached, several of us ran down the stirway to meet it. Two men from Gunnison—a white man and a Negro—sat on the board seat, their legs covered by a fur lap robe. The white man was driving.

"What brings you fellows away up here?" I greeted as they drove up.

"The people of Gunnison heard that you were pretty hard pressed, Doc," the driver said, "so they sent up these blankets, food, and medical supplies to help you out."

It was a pretty good feeling to learn that my deputies and I had not been forgotten, after all. This token of concern and affection from the people of Gunnison, whom I had served now for nearly eight years, was one of the most heart-warming experiences of my life.

"You must've figured we were in pretty bad shape," I said to the newcomers.

"We sure did, Doc," the Negro said. "The mine officials who came up with you in the other coach reported that you and your posse had been unexpectedly attacked by the strikers and probably all killed or wounded. Everybody is sure worried about you, Doc. A special train is on its way up now with thirty-five volunteer reinforcements and a doctor."

"So the mine officials got back to Gunnison all right?"

"Yes," the driver said, "apparently they was walkin' toward town when the shootin' started. Scared by the noise, they all returned to the depot, except for a young Catholic priest who was with them. He continued on uptown, believing that his services might be needed. When the engineer came down the tracks after he left you, he hooked on to the coach and backed the frightened bunch all the way to Gunnison. The engineer said he got mighty cold looking back out of the window with the temperature around twenty below."[16]

The sleigh-load of supplies, so generously contributed by the residents of Gunnison, restored the morale of my men and saved the day for me. An hour later the special train pulled up to our headquarters with fresh recruits, a doctor, and a number of mine officials, including William Grant—the superintendent, his assistant—Mr. Ramsay, and an attorney for the Colorado Coal and Iron Company by the name of E. M. Steck.

Steck told me that he considered the situation so critical that he had wired Governor John Routt to send in the state militia. I told him that he had jumped the gun, and I immediately wrote a note telling the governor to disregard the request since, in my opinion, no outside help was necessary. This message was taken back to Gunnison by return train and telegraphed to the governor.

I picked out replacements from the new arrivals and let ten of my less hardy deputies, who had suffered exposure and fright, return home. This left me with a force of about thirty men—six more than I had originally.

Relative to sending in the state militia, I was later shown an article on page one of the December 13th, 1891, edition of the *Rocky Mountain News* which read as follows:

> In conversation with a *News* reporter last evening Governor Routt expressed himself as entirely satisfied with the situation (at Crested Butte). From the start he has confidence in Sheriff Shores, whom he declares to be worth an army.
>
> "I have never for a moment entertained a thought of sending the militia to Crested Butte," he said, "and I have no intention of taking the first step in that direction until I receive word from Sheriff Shores . . . That hot-headed Steck was too nimble with his inflammatory telegram. Such exciteable men are dangerous in the face of a difficulty like that in Crested Butte . . ."

During all the time we had been up there, the mine had been rapidly filling with gas, and many of us were afraid of an imminent explosion. So, I told Mr. Ramsay, the assistant superintendent, to get the fans going right away or I would take my men and go down the tracks.

He, with the help of Superintendent Grant and several other company officials, soon had the engine started and the fans running. We all breathed more easily when we heard the welcome hum of the fans as they began clearing out the foul air in the mine.

That night half of us stood guard until midnight while the rest took over the watch until daylight. During the long vigil miners could be seen gathering in groups under the lights on Main Street, apparently to discuss the situation, but there was no violence.

The next day the train brought up the state labor commissioner, Mr. Bodine, and three newspaper reporters representing the Denver papers. The reporters wanted to talk with me, but I refused to make any comment to them at that time, since emotions were at the

Main Street of Crested Butte as it looked in 1891 at time of the big strike. *Photo courtesy of Denver Public Library Western Collection.*

breaking point and a misquoted statement from me could set off a holocaust. However, I told the newspaper men that they had my permission to interview any of the deputies.[17]

The regular train from Gunnison arrived each morning about ten o'clock, and when it pulled in, some of the strikers were usually on hand to see if any blacklegs (now known as "scabs") were being sent in by the Colorado Coal and Iron Company. In order to preserve the peace in case any showed up, I had three or four deputies meet the daily train also. Fortunately, no blacklegs ever arrived, or there might have been a free-for-all.

In returning to the mine from the station, the deputies would periodically go through town and pick up any mail which might have come in for us. Among the letters received one day was an anonymous message for William Grant, the mine superintendent, warning him that he would be killed if he did not leave town within one week.[18]

On the afternoon following the arrival of the state labor commissioner, another committee representing the strikers came to see me and the mine officials. It did so at the suggestion of Labor Commissioner Bodine, who addressed about two hundred of the striking miners that morning. This committee invited five representatives of the Colorado Coal and Iron Company to meet with their leaders at nine o'clock the next moning in the Elk Mountain Hotel to discuss differences. I was also asked to come along with four deputies to maintain order.

Shortly after the committee departed, the Crested Butte doctor, Mr. Rockefeller, made his appearance. He was an old friend of mine, and many was the time we had gone deer and elk hunting together.

"I thought maybe I should come up and see if I could do anything for you," he said.

"Well, it's about time," I said. "I thought you had forgotten all about this little bunch up here."

"No, Sheriff, I didn't forget you, but I've been kept busy night and day patching up the miners you shot up the other night."

"How many were wounded, Rocky?" I asked.

"Thirty-six were hurt, but, luckily, most of the wounds were minor ones—primarily leg wounds. You must've told your men to shoot low. How about you fellows?"

"Fortunately none of us got shot, but we've suffered quite a bit from exposure and lack of food. I let about ten of the worst-off go back home on the special train yesterday."

"Is there anything I can do to help?"

"No, thanks. A doctor from Gunnison came up and did what little that was needed. The men are in good shape, now that they've got food and blankets."

"I'm glad to hear that, Shores, and I hope things stay that way. Crested Butte is like an armed camp. Every man has a gun, and feeling is running high against you. The real reason I came up here was to warn you not to make any arrests down there without the help of the state militia. I want to go hunting with you again next year."[19]

"Well, I sure appreciate your coming up here to give me the low-down, Rocky, but I've got some pretty good gunmen with me, and if any arrests are made, I doubt if anybody in his right mind will want to go up against them."

"Remember that you and your deputies are outnumbered, and I sure don't want to miss that hunting trip next fall."

"You won't, Doc. I'll be around."

The next morning four deputies and I went with five mine officials down to the Elk Mountain Hotel for the conference. We were expecting trouble; so my men and I were each wearing two six-shooters under our overcoats, and the remaining deputies, carrying Winchester rifles, walked down behind us. They kept the hotel under close surveillance the entire day, ready to lend assistance in case things started popping.

While it was a stormy session, there was no serious trouble. I nearly got in a fight with a big Scotchman named Stuart Hurd, who started calling me names as we made our way down the street toward the hotel. Before we came to blows his fellow strikers persuaded him to shut up.[20]

We gathered in the parlor of the Elk Mountain Hotel. Representatives of the strikers included James Drympel, Stuart Hurd—

the Scotchman who accosted me on the street—and John Follette. They were the three primary instigators of the strike.

Drympel came from Gallup, New Mexico, where he had also been a labor organizer. He was a Welshman, I believe, with dark red hair, white-colored eyebrows, and a homely long nose. He looked like a pretty rough character, and I guess he was.

John Follette, on the other hand, was a popular, substantial citizen of Crested Butte. He and his wife ran a saloon there. Although it was generally believed that he sent the threatening anonymous letter to Superintendent Grant, I personally doubted if he did so. He was not the type of man who would write such a crack-pot message. However, I had learned not to be surprised at anything a man might do when under the influence of emotional stress or liquor.

Among the men representing the coal company were Superintendent Grant, Assistant Superintendent Ramsay, and E. M. Steck—the coal company's lawyer.

I was accompanied by my four best gun fighters. They included Jack Watson—a former Texas ranger whom I wrote about in the preceding chapter—and the Marlow brothers of Telluride, who were wanted in Texas but whom Governor Routt refused to extradite because of extenuating circumstances.[21]

Also present at the meeting were Mayor Tetard, two prominent business men of Crested Butte, and Labor Commissioner Bodine.

In opening the session the labor commissioner said, "Gentlemen, this conference has been called in the interest of peace, commerce, and labor. All factions are represented. It is called in hopes of a speedy settlement of the existing difficulties between the Colorado Coal and Iron Company and its employees. An idle mine of that magnitude does not line the pocket of an employer or buy bread for its employees . . . I don't want any inflammatory discussion at this meeting, and I will rule out of order any man who attempts to drag out the skeleton of the shooting affray last week. We came for settlement of the strike and not to hold any post-mortem over the Winchester chorus that belched forth its music last Friday. Now, then, gentlemen, proceed to business."[22]

I was appointed sergeant at arms, and a secretary was elected to keep the minutes. Labor Commissioner Bodine was chosen as permanent chairman, and he presided with an Italian interpreter on one side and an Austrian interpreter on the other.

The case for the Colorado Coal and Iron Company was presented by Steck, the company's lawyer. He said that wages had been lowered from seventy-five cents to sixty-five cents a ton because of increased competition and a reduction of fifty cents per ton in the price of coal.

Stuart Hurd and John Follette spoke for the strikers. They said that the cost of living in Crested Butte was higher than in most mining towns and that the miners could not make a living for less than the wages paid under the old schedule.[23]

James Drympel presented other grievances—namely, that there were too few mining cars and that the miners were having to push their cars and carry their props a lot farther than necessary.

The outcome of the all-day meeting was an offer by the company to reduce the number of men employed from 250 to 200 in order to increase the chances of those remaining to mine more coal a day per man. This, it was said, would offset the ten cent decrease in wages per ton. Also, the company agreed to correct all the minor grievances brought out by Mr. Drympel.

During the discussion the operators asked permission to move to market the 4000 tons of coking coal piled up on the dump. They said that they would pay the old scale of wages—seventy-five cents a ton—for this service.

At seven o'clock that evening 250 miners assembled in the Knights of Pythias Hall to hear the report of the joint conference. John Follette called the meeting to order, and the labor commissioner was once more elected permanent chairman. He was again assisted by two interpreters from the Austrian and Italian factions.

At the start of the meeting one of the miners stood up and said, "Mr. Chairman, I move that a keg of beer be brought in."

The labor commissioner banged his gavel in righteous indignation. "Sir," he cried out, "I rule your motion out of order. I don't want to see any intellect warped by liquor while such a serious matter is being considered. If anything stronger than water is brought into this hall, I will withdraw from the meeting."[24]

In spite of the labor commissioner's efforts to mediate, I was not at all impressed by him. He didn't seem to understand the men he was dealing with. He would have made a better boy scout master than a hard-boiled, down-to-earth labor negotiator.

After a tempestuous discussion of the company's offer, it was voted down. However, a resolution was passed, in spite of considerable opposition, allowing the coal company to load at the old wage the coke which had accumulated on the dump.

The following morning a group of Austrians came up to my headquarters at the mine entrance and offered to load the coke if I would furnish them protection. They were afraid of the Italian faction, which had violently opposed the resolution to let the company move the coke to market.

"Let me know when you want to start," I said, "and I'll be on hand to see that there's no trouble."[25]

After talking the matter over with Superintendent Grant, they informed me that they would begin work at one o'clock that afternoon. At the appointed time thirty deputies and myself, each carrying a rifle and fifty rounds of ammunition, marched down from the mine and took positions on top of the coke ovens, where we could get a good view of the town and the surrounding territory. This was the signal for twenty-five Austrians to come down to the dump and begin loading the coke.

As the work progressed, the town was ominously quiet, and the streets remained deserted all during the afternoon. The only evidence of life was the opening of an occasional door as grim faces peered out at us. The quiet was like the calm which precedes a storm, and I didn't like it.

By six o'clock twelve cars had been loaded. At that time my men and I escorted the workers to their different places of residence. The majority of the Austrian workers were staying at a boarding house owned by a fellow miner named Pruss.[26] Directly across the street on the other corner was an Italian boarding house, where twenty or thirty angry Italians had gathered. They had been drinking beer most of the afternoon and were in a dangerous mood.

Conditions were ripe for trouble, so that evening I placed two deputies near Pruss's house. I also stationed other men in strategic positions throughout the town, which under the peaceful surface was smoldering like an active volcano just before an eruption.

About eleven o'clock Pruss, the Autrian landlord, came running up to my headquarters. He excitedly displayed a letter which had been pushed under his front door. It was printed in English and said that his boarding house would be blown up during the night.[27]

"It's probably from some crank who is just trying to scare you," I said, "but we won't take any chances."

I put four deputies in the threatened boarding house, and as a further precaution, I placed a man in each of the other Austrian boarding houses. I also brought the main body of my posse closer to town.

At 11:45 three skyrockets streaked up through the night from the neighborhood of the Italian boarding house, where so many of the Italian strikers had gathered. Within two minutes every deputy in that area was at the scene to invesigate the occurrence. While it was apparent that some of the Italians in the house had set off the skyrockets, none of them would admit it. They were belligerent and arrogant, but I took them down a notch by warning them that if they made any more disturbance I would arrest the lot of them and throw them in jail.

This quieted them down somewhat, for I had the reputation of keeping my word. A short time later their boarding house was darkened, and the remainder of the night passed without further incident. The saloons had all been closed during the emergency, and no one was on the streets except the various patrols. All was quiet except for the fans at the mine, which could be distinctly heard creaking off their sixty revolutions a minute. An occasional camp fire sparkled on the mesa above town, built now and then by patrolling possemen to warm themselves.

The next morning forty more Austrians reported at the dump to load coke under our protection. This made a total of about seventy, and according to most of them, the entire Austrian faction was ready to go back to work in the mine under the company's terms. The fans had been running steadily since I had ordered them started, and the mine was expected to be cleared of gas within the next day or so.

The Italians, however, were continuing to hold out for the old wage scale, and it looked as if the controversy would be settled by the company hiring back the Austrians at the reduced schedule and letting the Italians go. This suited the Austrian faction since reduction of the working force would increase the daily output of coal per man, thereby helping to offset the decrease in wages.

Late that morning I took a group of my most experienced deputies and started out to arrest some of the ringleaders who had incited the attack on me and the posse. I had been advised against taking such action without the help of the state militia, but I thought that I could get away with it—especially with such well known gunfighters walking beside me as Jack Watson of Gunnison and the Marlow brothers of Telluride.[28]

Our first stop was at the depot where, as usual, a number of strikers had gathered to make their routine check for blacklegs or scabs. With the appearance of such a formidable array of gunmen, Crested Butte residents began to take notice, anticipating some sort of dramatic action.

Among the group of miners at the station I recognized one of the men I was after. He was a swarthy Neapolitan by the name of Jim Barto. I pulled a warrant from my pocket and walked over to him. The warrant charged him and about a dozen other strikers with conspiracy to commit a misdemeanor against the laws of the State.[29] After reading the warrant I had two of my deputies take him in custody. The crowd of spectators watched the proceedings curiously but without hostility. Things were breaking my way, but I kept my fingers crossed.

After the train pulled in and was duly checked, my men and I started up Main Street, which ran from the depot about a half-mile before entering town. All of the saloons and business houses were located on this street. We walked two abreast, each of us carrying a Winchester rifle. Jim Barto, our prisoner, brought up the rear of the procession between the two officers who had him in charge.

At sight of our approach the citizens of Crested Butte began appearing on both sides of Main Street. Whether they were just inquisitive or intended to cause trouble, I wasn't sure. Therefore, my deputies and I held our rifles in both hands as we entered town, prepared for any emergency.

Upon reaching the first saloon, owned by a man named Rozich, the posse halted outside the door while I entered. None of the men I was seeking were inside; so I walked out and continued on up the street at the head of my group.

By this time nearly a thousand people lined the street watching our progress with interest. When we came to John Follette's saloon, I went inside, carrying my rifle in one hand and a warrant in the other. Follette was a prominent man about town, and the spectators for the first time began showing some excitement. As they closed in around the posse to better see the show, Jack Watson and the Marlow boys raised their guns and ordered the onlookers back. They complied without hesitation.

The saloon was empty except for its proprietor who came forward and asked good naturedly, "Well, Doc, what can I serve you this morning?"

"This is a business call, John," I replied, handing him the warrant to read. "I've come to arrest you for helping to incite the ambush on us the other night."

As Follette and I walked outside to join the procession, a woman emerged from a side entrance of the saloon and rushed up to my prisoner.

"This is my wife, Sheriff," Follette explained. "May I speak to her a minute?"

I stepped aside to let them talk in private. The woman was greatly upset at her husband's arrest and created quite an emotional scene before she withdrew in tears.

When First Street was reached, one of my deputies informed me that he had seen Joe Papish, another of the men we were seeking, go into Rozich's Saloon. We reversed our course and arrested Papish before he had a chance to make his exit. We also visited the house of Jake Kinnick, but, like so many of the other leaders of the ambuscade, he had made himself mighty scarce when we were seen coming into town.[30]

"We'll get Kinnick and the others on payday," I said. "That's one affair they won't miss—even if it does mean getting arrested."

As we escorted our three prisoners to the depot, some women hurled a few invectives at us from their doorways. Otherwise, the townspeople were quiet and peaceable. We had expected a lot of resistance so were pleasantly surprised at the peaceful reception. Perhaps this was due to the well-known fighting men who accompanied me, since they presented quite a show of force.

At one o'clock that afternoon I boarded the return train for Gunnison with the men I had arrested, while my deputies went back to the mine. Upon arriving in Gunnison, warrants were sworn out before Justice W. S. Rainbow, and the three men were placed in jail pending trial.

The next day was payday at the mine, and it offered me an ideal opportunity to pick up the other men I was after. For several days previously the Colorado Coal and Iron Company had posted notices about town notifying the miners to report at the company's main office on this day to receive their November pay checks.

At two o'clock the long stream of miners began moving through the main office to receive their pay. I stood nearby to observe each man as he passed. Several of my guards were close at hand to help out.

Many of the strikers who had been wounded came hobbling by on crutches, canes, or pick handles. A few who were unable to attend were represented by their wives or friends.[31]

Whenever a man I had a warrant for showed up, I searched and placed him under arrest. Before long I had made quite a haul. The only person who stirred up any fuss was James Drympel. Shortly after his arrest, be began to complain and talk loudly with the obvious intention of starting a riot. Fortunately, his antics caused little, if any, commotion.

At six o'clock that evening several of the deputies and I set out for Gunnison with our prisoners on a special train. We got off at the La Veta Hotel, where we were met by County Judge McDougal. He told me then that Perham, the Gunnison telegraph operator, was the one who had tipped off the strikers about my coming on the night of the attack.

"I think I'll go over and have a little talk with Perham," I said. "My deputies can take the prisoners to jail."

La Veta Hotel where the railroad ticket office was located at time of the big Crested Butte strike.
Photo courtesy of Library, State Historical Society of Colorado.

"No, I wouldn't go down there, Doc," the judge advised. "Let me go, and I promise to tell him anything you say."[32]

"Then, tell him to stay out of my way, or I might take a notion to kill him."

That was pretty strong language, but this telegraph operator had really got my goat. By disobeying my orders not to relay any messages to Crested Butte, he was responsible, in my opinion, for the entire trouble in which a lot of men had got hurt and a lot more could just as easily have been killed.

County Judge McDougal sat as examining magistrate and had the prisoners bound over to the district court for attempting to kill me and my posse.

My term of sheriff expired before the trial and I did not run for office again. Instead, I accepted the job of special investigator for the Denver and Rio Grande Express Company.

Just before the trial, the Gunnison County attorney came to see me in Grand Junction, where I was living at the time. He asked me if I still wanted to prosecute the strikers.

"The decision is entirely up to you, Doc," the county attorney said. "You're the star witness, and I'll do whatever you advise."

"In that case, let 'em go," I replied. "Fortunately no one was killed, and anybody ought to be excused for losing his head once in a while."[33]

FOOTNOTES

[1]C. W. Shores, "The Coal Strikes I Have Been Connected with–", original manuscript, Denver, Colo., Mar. 30, 1929, p. 2. In possession of Western History Dept. of Denver Public Library.

[2]*Rocky Mountain News,* December 26, 1891, p. 3.

[3]Shores, *op. cit.,* p. 3.

[4]*Ibid.,* p. 2.

[5]*Rocky Mountain News,* Dec. 26, 1891, p. 3.

[6]Shores, *op. cit.,* p. 4.

[7]*Ibid.,* p. 12.

[8]*Ibid.,* p. 5. Also see *Rocky Mountain News,* Dec. 26, 1891, p. 3, for description of mine.

[9]Shores, *op. cit.,* p. 4.

[10]*Ibid.,* pp. 4-5.

[11]*Ibid.,* p. 5.

[12] *Ibid.*
[13] *Ibid.*
[14] *Rocky Mountain News,* Dec. 26, 1891, p. 3.
[15] Shores, *op. cit.,* p. 6.
[16] *Ibid.,* p. 7.
[17] *Ibid.,* p. 8.
[18] *Rocky Mountain News,* Dec. 13, 1891, p. 1.
[19] Shores, *op. cit.,* p. 9.
[20] *Ibid.,* p. 8.
[21] *Rocky Mountain News,* Dec. 19, 1891, p. 1.
[22] *Rocky Mountain News,* Dec. 14, 1891, p. 1.
[23] *Ibid.* Also see Shores, *op. cit.,* pp. 8-9.
[24] *Rocky Mountain News,* Dec. 16, 1891, p. 1.
[25] *Rocky Mountain News,* Dec. 18, 1891, p. 1.
[26] *Ibid.*
[27] *Ibid.*
[28] *Rocky Mountain News,* Dec. 19, 1891, p. 1.
[29] *Ibid.*
[30] *Ibid.*
[31] Shores, *op. cit.,* p. 10.
[32] *Ibid.,* p. 11.
[33] *Ibid.,* p. 13.

Chapter V

One October afternoon in 1890 a large man dressed in the garb of a prosperous cattle rancher strode into my office. He introduced himself as George Strachn and said that he owned a ranch on Cochetopa Creek in the adjoining county of Sagauche.

"Twenty-four head of horses were stolen on my fall range recently," he said. "Some were mine and the others belonged to the Cuenin Estate. Here's two hundred bucks in advance if you'll take the case."

He pulled a wad of bills from his pocket and handed it to me.

"I'm pretty busy right now," I said, "and may not have time to do anything for you. So, you'd better keep this money for the time being. If I decide to take the case, you can pay me after I've finished."

"I know your reputation, Sheriff," he said, reluctantly accepting back the roll of greenbacks, "and we need your help real bad over in our county. Cattle rustlers and horse thieves have practically taken over, and it's high time an example was made of some of them. You're the man to do it, and if you don't mind, I'd like to draw up a little agreement."

Picking up a pencil and a sheet of paper from my desk, he scribbled down a few words which read:

> This is to certify that I hereby agree to pay to C. W. Shores, Sheriff of Gunnison

County, Colorado, the sum of $200 for doing
the best he can toward locating the
thieves who stole my horses and the
horses of the Cuenin Estate.

George Strachn[1]

The brands of the stolen animals were drawn under the signature for identification purposes.

"It's strictly a one-way contract, Sheriff. The only person it puts under any obligation is me."

"Where were the stolen horses last seen?" I asked, folding the sheet of paper and putting it in a drawer.

"I seen their tracks up near Saw Tooth Mountain. They made quite a trail as they were being driven down the divide, and it shouldn't be hard to follow."

"Your offer interests me," I said, "and if I get some spare time, I'll scout around."

Since a sheriff in those days had to depend on rewards and fees from extra-curricular jobs to round out his income, the offer was tempting. While the horse stealing did not come under my jurisdiction as sheriff of Gunnison County, it did come within my authority as a deputy United States marshal.

A couple of days after Strachn had come to see me, I took a pack outfit and rode over to Saw Tooth Mountain, which was about twenty-five miles south of Gunnison. I was not long in finding the tracks made by the stolen horses. They had torn up quite a bit of ground as they stampeded southward down the Continental Divide. I was not surprised at the direction they were taking, since a big bunch of horses stolen in Western Coolrado during the late fall or winter were usually herded south into Arizona or New Mexico where there was plenty of forage. On the other hand, horses stolen in the spring after the grass had started were customarily driven northward into Wyoming. When only a few head were involved, a horse thief might go in any direction.

I followed the comparatively fresh trail nearly to the mining town of Creede. Among other observations, I noticed that only two of the horses I was trailing were wearing shoes. Since these were undoubtedly the mounts of the rustlers, I judged that there were only two men involved. By the time I got to Creede I was convinced that the horse thieves were following the usual pattern and were on their way to New Mexico or Arizona. Having determined the general direction that the two outlaws were taking, I returned to Gunnison.

As I went about my other duties, I inquired around as to whether anybody had left the Gunnison area recently. From these queries I learned that two transient cowboys of questionable character had disappeared about the time the horses were stolen. One of them was known as Jim Wylie and the other as Mat Edmiston. They were frequent patronizers of the local saloons; so, whenever I had a little free time, I made a point of dropping into their favorite hangouts. I would order a drink or two and try to strike up casual conversations with some of the drinking comrades of the missing cowboys.

In this manner I learned that Jim Wylie had been seen a number of times with a prostitute from the neighboring town of Pitkin. I looked up this girl the next time I was there, and, true to type, she was not at all reluctant about betraying her former lover. She told me that shortly before Wylie left the country he had said something about taking a bunch of horses south across the Colorado border. She also gave me a picture that had been taken of her and Wylie together. This was a real break, and I took full advantage of it.

I cut the girl out of the picture and had a photograph made of the suspect. Then, I made up a small poster which would fit in a regular sized envelope. This poster featured Wylie's picture and his description as well as a detailed description of the other wanted man—Mat Edmiston. It also contained the brands of the stolen animals.

I had a lot of these posters printed, and with the help of a Rand and McNally map of Arizona, New Mexico, and southern Colorado, I sent them to the sheriffs and postmasters in key county seats of this general area.[2] Since this country was sparsely populated, any stranger coming into the region would likely be noticed. So, if the two outlaws should be wintering in any of these sections, I figured that the chances of getting a response from my wanted cards were good.

Finally, in December a letter arrived from the postmaster of Solomonville, a small town in southeastern Arizona. He wrote that the man whose picture I had sent him was in the region and came to the postoffice occasionally to get his mail. He went on to say that besides being postmaster he and his brother owned a big cattle spread known as the Dunlap Brothers' Ranch, and that their foreman, Tom Horn, had reported seeing the other horse thief whom I described in the poster. He concluded by saying that being in the cattle business himself, he appreciated what I was doing and would have his foreman appointed as deputy sheriff to assist me in making the arrests. He praised Tom Horn highly as a capable cattleman, rodeo star, and a former Indian scout.[3]

I immediately answered this letter, telling Mr. Dunlap that I would like to meet him or his foreman, Tom Horn, at the nearest railroad point. By return mail he wrote that Tom Horn would meet me at Willcox, forty miles south of Solomonville, on the Southern Pacific Railroad.

Upon leaving Gunnison, I wired Dunlap when I was scheduled to arrive in Willcox. It was about a seventy-two hour trip, and I was pretty tired when my train finally pulled into town at one or two o'clock in the morning. I registered at the only hotel as John Wells from Kansas City. I always made a practice when on the outlaw trail of not revealing my real identity except when necessary.

I arose early the next morning, and after breakfast went into the hotel lobby to await the arrival of Dunlap's foreman—Tom Horn. About eight-thirty a tall, dark-complected man with a black mustache walked into the hotel. He was around thirty years of age and presented an imposing figure of a man—deep chested, lean loined, and arrow straight. He was wearing a plaid shirt, woolen trousers, and high-heeled boots. A wide-brimmed sombrero covered his head, and he didn't bother to remove it as he strode up to the desk and looked at the register. Then, he turned around and started back out, glancing at me as he did so.

"Is your name by any chance Tom Horn?" I asked, getting up and walking toward him.

"That's right," he answered, looking at me questioningly through black, shifty eyes.

"Well, I believe I'm the man you're looking for. Doc Shores is the name."

Tom Horn in December, 1890, when Doc Shores first became acquainted with thim. *Photo courtesy of Mrs. Lucille B. Hartman.*

"I didn't see your name on the register," Horn said as we shook hands.

"No, I was that fellow Wells from Kansas City."[4]

That was my introduction to Tom Horn, who was destined to become a legendary figure within the next thirteen years. Although he held the world's record in calf roping and was chief of scouts in the several campaigns against the great Apache Chief, Geronimo, he was not well known outside of Arizona. His real fame and immortality in cowboy legends was to come later when in 1892 as a "stock detective" he began to kill off cattle rustlers and sheepmen for the cow barons in Utah, Colorado, and Wyoming.

While Tom Horn was universally praised for shooting down Indians in the Apache wars, he was tried and hanged at Cheyenne in 1903 for using the same talents to shoot white men for the big cow outfits. Although many other so-called "stock detectives" were also riding the ranges for the cattle kings, Horn stood out from all the rest because of the small value he placed upon human life when dealing with men in the opposite camp.

He became a professional killer or "cattle rustler exterminator," as he called himself, shooting victims from ambush for his customary price of $600 per head. As a result, for years after Tom Horn died whenever a man was found mysteriously murdered on the range, it was said that he had been "Tom-Horned." The terms "drygulched" —so popular in western fiction—and "Tom-Horned" became synonymous.[5]

This then was the enigmatical, interesting man with whom I was to be associated in my pursuit of the horse thieves, although at the time I was not aware of his dubious attributes.

"I understand that you know the whereabouts of Wylie and Edmiston," I said as we walked out of the hotel.

"I know where two men are who answer to their descriptions, but they're goin' under different names. I suppose you've got a requisition for them?"[6]

This question sort of took me aback since I didn't have any requisition nor did I intend to get any. Not liking the delay or red tape that one had to go through to obtain extradition papers, I intended to kidnap the fugitives, so to speak, and bring them back to

Colorado where I did have jurisdiction. I had done this many times before and got away with it.

However, I didn't tell Tom Horn this since from the matter-of-fact way he asked the question I was afraid that he would refuse to help me if he knew I had no papers. So, I replied, "Yes, I've made arrangements to obtain a warrant, and it should be here by the time we get back with our prisoners."

"Good. I've been sworn in as a deputy; so I'm ready to take off whenever you are."

"How are we travelling?"

"I've got a team and two-seated buckboard over at the livery stable. Have you had breakfast?"

"Yes, and I'm ready to leave now. While you're hitching up, I'll run over to the drug store and get some quinine. I feel like I'm coming down with the grippe."[7]

Main Street was situated on the north side of the railroad tracks and ran parallel with them. So, in order to avoid being seen by a chance acquaintance, I walked up the tracks until I was opposite the drug store. Then I re-entered town and went inside the store to procure the needed medicine. There were several customers ahead of me, and it was such a long time before I got waited on that to save time I decided to take the shorter route down Main Street back to the stable. I didn't want to keep my partner waiting too long, or he might take off without me.

The street was lined with a long string of low buildings, including saloons, gambling houses, barber shops, and general stores. As I hurried along, I passed a number of cowboys, Indians, and Mexicans standing around in various groups. They eyed me curiously, but I saw no one that I knew. After all, Willcox was a long way from home, and the chance of meeting an acquaintance was slight.

"Hello, Doc," a voice greeted from behind. "What are you doing away down here?"

Startled, I whirled around to see who had spoken. The man was walking out of a barber shop. He was wearing a barber's apron and was apparently the proprietor of the place. I scrutinized him carefully, but he didn't look like anyone that I had ever seen before. Nevertheless, he apparently knew me. Such is the price of fame.

"You're Sheriff Doc Shores, ain't you?" he asked me hesitantly as I glared at him in non-recognition.

Several people were listening; so I answered, "No, my name is Wells. I'm afraid you've got me confused with someone else."

I grabbed his arm and led him back into the barber shop. Fortunately, no one else was inside; so I took him into my confidence.

"You are right," I said. "I am Doc Shores, but I'm down here after some outlaws, and I don't want them to find out I'm in the country. So, I'd appreciate it if you didn't tell anyone about seeing me. Such information has a way of getting around to the wrong persons."

He assured me that he would keep my secret, and although I was pressed for time, I bought a dollar's worth of cigars from him and visited a few minutes in order to win his good will and cooperation.

After this brief interruption, I continued on to the livery barn where Tom Horn was impatiently awaiting me. The team was hitched up and ready to go. There were two other men in the stable, and as I climbed into the wagon, I noticed that one of them was looking at me intently. He was a big, long-nosed fellow with bushy red hair partially concealed by a slouchy sombrero pulled down low over his forehead.

I remembered the other man as being a former resident of the Gunnison area. His name was John Harr; and he used to be quite a bear hunter. Since he was only a casual acquaintance, however, I didn't speak to him, hoping that he wouldn't recognize me and spread word of my whereabouts. This was the second acquaintance I had run into that morning six hundred miles from home. It was indeed a small world.

Horn drove the wagon up to the hotel where I obtained my suitcase and other paraphernalia, including handcuffs, shackles, Winchester rifle, and an old regulation six-shooter. Horn's rifle and sack of plunder were already in the buckboard along with some grub, a mess outfit, and a roll of blankets which the Dunlap brothers were donating to the cause.

As we rattled out of town, I said, "Who was that big, red-headed jasper in the stable who kept looking at me?"[8]

"I don't know. I never saw him before."

"I recognized the other fellow," I said. "He used to hunt bear around Gunnison."

"You mean John Harr?" Horn asked in some surprise. "He's a mining partner of mine. I had a talk with him while you were at the drug store. Why didn't you speak to him?"

"I never speak to anyone on official trips like this unless I have some business with them."

When we were a few miles out of town, I said, "Tom, I've got a quart bottle of whiskey in my valise that I've carried all the way from Gunnison. Would you like to wet your whistle?"

Horn surprised me by refusing; so I said, "All right, in that case we'll save it for future reference."[9]

We passed through level country that first day and made good mileage. My companion proved to be an interesting conversationalist and told me about some of his experiences while serving as an Indian scout under General Crook and General Miles during their expeditions against Geronimo.[10]

"Geronimo's Indian name was Goyothay," he commented, "but the Mexicans called him San Geronimo after Saint Jerome, the orator, because that old Apache liked to make speeches even more than he liked to fight."

During the conversation Horn showed me an old arm wound that he had received while pursuing Geronimo through the Sierra Madres of Old Mexico.

"Captain Emmett Crawford was standing beside me at the time, and he was killed."

This reference to Captain Crawford interested me because Fort Crawford—a military contonment eight miles south of Montrose, Colorado—had been named in honor of this officer. The post had just recently been abandoned and was well known to me.

We spent the first night of our journey at a cattle ranch owned by two brothers named Parks. When Horn introduced me, he told them that I was from Gunnison. One of the brothers then asked if I happened to know John Parks of that city. I said that John was a good friend of mine and that I knew his brother Cliff Parks also.[11] This gave us something in common to talk about, and we had an enjoyable visit before hitting the blankets.

Late on the second day we reached Arvaipa Canyon, where Tom Horn and John Harr had a galena lead mine. We stopped at an old cabin which they used for their headquarters when working the mine. Unhitching the team, we staked them out near a little stream where there was plenty of good pasture. Then, taking some grub, a mess kit, and our blankets we entered the cabin and built a fire in an open fireplace at the rear of the room.

We remained here all night, and the next morning we walked down the canyon to another cabin where Horn said that Jim Wylie had been staying for several weeks while prospecting for galena ore. We knocked on the door but no one answered. The cabin showed signs of having recently been used; so we waited around for a while hoping someone would appear.

"He's probably out prospectin' and won't be back until evening," I commented.

"There's a Mexican who lives further down the canyon," Horn said. "Wylie might be down there with him. I'll go down and check. Maybe you'd better stick around here in case Wylie should show up before I get back."[12]

After Horn left, I hid behind a convenient bush and kept my eyes on the various trails leading down to the cabin. However, no one came into view until several hours later when I caught sight of two men in the distance coming up the canyon trail. As they came nearer, I recognized Tom Horn, and I assumed that the other was Jim Wylie—the horse thief.

I walked out into the open and waited for them to arrive. When they finally did so, Horn said, "Wylie, this is your friend that I was telling you about—Sheriff Shores of Gunnison. He's come a long ways to meet you."

"Glad to see you, Jim," I greeted, clapping the handcuffs on his wrists. "Did you frisk him, Tom?"

"No, I just took his six-shooter."

Tom told me later that when he entered the Mexican's cabin, Wylie and the Mexican were eating lunch. The Mexican was unarmed, and Wylie's gun and holster were hanging behind him over his chair.

"Hello, gentlemen," Horn said as he stepped inside. "It looks like I'm just in time for dinner."

"Hello, Tom," Wylie said. "Draw up a chair."

Since Wylie and the Mexican both knew the big newcomer, they were not alarmed at his unexpected appearance. Wylie did not reach for his gun, and Horn picked it up as he walked by. Only then did Wylie become suspicious.

"I hate to interrupt your meal," Tom said to Wylie, "but there's a fellow waiting to see you up at your cabin, and I don't think we ought'ta keep him waitin'."

"What's all this about, Tom?" Wylie asked indignantly.

"I'm arrestin' you for horse stealin'," Horn said. "Now, get movin'."

Horn was not the type of man one liked to argue with; so Wylie got up from the table and walked outside without registering further protest.

In going through Wylie's pockets I found some letters which had been written to him by the foreman of a big cattle ranch in Saguache County. The rancher's name was Snyder, and his foreman was apparently a close personal friend of both Wylie and his accomplice—Mat Edmiston. In one of the letters Jones, the foreman, had written:

> You boys had better come back here and kill Snyder since he is no doubt giving information about your stealing those horses from Strachn and the Cuenin Estate.[13]

This and other information I found in the letters was nearly as good as a confession. In fact, after I read them, Wylie realized I had the goods on him and made no further attempt to cover up.

"Where are the horses that you and Mat Edmiston stole?" I asked.

"We got in a box canyon along the South Fork of the Rio Grande," Wylie said frankly, "and were only able to get three head out. Them three are foraging around here somewhere."

"You mean that you lost twenty-one head in the canyon?" I asked in surprise.

"That's right. We could have driven them back through the open end but thought we saw some horsemen following us a mile or so back."[14]

"As soon as we get a bite to eat," Horn said, "I'll round up the three head and drive them down here for you to see. I've seen 'em around, and they ain't much to look at."

We proceeded on up Arvaipa Canyon to Horn's cabin where we had left our team, wagon, and gear. Horn started a fire in the old fireplace while I put shackles on the prisoner's ankles. We cooked our meal over the open fire, and since there were no chairs or furniture in the place, we sat on some blocks of wood to eat. The meal served as both dinner and supper, for the afternoon was well along. When we finished, Horn jumped on one of the team and rode out bareback in search of the stolen horses.

The grippe or flu that I started coming down with at Willcox had become progressively worse. In the excitement of the hunt, I hadn't noticed how badly I felt. But sitting there in the overheated cabin, I began to feel light-headed and sick. Fearing I might faint, I got to my feet and opened the door. The cool fresh air helped clear my head, but still feeling faint, I walked about the room to keep from losing consciousness.

"Do you feel bad, Sheriff?" Wylie asked, noticing my discomfort.

"No, just a little tired."

Wylie knew I was lying and glanced around the cabin to size up the situation and determine the best means of escape in case I should keel over. My Winchester was leaning against the wall beside the door. However, I was wearing my six-gun, and the prisoner was handcuffed and shackled. The odds were all against him if he tried to make a break for freedom unless I should pass out completely.

I took some more quinine and continued to move around. Finally after an interminable wait I heard the pounding of horses' hoofs as Tom Horn brought in two of the stolen horses. I went over to the door and watched them approach. They had not been wintering well and were about the sorriest looking animals that I ever laid eyes on. They were so thin that you could count every rib in their bodies, and their long tails and manes were full of burrs.

"I don't think much of your remuda, Wylie," I remarked. "Why did you bother to steal those bags of bones?"

"They looked better when we took them. This Arizona grass don't seem to do 'em any good."

"What do you want to do with these broomtails?" Horn called out to me.

"Let 'em go," I said. "They're not worth the trouble or expense of taking them back to Colorado."

When Horn entered the cabin, he said, "I'm plumb tuckered out. I could use a drink of that Colorado whiskey you offered me a while back."

"You've got nothin' on me," I said. "I could use a drink, too."[15]

I opened my valise and took out the treasured quart of whiskey which I had been carrying unopened ever since leaving Gunnison. I passed the bottle around to Horn and the prisoner before taking a long swig myself. Within five minutes we all decided that life wasn't so bad, after all. That was one time when I know whiskey did me some good. It brought about a quick recovery from whatever was ailing me.

Shortly after dark we heard someone ride up. It proved to be John Harr, Horn's mining partner whom I had seen in the livery stable at Willcox.

"I figured I'd find you here," he said to Tom. "Who are your friends?"

"This is Doc Shores, Sheriff of Gunnison County, and our prisoner there goes under several names. Up in Gunnison he is known as Jim Wylie."

"Glad to see you, Doc," Harr said, shaking hands with me. "I thought that was who you were but I wasn't sure. That big redheaded fellow who was in the stable back at Willcox spotted you also. When you and Tom drove out, he turned to me and said, 'That tall, slim feller looks like a sheriff I once seen in Colorado, and I'll wager he's after a couple of horse thievin' friends of mine.' After patronizin' several of the saloons he got on his horse and galloped out of town. I thought he was probably headin' out to warn his pals so decided to come up here and let you know."

"That was mighty nice of you, John," Horn said. "Your red-headed friend will be a little late to do Wylie here any good, but it might be a little embarrassin' if he reaches Mat Edmiston before we do."

"In that case," I observed, "maybe we'd better get goin'. We could use a little sleep, but, under the circumstances, I guess we'll have to postpone it."

"Edmiston should be at the Iron Springs Ranch about twenty miles from here," Horn said. "If we don't let any grass grow under our feet, we should make it by nine o'clock."

We hitched up the team, and throwing our equipment into the wagon, we were soon on our way. I put Wylie on the front seat beside Tom Horn, who was driving, and I sat on the back seat where I could keep an eye on the prisoner. John Harr spent the night at the cabin, intending to return to Willcox the next day.

"Suppose we meet that red-head and Mat Edmiston riding down here to warn you?" I asked Wylie as we rattled along.

"There would probably be trouble," Wylie admitted.

"If you see them comin'," I said "tell them to stop quick because if there is trouble, you'll probably be the first to get it." To emphasize my remark I pushed the muzzle of my six-shooter between his shoulders.

"You wouldn't shoot an unarmed man in the back, would you, Doc?" Wylie asked slyly.

"Try me out and see."

We really turned a wheel and arrived at the Iron Springs Ranch a little sooner than we had expected. The cow hands had just finished a late supper and were lounging around the bunk house playing cards, reading, and doing odd jobs before blowing out the kerosene lamps. Horn was acquainted with them and went inside while I remained in the wagon with Wylie.

After a few minutes Horn returned. "Mat Edmiston is up at the main house washing dishes," he said.

"Let's go help him out," I said. "He'll be surprised to see you, Wylie."

"He'll be more surprised to see you, Doc."

I unlocked Wylie's shackles, and the three of us walked over to the main house.

"You wait here," Horn said as we neared the back door. "Mat knows me and won't suspect nothin' if I go in alone. Incidentally, he's known around here as Jack Smith."

Opening the door he strode into the kitchen. "Hello, Jack," he greeted. "What're my chances of gettin' a cup of coffee?"

Edmiston looked up from a pan of dishes. "Why, Hello, Tom. Ain't you a little off your range?"

Through the open door we saw Horn pick up the outlaw's gun and cartridge belt, which were hanging on the wall. I had never seen the rustler before, but from descriptions of the wanted man I knew he was Mat Edmiston.

"There's a fellow outside who's come a long way to meet you," Horn said. "Let the dishes go for a minute while I introduce you to him."

Edmiston looked a little puzzled as he accompanied Horn outside, but he showed no alarm at his friend's unusual request. In the darkness he did not immediately recognize Wylie or me until Horn said, "Jack, I'd like to have you meet Sheriff Doc Shores of Gunnison. Doc, this is Jack Smith alias Mat Edmiston."

Upon hearing my name, Edmiston realized what was happening. "God damn you, Tom. I thought you were a friend of mine."

"Now, take it easy," I said, grabbing him by the arm and handcuffing him to Wylie. "I'm in a hurry, and we don't have time to argue, especially if you want to get your gear and pick up your wages before we take off."

Edmiston quieted down, and after getting some kind of settlement from his boss, we drove away, not wanting to take the risk of spending the night at the Iron Springs Ranch where Edmiston had friends who might help him escape. We drove on until daylight and then stopped at a ranch house to obtain food for ourselves and hay for the horses. After a short rest we continued on to Willcox, arriving an hour or two before train time; so leaving the two prisoners with Horn at the station, I hurried over to the postoffice as if to obtain the warrant that I had told him about. Of course, no warrant had arrived, and upon returning I said, "The warrant has been delayed, but I believe I'll take the prisoners out of here on the next train, anyway."[16]

Horn appeared satisfied, and I gave him fifty dollars to pay him for his valuable assistance in making the arrests. I had, of course, taken care of all expenses, and in those days fifty bucks was the equivalent of a month's wages.

As we awaited the train, I said, "Tom, you ought to go into the law enforcement business. You sure have done a good job for me, and with your background as an Indian scout and understanding of the Mexican lingo, I believe I could get you a job with the Pinkerton National Detective Agency. I'm pretty well acquainted with Jim McParland, superintendent of the Denver office."

"It is sort of along my line," Horn said enthusiastically. "I'd sure like to give it a try."

"Then, I'll put in a good word for you."

It was a three-day and three-night trip back to Gunnison, which was quite a strenuous journey for one man with two prisoners. I kept them handcuffed to their seat during the nights so that I could get a few winks of restless sleep. In my profession a person had to be a light sleeper if he was going to live very long, and any unusual sound awakened me instantly. Although I managed to sandwich in a few cat naps at various intervals, I remained awake for the greater part of the trip.

During each day I took my charges to the diner and to the washroom whenever they wanted to smoke or wash up. Since the outlaws were handcuffed together, they created considerable attention whereever we went. However, I followed out my usual policy of never letting anyone talk to them or myself. But I made a point of treating them considerately, visiting with them and giving them plenty to eat and drink, whether the drink was coffee, water, or whiskey.[17]

During the course of one of our conversations, Mat Edmiston told me that he had nearly got killed trying to drive the stolen horses out of the box canyon. While riding along a narrow ledge which only a mountain goat or trained burro could have negotiated, his horse slipped and fell backward over the precipice. The horse plunged several hundred feet to its death on the rocks below, but Edmiston during the descent grabbed hold of a sharp jutting rock and was miraculously left dangling in mid-air. Wylie, who was coming along behind, threw him his lariat rope and managed to pull him back to safety. The next day Edmiston stole another saddle to replace the one that he had lost and replaced his dead mount with one of the stolen horses.

When we finally arrived in Gunnison, I locked my two prisoners in jail. After a few days rest I took them to Saguache where I turned them over to the Saguache County Sheriff. When the district court convened I went before the grand jury, and as a result of my testimony they were both indicted and went on trial. They were convicted and given terms in the state penitentiary.

I gave the district attorney the incriminating letters which I had found on Jim Wylie. The writer of these letters was also indicted and convicted for telling Wylie and Edmiston to kill his employer.

I received a good-sized reward for rounding up the two horse thieves. Mr. Strachn, the cattle rancher who asked me to take the case, gave me his promised two hundred dollars. The trustee of the Cuenin Estate, whose horses were also involved, contributed a good deal more. The Saguache County Cattlemen's Association took up a collection of several hundred dollars, which it presented to me. Even the Saguache County commissioners gave me a reward.[18] I believe it was the first time that anyone had really cracked down on outlaws and rustlers in that county, and it was widely appreciated.

I did not forget the invaluable assistance of my associate Tom Horn. Right after I delivered my prisoners to the Saguache County authorities, I wrote a letter to James McParland, superintendent of the Pinkerton National Detective Agency in Denver. In this letter I told about Horn's background as an Indian scout and of his capable help in running down the two horse thieves. I concluded by recommending him for the job as a Pinkerton agent in the Denver office. McParland sent my letter on to William Pinkerton in Chicago, and, as a result, Tom Horn was shortly afterward taken into the employment of the world-famous detective organization. He worked as a Pinkerton investigator for two years when he quit in 1892 to start work as a stock detective for John Clay, grand old man of the Union Stock Yards in Laramie, Wyoming. Clay, a Scotchman, was also president of the Wyoming Stock Growers' Association and manager of the Swan Land and Cattle Company, which was a Scotch syndicate capitalized at four and one-half million dollars. On the surface Clay

Tom Horn's grave in Boulder, Colorado. Tom Horn's brother drove a brewery truck in Boulder. *Photo courtesy of L. B. Dean.*

hired Horn as a horse breaker, and, in this capacity, he could ride around and check on rustling activities without being suspected.[19] When Horn ran across a rustler, he was paid for bushwhacking him.

For the next decade Horn worked in such manner for most of the established cattle barons. His record during this time until he was hanged in 1903 at Cheyenne for the killing of Willie Nichol is part of cowboy folklore. However, I had no further connections with him after he quit the Pinkerton Agency.

Shortly after starting to work for the Pinkertons, Tom and I ran down a couple of train robbers who held up the Denver and Rio Grande at Cotopaxi near the Royal Gorge. But therein lies another story.

FOOTNOTES

[1]C. W. Shores, "A Story of the Stealing of Twenty-four Head of Horses," original manuscript, Denver, Colorado, Mar. 21, 1927, p. 1. In possession of Western History Dept. of Denver Public Library.

[2]*Ibid.,* p. 2.

[3]*Ibid.,* p. 3.

[4]*Ibid.*

[5]For more information about Tom Horn see Jay Monaghan, *Last of the Bad Men,* The Bobbs-Merrill Co., Indianapolis and New York, 1946.

[6]Shores, *op. cit.,* pp. 8-9.

[7]*Ibid.,* p. 4.

[8]*Ibid.,* p. 5.

[9]*Ibid.,* p. 6.

[10]*Ibid.,* p. 8.

[11]*Ibid.,* p. 5.

[12]*Ibid.,* p. 6.

[13]*Ibid.*

[14]*Ibid.,* p. 10.

[15]*Ibid.,* p. 7.

[16]*Ibid.,* p. 9.

[17]*Ibid.,* p. 10.

[18]*Ibid.*

[19]*Ibid.,* p. 11. Also, see Monaghan, *op. cit.,* pp. 152-154.

Chapter VI

Upon returning to Gunnison in early September, 1891, after a short absence, I found an important telegram awaiting me. The message was from H. G. Kramer, general manager of the Rio Grande Express Company, and said:

> Wire me at Cotopaxi earliest possible date you can meet me in Salida. Urgent.[1]

The telegram was several days old; so I wired back immediately that I would leave for Salida on the next train. Kramer was there to meet me and invited me to join him in his private car, which was standing on the main line. I told him that I had a saddle and some other luggage in the baggage car; so he instructed his expressman to make the transfer. We then walked over to his coach where I was introduced to J. J. Burns, superintendent of transportation; Anthony Sneve, auditor; and two special express company investigators—a Mr. Lay and a Mr. Dickey, who were interrogating a young man by the name of Hallack.

"I suppose you know why I wanted to see you?" Kramer asked as soon as we were sitting alone in the back portion of the car.

"I presume it has something to do with the big train robbery," I said. "I heard about it indirectly, but I've been away and haven't had a chance to study up on the case."

"Then I'll give you the details since we want you to help us out."

"I don't believe I'll have the time to help you," I said. "My term as sheriff expires the first of the year, and I've got a lot of loose ends to tie up before I leave office."[2]

"You wouldn't be gone more than a couple of weeks," he pleaded.

"In a case like this, Mr. Kramer, I couldn't even get started in a couple of weeks."

"I know these investigations take a lot of time," he admitted, "but, in my opinion, you're the one man who can run down these train robbers, and we've got to make an example of them or we're apt to have an epidemic of holdups. As a personal favor to me, I hope you'll take this case."

He looked at me so imploringly through his expressive brown eyes that I didn't have the courage to turn him down.

"All right," I said, "I guess I can work it in. Go ahead and tell me what happened."

From Kramer's account I learned that on the night of August 31st the flagman at Texas Creek, a little station about seven miles east of Cotopaxi, was held up in his office by four masked men. They took all of the torpedoes in his possession and forced him at gun point to accompany them up the railroad tracks a mile or so from the town of Cotopaxi.[3] Here the Arkansas River Canyon, through which the railroad runs, is narrow and steep—an ideal location for a holdup.

The little group waited behind a clump of brush until they finally heard the eastbound Rio Grande passenger train approaching in the distance. When it drew near, thundering down the canyon, the outlaws with the assistance of the kidnapped flagman shot off three torpedoes at short, regular intervals. Responding to these warning signals, the engineer began letting up on the throttle. Then, when he spied the flagman waving his lantern directly ahead of him, he applied his brakes, and the ponderous wheels of the onrushing locomotive ground noisily to a stop.

The four train robbers wasted no time. Two of them scrambled aboard the engine and covered the engineer and fireman with their rifles, while the other two stood guard, shooting volley after volley down the length of the train to discourage any of the passengers or crewmen from coming out and interfering.

The engineer and fireman were told to climb down out of the cab, and when they had done so, they were lined up beside the flagman who was being kept under surveillance by the two bandits on watch.

Most of the passengers were asleep, and in spite of the commotion they slept through all of the excitement. John C. Roberts of Fort Garland, a passenger on the day coach, was one of the few who awakened. He heard the shooting and walked to the door to see what was happening. As he opened it, he was met on the platform by one of the masked men patrolling the train who said, "Don't come out here if you wanta stay out of trouble."[4] Roberts returned to his seat without argument, and shortly thereafter the brakeman came through, warning the few travelers who were awake that the train was being held up and advising them to remain inside.

The conductor, A. M. Sadd, was in the rear of the train when it came to its unscheduled stop. He had heard the three torpedoes, and having visions of broken rails, washed out bridges, and landslides, he rushed on to the platform and peered out into the darkness. At that moment a volley of shots flashed up ahead, and bullets began whizzing all around him. He realized then what was happening and ducked back inside.

After turning the engineer and fireman over to their comrades, the pair who seemed to be running the show proceeded to the mail car and pounded on the door with the butts of their Winchesters, demanding admittance. The mail agent, Frank Donahue, suspecting that a holdup was in process, was busily engaged hiding several large packages of registered letters under the mail sacks. He hurried on with his task, paying no heed to the racket. When there was no response to their requests, the outlaws began firing into the door. The agent lay down on the floor to keep from getting hit.

"Open up in there," one of the robbers yelled, "or we'll set fire to the car."

Fearful that they might carry out this threat, the mail agent finally capitulated and let the two men in.

Seeing the mail sacks, the bandits realized at once that they had made a mistake. "We're in the wrong place," one of them commented. "The safes are in the express car, not in here."

The mail agent was ordered outside, where he was placed in the company of the three other prisoners. The only item that was taken in the mail car was the agent's gold watch, which was lying in plain sight on the table. In his haste to hide the registered letters, the conscientious agent had forgotten about his own property.

The express car was tackled next, and by threatening to use dynamite, the robbers persuaded the messenger to open the door. There were two safes in this car—a small way safe and a large through safe. The way safe, which the messenger had access to, contained several hundred dollars in cash and a gold retort worth around six hundred dollars. The through safe, which only the station agents at the larger depots could open, contained a much larger amount of money.[5]

The messenger was told to open both safes, but after working the combination to the smaller one, he explained the situation, and the two train robbers made no comment, apparently taking him at his word.

After taking the cash and gold retort from the opened safe, the bandits jumped out of the express car, and shouting to their two accomplices, the group ran down the steep incline toward the Arkansas River, disappearing into the night. A few minutes later there was another volley of shots, followed by a pounding of hoofs as the desperados galloped away.

While Kramer was reconstructing the crime for me, an engine hooked on to our car and began pulling us toward Texas Creek Station, headquarters for the manhunt, which had already been in progress several days.

"Did you get any description of the robbers?" I asked when he had finished his account.

"I talked with the trainmen who were involved, and they all agreed that the leader of the gang was a powerfully built man of about forty. The most noticeable charcateristic about him was that he had a peg leg, although he was remarkably active for a cripple. His right-hand man, who helped him engineer the robbery, was about the same age but more slender. His most distinctive feature was the dark derby hat he wore, which bobbed around conspicuously among the broad-brimmed sombreros of his associates.[6] The two robbers who stood guard stayed in the background and were not so clearly seen. However, they appeared to be quite a bit younger than their accomplices. One of them, in particular, looked like a gangling willow of a kid not over eighteen or nineteen. He was wearing a weather-worn floppy hat and a checked shirt."

"Well," I commented, "outside of the peg leg and the derby hat, we don't have much to go on. Have you run across anything else during the investigation?"

"Not much. The robbers' horses were trailed into Wet Mountain Valley, about twelve miles from Cotopaxi, and then their tracks were lost. But something or other should break soon. There are around sixty men in the field, including U. S. marshals, sheriffs, special investigators, Pinkerton detectives, and even bloodhounds. All of the mountain passes are being watched, and the Wet Mountain Valley is surrounded. The case has, of course, received a lot of publicity, and the entire state is on the alert."

"I notice that you've already picked up one suspect," I said, nodding toward the youth who was being questioned by the express company investigators.

"That's right. He was found the morning after the robbery in the Wet Mountain Valley area on horseback, and he fits the description of the gangling young robber with the slouch hat and checked shirt. Let's go on over and listen in. I'd like to get your impression of the kid."

We got up and walked up the aisle to the other end of the car where the interview was taking place. After we arrived, the interrogation only lasted a few more minutes, but it was long enough to pretty well convince me that the boy was innocent. In dealing with criminals as much as I had, one sort of develops a sixth sense or intuition as to whether a person is telling the truth.

"Doc," Kramer said, "would you like to ask Hallack anything?"

"Yes," I replied, "I would like to ask him one question. Son, where were you last Monday night?" That was the night of the robbery.

"I spent the entire night in the Wet Mountain Valley with Reverend Richards and his family."[7]

I said no more, and a little later when Kramer and I were alone, he asked, "Well, what do you think about that young fellow?"

"I don't believe he knows anything about the holdup."

"Well, your opinion is good enough for me, Doc. I'm going to tell Lay and Dickey to let him go."

"Maybe they won't like it," I commented. "They might not agree with me."

Kramer did not answer as he got up and walked over to where the prisoner and two investigators were sitting.

"I believe that you can turn Hallack loose." I heard Kramer tell them.

The special agents turned toward their superior in surprise. "If you let this fellow go," one of them said, "you'll never see him again."

"That's all right," Kramer said decidedly. "You can turn him loose. I'll take the responsibility."

Lay and Dickey shook their heads in disapproval, but they had no choice in the matter. They removed the handcuffs, and Hallack was a free man. Kramer's decision did not enhance my popularity with them, but I hoped that time would prove beyond any doubt that the boy was innocent.

At Cotopaxi Hallack bid us goodby and got off the train. A few miles further on Kramer called my attention to the place where the train robbery had taken place. By this time, however, it was dark; so we didn't stop to make an examination. The others in the car had already combed over the area, and I told Kramer that I preferred looking around when it was daylight.

The scene of the robbery was familiar to me since I had often passed by there when taking prisoners from Gunnison to the state penitentiary at Canon City. It occurred to me as we rattled by that directly across the Arkansas River from the locality stood a log ranch house, owned by a notorious horse thief and cattle rustler by the name of Dick McCoy. His cabin had for many years been a hideout and headquarters for all kinds of badmen. I had seen some of these unsavory characters, since it was a common practice for representatives of the McCoy gang to check the smoking car of passing trains at the Cotopaxi stop to see what peace officers might be going through. They usually carried big six-shooters dangling on their hips and were often drunk and looking for trouble. While I had seen them pick fights with conductors and fellow officers, none of them as yet had bothered me.

"It seems strange to me," I remarked to Kramer, "that the train was held up in full view of the McCoy ranch over there across the river, unless the robbers stood in somehow with the McCoy outfit. Have any of your men talked with Dick McCoy or his family?"

"No," Kramer answered, "we haven't got around to it yet."

"Let's you and me run up there tomorrow then," I suggested, "and pay them a little visit."

"Sounds like a good idea," Kramer agreed.

When we arrived at Texas Creek that night, Kramer and his associates took up where they had left off in directing pursuit of the train robbers. Men were converging there from all directions to report their findings. The usually quiet and deserted railroad stop had taken on all the aspects of a wild west boom town. The place was overflowing with cowboys, sheriffs, posses, detectives, and special investigators. One of the first persons I ran into was my old partner, Tom Horn, who was representing the Pinkerton Detective Agency.

"Well, Tom," I greeted, "it looks like we're gonna be working together again."

"That's right, Doc," he said, as we shook hands. "I hope we do as well chasin' train robbers as we did chasin' horse thieves." He was referring to the two horse thieves that he and I had picked up a year previously in southern Arizona.

Kramer's private car was a mad house with officers coming and going all during the night. I sat in on most of the conferences. According to the latest reports, the train robbers had apparently slipped out of the Wet Mountain Valley where they were at first believed to be surrounded. However, no one had been able to find their trail leading out of the area.

Shortly after midnight Sheriff Stewart of Fremont County shouldered his way into Kramer's compartment, which the express company manager was using for an office. Stewart told us that while searching for the fugitives he had discovered a deep cave a few miles distant from the Wet Mountain Valley, and he was convinced that the four bandits were hiding out in there. He asked for volunteers to accompany him up to investigate.

"We'll take some dynamite along," he said, "in case they decide not to come out peaceable-like."

"What makes you so sure they're in that cave?" I asked. "Did you see their tracks leading into it?"

"No," Stewart said, irritated at my skepticism, "but that canyon where the cave is located is so full of rocks and boulders you wouldn't expect to find any."

"Then, on what evidence do you base your belief that they are in there?" I persisted.

"Because if they're in that vicinity, as we have reason to believe since it's not far from where we lost their trail, it would be a natural place to hole up."

"I don't want to dampen your enthusiasm, Sheriff," I said, "but only a bunch of amateurs would hole up in a cave where they could be so easily cornered. I believe that the men we're after are experienced enough to get out of this country just as fast as they can travel."[8]

"Well, no one is asking you to go along, Doc," Stewart said in exasperation.

"Shores here has had more experience than any of you in trailing outlaws," Kramer said, "so he probably knows what he's talking about. Anyway, tomorrow he and I plan to visit the McCoy ranch."

"My name is Lloyd," a man in the crowd spoke up, "and as deputy sheriff from this county, I know the McCoys and their henchmen. I'd be glad to go with you fellows up to the McCoy ranch if you want me to."

"I'm Ed Farr," another young man said, "deputy sheriff from Walsenburg, and I lost a couple of saddles which I think the McCoy gang might have stolen. I'd like to go up there with you also and have a look around."[9]

"You can count me in too, Doc," Horn said. "We make a good team."

"That's all I can take," I interrupted. "I can't learn anything if I go up there with a crowd."

"So long as you've got so many volunteers, Doc," Kramer said, "why don't you count me out. That long walk up the river would be pretty hard on an old man like myself. Isn't there anybody here who would like to check over the cave with Sheriff Stewart? We shouldn't leave a stone unturned." Six men volunteered.

The next morning Stewart and his followers set out on horseback to inspect the cave while I and my party set out on foot to visit the McCoys. We crossed the Texas Creek bridge over the Arkansas and turned up the shoreline. As we plodded along, Deputy Sheriff Lloyd gave us the lowdown on the McCoy family.

"They're a pretty tough bunch," he said. "Dick McCoy, the old man, is out on bail and will soon go on trial for killing a stock detective named Arnold. Dick has two daughters and four sons, and they're all chips off the old block with the single exception of the oldest boy, Charles, who runs a saloon in Cotopaxi. The next to the oldest boy, Joe, already has a record. He recently broke jail and is still at large. The two youngest boys, Tom and Street, ain't served time yet, but at the rate thy're goin' they soon will be."[10]

We arrived at the ranch about one o'clock. Lloyd knocked on the door, and a big, full-bearded man appeared. He was unkempt, shifty-eyed, and his breath reeked of whiskey, although he was not drunk. A big six-shooter dangled from his hip.

"Hello, Dick," Lloyd said, "we were just on our way over to see where the train was held up and thought we'd drop in and get a drink of water."

"You're just in time for dinner, Sheriff," the big cattleman said amiably, glad of an opportunity to get in good with the strong arm of the law. "Bring your friends and come on in."

As we entered, I glanced curiously at the clan. Mrs. McCoy was a large, coarse looking woman whose lined, weather-beaten face made her age indeterminable. Two tall youths, who proved to be Tom and Street McCoy, were sitting at the table. McCoy's buxom daughters were helping to set the table. They were quite attractive, in striking contrast to the rest of the family. The younger was about eighteen while the older girl was in her early twenties. During the course of the conversation I gathered that she had only recently been widowed. Nevertheless, she was already keeping steady company with one of the Price brothers. The Price brothers, I learned, were two young men who owned a small ranch some twelve miles away in the Wet Mountain Valley, where the train robbers' trail had been lost. They were both members of the McCoy gang, and I decided to pay them a visit in the near future.[11]

For a time the conversation proceeded spontaneously and without effort. The train robbery was purposely avoided in much the same manner as a salesman will make a lot of small talk with a prospective victim before coming down to the real purpose of his visit. Apparently the McCoys liked Deputy Sheriff Lloyd, even though he wore a badge, and accepted the rest of us at our face value. No introductions had been made.

Street, a boy of about fourteen, and Tom, around seventeen, sat on each side of me, and I soon had Street talking a blue streak about trivial matters that a young ranch boy is interested in.

When I thought the time was ripe, I guided our conversation around to the robbery. Street abruptly clammed up.

"Since it all happened just across the river," I went on casually, looking at Street to observe his reaction, "I'll bet you heard some of the commotion, didn't you?"

The blood drained from the boy's face, and he was obviously rattled. He hesitated, glancing in the direction of his father, who was sitting at the head of the table. Everyone was busily eating and talking; so no one noticed the boy's embarrassment.

Seeing that no help was forthcoming, Street finally muttered, "I—I guess I was asleep at the time."

That was a good answer, but his hesitation and discomfort convinced me that he was lying. Apparently the McCoys knew more about this robbery than they wanted to admit. It was not beyond the realm of possibility that one or more of them had even participated in it. They were certainly not above such things, and Joe McCoy, the fugitive from justice, and even Tom McCoy, the quiet seventeen-year-old lad sitting next to me, both fitted the vague description of the willowy youth who wore the droopy cowboy hat.

"It looks like all the shooting would've awakened some of you," I said, pushing my advantage.

Before he could answer, his father broke in, "Street, you'd better quit talkin' so much and git to eatin'." The boy took advantage of his reprimand to say nothing more for the remainder of the meal.

"Where are you from?" Mrs. McCoy asked me to bridge the ensuing silence. She was sitting at the foot of the table, and everyone heard the question.

"I'm from Gunnison, ma'am."

"Do you happen to know Doc Shores, the sheriff who lives there?" she asked with more interest.

"Yes," I replied quietly, "that's me."[12]

The impact of this admission on the McCoy family was so pronounced that it surprised me. They all paused in their eating to stare at me. Although they quickly regained their composure, it definitely put an end to their camaraderie. Thenceforth, the atmosphere around the table was tense and strained. Apparently my name was not a popular one with them.

After dinner Deputy Sheriff Lloyd complimented Mrs. McCoy and her daughters on their good cooking and offered to pay her for the dinner. She, of course, refused but was obviously pleased by his gesture. I was beginning to see why Lloyd was so well-liked among his constituents. He was apparently a good politician as well as an efficient peace officer.

While the women began clearing the table, the rest of us walked outside onto the cobble-rock river bank. The canyon wall towered above the log house, allowing only a few hours of sunlight to reach it each day. Smoke from passing trains had stained the bluffs and the dwelling, making the place a gloomy and depressing spectacle.

"Mr. McCoy," I said, "could we rent some horses from you to ford the river and take a look at the place where the holdup occurred? Maybe Street could be our guide?"

"Oh, I'll go with you myself," McCoy replied, apparently believing that his youngest son had talked too much already. Turning to Street and Tommy, he told them to saddle up five horses.

The boys walked over to the corral and returned shortly with the horses. As they approached, Ed Farr nudged me and said very quietly, "The saddle on that pinto is mine. I'd recognize it anywhere."

"Well," I said, "go ahead and tell McCoy it belongs to you. We'll back you up in case he starts anything."

Farr walked up to the pinto and examined the saddle. "Mr. Mc-

Coy," he said finally, "this saddle is mine. It was stolen from my place about a month ago."

Not knowing just what McCoy's reaction might be, I braced myself.

"I don't doubt it," McCoy replied with surprising docility. "Kirkendall, one of my cowhands, came in with it the other day. He's not always too particular where he gets things."[13]

I had heard of Kirkendall. He had the reputation of being one of the worst in the gang. Among his many escapades which had reached my ears was the time he got into a fight with a conductor while looking through the smoking car of a train stopped at Cotopaxi. He was drunk and tried to pick a fight with one of the peace officers who was taking a prisoner to Canon City. The conductor ordered him to get off the train, and when he refused, the conductor knocked the outlaw down, took an ivory-handled revolver away from him, and threw him off the train. Since the McCoy outfit usually got away with their bullying antics, the conductor became quite a popular hero for getting the best of them.

As we were fording the river, McCoy once more brought up the subject of the stolen saddle. "How much did it cost you?" he asked Farr.

"Thirty dollars. I had it made for me by Frazier of Pueblo."

"I'll give you what you paid for it," McCoy said. "I have a trial comin' up in a few weeks, and it wouldn't help my cause none to have it said that I was in possession of a stolen saddle."

"Do you think I should sell it to him, Doc," Farr asked. "I don't want to allow anything to stand in the way of a man's good name." He turned in his saddle and winked at me. Fortunately the irony of the remark and the wink went unnoticed by McCoy.

"It's up to you, Ed," I said.

"I don't have the cash with me now," McCoy explained, "but if you sell it to me, I'll send you the thirty bucks in a few days."

"What do you think about it, Horn?" Farr asked.

"If you don't need the saddle, why don't you sell it to him?" Horn commented. "He'll pay you for it all right. With his trial coming up he couldn't afford not to."

"All right, McCoy," Farr said. "You can keep the saddle, but send me the money soon or I'll be back to get it."

"Where shall I send it?" McCoy grunted.

"To Ed Farr, Walsenburg, Colorado."

I learned later that the old scoundrel sent Farr the thirty dollars as promised. It was perhaps the only time that he ever honored an obligation.

After riding across the Arkansas River we followed McCoy up the steep grade to the railroad tracks where the train had been flagged down and robbed. Leaving our guide with the horses, we dismounted and scattered out to inspect the trampled sand and cinders for evidence. The various posses had obliterated most of the tracks and signs near the scene of the crime. However, we examined the ground carefully, trying to sift out the marks of the outlaws from those of the investigators.

I had learned from past experience that when holdup men are waiting for their victim, be it a train, a stagecoach, or a person, they nearly always use tobacco to relieve the nervous tension. So, I kept my eyes open for any such tell-tale signs. After a time I discovered a pipe with a wooden bowl and a crooked stem lying under a log in a bunch of cedars. Scattered around in the same vicinity were some cigarette stubs and a lot of burnt matches.[14] Since the spot where I found these articles was some distance from the railroad where the ground had not been trampled by the posses, I assumed that they had been left there by the train robbers.

I put the pipe in my pocket and got down on my hands and knees to look at the tracks more carefully. It appeared as if a number of men had crouched and stood around the immediate area. I judged that this was where the robbers and flagman had been hiding just prior to the holdup. I became sure of it when I noticed circular indentations scattered among the footprints. Such imprints could have been made by a peg leg.

Encouraged, I ascended the hill still further. I had proceeded upgrade about another fifty yards when I came to a clump of cedar and pinon trees. In this shady alcove I found where two horses had been tied. I called the attention of my companions to the comparatively fresh tracks, and we agreed that they had probably been made by the horses of the train robbers.

We returned to where McCoy was holding our horses, and mounting up, we followed the suspicious-looking tracks down to the river. Crossing the stream, we found where they came out of the water and entered a narrow gulch. Numerous other horse tracks converged on them here, where some posse had picked up the trail. We rode back to the railroad grade, where I paid McCoy for the use of his horses, and we started walking down the tracks to Texas Creek.

"Those horse tracks leading up the gulch," Farr observed after McCoy had departed with his horses, "could be the ones that the posse followed into Wet Mountain Valley."

"Why don't we hit that trail tomorrow, Doc?" Horn said. "It looks like a good lead."

"Maybe so, Tom," I said, "but in this game a fellow must go slow. I'd like to take another day or so assembling all the known facts before we go blundering off half-cocked."

"What kind of facts?" Horn asked impatiently.

"Well, for example, I didn't like the way McCoy acted. It might help us to find out more about him and his recent activities. I suggest that we ride up to Cotopaxi tomorrow and talk with some of the people there who know him."

"The train robbers will be clear across the border," Horn muttered, "before we even get off our butts."

The next morning Horn, Farr and I rented three horses and rode up to Cotopaxi. We put them in the town's livery barn and went over to the grocery store, which was usually the center of local gossip and news. There were several loafers lounging around, and we struck up a conversation with them.

After a preliminary amount of small talk, we directed the topic of discussion around to the McCoys. One of the visitors was garrulous and volunteered most of the information. He said that a term of court never set without old Dick McCoy being brought to trial for cattle rustlin' or horse stealin'.

"Do you think the old boy had anything to do with the recent train robbery?" I asked, bringing up the holdup for the first time.

"No question about it," the talkative one continued. "He and his boys prob'ly done the whole thing. Dick will soon go on trial for murder, and that's their way of raisin' enough money to hire a good lawyer."

"A most interesting motive," I commented. I could see that we weren't going to learn anything so long as this opinionated fellow was around; so I suggested to my comrades that we'd better be moving along. A few hours later we returned to find the store empty except for the proprietor.

We bought a box of cigars and some other items to get the storekeeper in a friendly, communicative mood, all the time pleasantly talking about the weather and other casual subjects.

"That was quite a talker you had in here a while ago," I remarked with a laugh. "Do you think he was right about the McCoys being back of the train robbery?"

"No, that feller is just a bag of wind."

"I figured as much," I said, lowering my voice in a confidential tone, "but the McCoy place is located so close to the holdup that it makes a fellow sort of wonder whether the old sidewinder had something to do with it."

"I reckon the McCoys knowed who pulled the job all right, but I don't believe they done it."

I bought another box of cigars to keep the storekeeper cooperative, and then I turned to him and said with admiration in my voice, "I can see that you really know what's goin' on in this man's town."

I could tell by his pleased expression that my flattery had the desired effect. "All I have to do in my business," he said knowingly, "is just keep my eyes and ears open."

"That's right," I agreed, continuing to pour it on thick, "but it's surprising how few people have learned to observe what's going on around them. Now, a fellow like you, who has trained himself to be alert, notices things that most others don't. For example, if you told me that you suspected somebody of robbing that train, it would mean something."

Swallowing the bait hook, line, and sinker, the gullible storekeeper walked out from behind the counter and took the three of us into his confidence. "As a matter of fact," he said quietly, "I do have some suspicions, and now that them loafers is gone, I'll tell yuh what I think."

Horn, Farr, and I gathered around him, listening attentively, and he obviously enjoyed being the center of attraction. He spoke softly and emphatically as if he were revealing a secret of world-shattering significance.

"A few months ago," he said, "two prisoners was let out of the pen down at Canon City, and they came up here and throwed in with the McCoys. They traded with me a lot, and I got to know 'em pretty well. Now, ever since the train robbery, I ain't seen hide nor hair of 'em. It looks mighty funny to me, mighty funny."

"Can you describe these two fellows?" I interrupted.

"Well, one of 'em looked sort of like a slicker from the city. He liked the ladies and was quite a dresser, usually wearing a celluloid collar and a derby hat."[15]

"What did he call himself?" Horn asked with growing interest.

"Burt Curtis."[16]

"What did his partner look like?" Horn went on.

"He was a husky feller with a peg leg, and he was known around here as Peg Leg Watson."[17] Mention of the peg leg brought us all up with a start. It was beginning to look as if we had stumbled on pay dirt.

"A peg leg?" I asked to make certain I had heard right.

"According to Watson," the storekeeper continued, "he lost the lower part of his leg during the war while fightin' for the Union. More'n likely, though, it was shot off in some holdup. But in spite of his peg leg he was as active as a cat. He could ride a horse with the best of 'em, and he cut quite a figure at the community square dances, bowing to his partner, 'chasing the squirrel,' and pointing his peg leg like a young dance master."[18]

A customer entered the store, and the storekeeper cut short his account to wait on him. I nodded to my companions, and we walked outside and headed for the stable.

"Well, we sort of got an earful," I commented. "Things are beginning to take shape."

"It looks like Watson and Curtis are two of our men, all right," Farr said. "What do you thing about McCoy?"

"He's still a question mark," I said. "Apparently he's got inside dope about the robbery, but my hunch is that if any of the McCoys took part, it was one of the boys rather than the old man."

"Do you think we've got enough facts now, Doc," Horn asked, "to get down to business and pick up those tracks before they get any colder?"

"There's still some loose ends," I replied, "but I think we've gathered about all the information we're gonna get around here. I'm ready to set out in the morning. That is, if you can be persuaded to leave." I winked at Farr.

"Well, it's about time," Horn grumbled. "I was afraid that Sheriff Stewart or somebody would bring in the robbers before we even got goin'."

After returning to Texas Creek we made preparations to head out the next day. We procured three fresh saddle horses and a pack horse, ready for a long trail. That evening I checked with Kramer to see how Sheriff Stewart and his posse had fared on their cave expedition, but no word had been received from them as yet.

Early the following morning Horn, Farr, and I picked up the tracks of the two train robbers, where they had ridden up the narrow wash across the river from the scene of the robbery. We followed the hoof-prints into the Wet Mountain Valley, where they were obliterated by those of the pursuing posses and bloodhounds. Since the trail was pointed westward in the direction of the Sangre de Cristo Range, we assumed that the fugitives had proceeded over this mountain range down into the San Luis Valley. From here they could have turned southward down the valley into New Mexico or continued westward over the Continental Divide into the formidable San Juan Mountains of the Western Slope. Between these two alternatives the easiest and most logical route for them to have taken was the former, for if winter overtook them in the rugged San Juans, they would never get out alive. So, after a consultation we decided to strike over the Sangre de Cristo and try to re-discover their trail in the San Luis Valley.

First, however, there were a couple of details I wanted to check on before leaving the Wet Mountain Valley. The first of these was a visit to the Price brothers' ranch. One of them was going steady with the older McCoy girl, and both were members of the McCoy gang. As such, they were definite suspects.

Nobody was at home when we arrived, but we could see a couple of men working in a nearby hay field. We dismounted and led our horses into the barn where we tied them. As we started back out, Farr stopped to look at a comparatively new saddle hanging on one of the mangers.

"This is that other saddle of mine which was stolen," he said. "You seem to bring me luck, Doc. I'm sure glad I decided to go along with you."

We walked out into the field where the Price boys, John and Henry, were pitching hay onto a wagon. They were friendly and we visited with them for some time. Among other subjects, we talked about the robbery, but, unlike the McCoys, they were perfectly relaxed and betrayed no appearance of guilt.

Before we left, Farr said, "A saddle of mine is hanging up down there in your barn."

The brothers looked at each other in surprise, but after a moment's silence, one of them said, "Well, if it's yours, go ahead and take it. Somebody down the river left it here the other day."

"Kirkendall, maybe?" I couldn't resist asking.

"Oh, do you know him?" John countered evasively.

"Who doesn't?" I replied. "But we're after train robbers, not saddle thieves; so I guess we'd better be makin' tracks. Can you tell us where the Reverend Richards lives?"

"He lives in a little white house a quarter of a mile south of here next to the Rockhill place," Henry said, pointing in the general direction. Then, with a sudden twinkle in his eye, he added, "You never can tell about these preachers, can you?"

As we walked back to the barn, Horn asked, "What in hell do you want to see the preacher for? Do you think he's mixed up in the holdup?"

"A young suspect by the name of Hallack claimed he spent the night of the robbery at Reverend Richards' house," I explained, "and because I thought the boy was tellin' the truth, Kramer made two of his special investigators turn him loose. I just wanted to make sure that I didn't give Kramer a bum steer."

Upon reaching the barn, we untied our horses and Farr tied the stolen saddle on top of our pack outfit. We arrived at the minister's house around noon, and Richards invited us to have dinner with him and his family.

While we were eating, I stated the purpose of my visit. "I was in Salida several days ago," I said, "and I happened to hear a couple of officers interrogating a lad by the name of Hallack concerning the recent train robbery. His alibi was that he spent the entire night of the holdup, August 31st, in the Wet Mountain Valley with the Rockhill family."

One of the Price boys had mentioned this name as we were leaving, and I used it now to see what Richards' reaction would be.

"Well, that's funny," the minister said thoughtfully, "for I'm sure that was the night he stayed here with us." He looked questioningly at his wife and daughter.

"Yes," Mrs. Richards agreed, "he spent last Monday night with us. Was that the night of the robbery?"

"That's right," I replied, pleased to see the boy and myself vindicated in this roundabout manner. "On second thought Hallack did say that he spent the night here with you folks. I got the names twisted, maybe because they both begin with the letter R."[19] I laughed lamely. The preacher glanced at me piercingly. He apparently saw through my little ruse.

Having completed my two projects in the Wet Mountain Valley, my associates and I started over the Sangre de Cristo Range. In the foothills we came across a small potato patch. We took advantage of this opportunity to paw enough spuds out of the ground to fill our saddle pockets, thereby increasing our limited supply of grub.

We made camp that night near timberline. The September nights are bitterly cold on the Sangre de Cristo at this altitude; so we gathered some dry wood and built a big fire. That evening we rounded out our usual diet of coffee, biscuits, and salt pork with roasted potatoes, which really hit the spot.

We retired early, sleeping with our feet toward the fire. It grew so chilly during the night that we nearly burned the soles off our boots trying to keep warm. Under the conditions none of us slept well, and we were anything but refreshed when we broke camp and set out in the early morning.

The top of the range was above timberline, and we picked our way across it through the rocks and boulders. Descending the other side, we once more entered forests of spruce and pine, which gradually gave way to quaking aspen in all of their autumn splendor.

On our way down the grade we shot three grouse, which we tied to our saddles. Around mid-morning we rode out onto the broad, grassy expanse of the San Luis Valley. Spreading out somewhat to look for tracks, we turned directly south toward the Rio Grande River. If the fugitives had passed through the valley, as we assumed they had, it would be comparatively easy to find their trail in that wide open country.

Early that afternoon we came to the Mineral Hot Springs Ranch.[20] This was a small resort with several cabins, a store, and a granary. We bought some oats from the caretaker to feed our tired horses and asked if he would cook the three grouse we had shot. He agreed to do so, and while he was preparing the meal, I asked if he had seen any horsemen pass by in the last week. He replied in the negative, which, along with our failure to discover any recent horse tracks, pointed strongly to the possibility that we were on the wrong scent. After reaching the Wet Mountain Valley the outlaws, instead of continuing westward over the range, had apparently reversed their original course and turned eastward through the plains country to throw us off the track. They could still be hiding out in the Wet Mountain Valley, but I doubted this since these outlaws were nobody's fools, and with an intensive manhunt going on, it was definitely to their advantage to get out of the area as quickly as possible. At any rate, they had given us the slip and won the first round. All we could do now was to admit our mistake and start over.

I returned from the kitchen to the living room, where I found my two companions taking a needed nap. Farr was stretched out on the floor, while Horn was dozing in a big arm chair. Following their example, I lay down beside Farr and was soon fast asleep.[21]

Our host awakened us when the grouse were ready, and after washing, we ravenously fell to. We were hungry after our long morning in the saddle, and the fried birds were a rare treat.

"I hate to admit it," I said to my companions as our host went into the kitchen to warm up the coffee, "but if the train robbers had come through here, we should have found some evidence of it by now. I'm ready to go back to Texas Creek or Cotopaxi and pick up a new lead."

"You may be right," Horn said, "but on the off-chance that they did come this way, I'd like to ride on down as far as Monte Vista. If I don't find any sign by then, I'll meet you fellers at Texas Creek in a couple of days."

So, after completing our meal we parted company. Horn continued on south toward Monte Vista while Farr and I went north on our way back to headquarters. We rode through Hayden Pass and spent the night at a ranch house belonging to an old German family. The next day as we were approaching Cotopaxi, Special Agent Lay intercepted us.

"You got here just in time," he said with suppressed excitement. "We are just getting ready to pull out in that freight train over yonder. Why don't you put up your horses and come along with us? We'll wait for you."

"Where are you going?" I asked.

"Down into the San Luis Valley. We just received word from the caretaker at the Mineral Hot Springs Ranch that three of the train robbers took dinner there yesterday."

"Well, I'll be darned," I said, amazed at this unexpected development. Could the outlaws have shown up after we left? "What did the caretaker say about them?"

"He said that they were all armed with Winchester rifles and six-shooters. They were so tired out that while he cooked their dinner, two of them lay down on the floor and went to sleep while the third sat up and kept watch."[22]

This account clarified the situation. Apparently our host at the resort had mistaken Horn, Farr, and me for the bandits.

"Two of those train robbers are right here," I said, pointing to Farr and myself. "Ed, Tom Horn, and I were the three men who took dinner at the Mineral Hot Springs Ranch yesterday."

"Well, that's another good lead gone plumb to hell," Lay said bitterly, turning back toward the freight train to call off the trip.

"I don't believe you are very popular with Lay," Farr remarked with a laugh as we rode on. "That's the second time you've taken the wind out of his sails."

In Cotopaxi we learned that Kramer was in town; so after leaving our horses at the livery stable, we went over to his private car which was standing on a siding. We reported the failure of our mission and set Kramer straight on the mixup at Mineral Hot Springs. We then asked if anything had happened during our absence and were told that nothing of significance had occurred. Sheriff Stewart and his posse had still not shown up, and their delay caused some to speculate that they might have run into something important.

These hopes were dispelled the next day when the saddle-weary group rode into town. I was present when Stewart gave his momentous report. After finding no evidence of the train robbers ever having been in the cave, Stewart, not wanting to admit defeat, had taken his posse up into the Sangre de Cristo mountains on the remote chance of finding some trace of the elusive fugitives in that locality. In the foothills they ran across the recently made tracks of three shod horses, which they assumed to be the mounts of the outlaws. The eager manhunters followed these tracks over the range and down into the San Luis Valley as far as the Mineral Hot Springs Ranch. Here Stewart was informed by the caretaker that three suspicious-looking characters had dined with him the previous day and upon leaving had split up, two riding north and the other south.

Some of the listeners were beginning to smile when the narrator reached this stage of his account.

"So, I divided the posse," Stewart continued, not noticing the amused expressions which were spreading through his audience. "I sent Deputy Lloyd with three men after the outlaw headin' south, while the rest of us struck out after the two goin' north. Their tracks led straight back here to Cotopaxi. So, gentlemen, the old parable that a criminal always returns to the scene of his crime may again be proving true. At least," he concluded with a dramatic gesture, "two of the train robbers are right here in our own back yard."

There was a moment of embarrassed silence as many in the group who knew the score began glancing at Farr and me.

"They're even closer than that, Stewart," I spoke up suddenly.

"As a matter of fact, your two outlaws are standing on each side of you." I pointed toward Farr and me as Kramer and the others broke out laughing. Stewart looked at me in bewilderment until the truth gradually dawned upon him.

"Our associate who headed south is Tom Horn," I continued. "Farr and I surrender, but I warn you that Tom is armed and might prove dangerous."

"I told Stewart that those tracks might have been made by you and your men, Doc," one of the posse commented lamely when the laughter had subsided, "but he said they couldn't be because you didn't know nothin' about that part of the country."[23]

"Well, Ed," I said to Farr, "this is the second time we've been mistook for train robbers. Maybe we'd better give up and go back home before we get killed or land in the hoosegow."

While Sheriff Stewart knew that I wasn't serious about giving up and going back home, I could tell by his expression that he wished I would. This was the second time that I had inadvertently locked horns with him.

The manhunt so far had been little more than a comedy of errors, and in spite of the laughter there was a strong undertone of discouragement. Having reached an impasse in the investigation, Kramer and his immediate staff returned to Denver, leaving instructions for those of us who remained to keep in touch with him through coded messages. Farr and I hung around Cotopaxi and Texas Creek for a couple of days, resting up and hoping for some new break in the case.

It soon came in a long coded telegram to me from Kramer saying that four armed suspects were recently seen riding south near La Veta Pass, thirty-five miles east of Alamosa. He asked Farr and me to meet Investigator Lay in Salida, where a special train would take us down through the San Luis Valley to Tres Piedras in northern New Mexico. En route the train would stop at Monte Vista to pick up Tom Horn. At Tres Piedras the four of us were to procure horses and try to intercept the fugitives in a little Spanish American village between there and Taos.[24]

"Sounds like another false lead," I remarked when I showed the message to Farr, "but we've got to check them all until we wind up with the right one. It's sort of frustratin' until you realize it's all part of the game."

Horn was awaiting us at Monte Vista, having made contact there with the Pinkerton Agency in Denver, which was working with Kramer. I asked Tom if he knew that a posse had been on his trail. That was the first he had heard about the fiasco; so apparently the posse had been notified of the mistake and turned back before overtaking him.

At Tres Piedras, New Mexico, we borrowed some saddle horses from an old sheriff of Mexican descent who volunteered to go along and help. He took us to the tiny settlement where we were supposed to intercept the horsemen. We spent the night on the roofs of various adobe buildings, waiting for the outlaws to ride into town. However, they did not show up.

During the night Lay, the special investigator, came down with the grippe; so the next morning he returned to Tres Piedras for medication while the rest of us went on to Taos. From here we decided to move in a big circle in order to head off or pick up the trail of the four horsemen, who were supposed to be riding southeastward through that area.

On the following day we rode to Cimarron, a town sixty miles northeast of Taos. Our horses were in good shape, and we jogged along at a steady, mile-consuming pace. We spent the night at Cimarron, and the next day rode north for some distance before turning southwest to complete the circle trip back to Taos. Our strategy was successful, and before dark we came upon the fresh tracks of the four suspects.

We soon caught up with them, but they proved to be four Colorado cowboys on their way south looking for strays. As was the custom when hunting cattle a long way from the home range, they went armed. Probably some rancher, seeing four strangers ride by with Winchesters in their saddle scabbards, had become suspicious and reported the horsemen as the Cotopaxi train robbers. The robbery had received a lot of publicity, and nearly everyone in the region was on the alert and interested in the manhunt. As a result, tips of all kinds were coming into headquarters, most of which were obviously of no value. After careful screening, only a few, such as this one, were deemed worthy of being acted upon.

After our return to Cotopaxi I took a short leave of absence from the chase to attend a term of court in Gunnison. Farr went back to Walsenburg to resume his duties as deputy sheriff of Huerfano County. Horn remained, continuing his investigation and sending regular reports in cipher to Kramer and the Pinkerton office.

Farr did not intend to work any more on the case; so Horn and I bid our friend goodby. My association with Farr had been very pleasant, and he told me several years later that as a result of it he had decided to make law enforcement his permanent career. He became exceptionally proficient in running down train robbers. In 1899 while pursuing the notorious Black Jack Ketchum's gang of outlaws near Cimarron, New Mexico, he was killed. He was sheriff of Huerfano County at the time. Strangely enough, he was shot in the Cimarron region not far from where he helped Horn and me intercept the four cowhands.[25]

I had not been in Gunnison long when I received an urgent message from Kramer asking Horn and me to report at once to his Denver office. I took the next train for Denver, picking up Horn at Texas Creek. We got off the train at the Denver Union Depot and proceeded on foot to Kramer's office, located in the old Cheesman Block on the corner of Seventeenth and Larimer Streets.[26]

The story that Kramer told us sounded like something out of a ten-cent detective magazine. A man by the name of Frank Owenby, who was known to us as a reputable character, had come to Denver from Walsenburg to report to Kramer that two vagabonds had told him they had run onto the train robbers' camp in a deep wash near Trinidad in southeastern Colorado. They claimed that they had sneaked up to the camp in hopes of picking up something to eat when they overheard the two occupants talking about participating in the train robbery. It was dark; so the eavesdroppers managed to creep away unseen. The next day they returned to the deserted camp site where they found some false whiskers. These were turned over to Owenby to corroborate their fantastic story. Kramer pulled the whiskers out of a desk drawer for Horn and me to look at.

"I know the story sounds crazy and like another dud," Kramer commented half apologetically, "but since Owenby is a dependable fellow, I think it's worth a check. So, I'd like to have you men go to Walsenburg and see him and his two informers."

Accordingly, Horn and I went to Walsenburg where we looked up Frank Owenby. He took us around to a nearby saloon and introduced us to the two bums. One of them was a supposedly reformed horse thief known as Black Bill Kelley. The other was a tinhorn gambler with a weak, pasty face whose name I don't remember.

They repeated their unusual story and agreed to accompany us to the alleged camp site near Trinidad. In agreeing to do so, Black Bill suggested that a small advance payment on the reward money be made to them to make the journey worth their time. Neither one had probably done an honest day's work in his life, and this reference to the reward was a further indication that they were lying in order to pick up some easy money and free publicity.

"None of the reward money can be distributed," I explained, "until one or more of the wanted men are actually captured. Now, unless you fellows are sure of what you're talkin' about, I advise you to call this whole deal off without wasting any more of our time."[27]

"That's good advice," Horn added, "for if we go down with you to Trinidad and don't find that camp site, we may decide to kill you."

"I'll go along with you on that," Owenby agreed. "I don't like to be doublecrossed either."

They assured us that they were telling the truth and would meet us at the livery barn in the morning to take us to the site. When it was time to leave, Black Bill's companion did not appear. He apparently got cold feet and decided to call off the deception while he still had a whole skin. Black Bill was on hand and seemed as confident as ever.

After renting a team of horses and a two-seated buckboard, the four of us started out for the Trinidad area. Darkness fell before we reached our destination; so we built a fire and dozed around it until daylight. In the morning Black Bill pointed to a wash where he said that the mythical camp had been located. But it was nowhere in evidence, and he wandered up and down the gulch, while Horn, Owenby, and I sat in the buckboard along the rim and watched him.

"Well, Owenby," I finally commented, "it looks like you got taken in all right. He's not gonna find any camp."[28]

"He must've been lyin' to me all the time," Owenby said. "Let's kill the bastard."

"That's a good idea," Horn agreed, "but let's make it look like we shot him in self-defense. That'll keep us in the clear."

"Oh, let the poor cuss go," I said, driving off. "Why should we take a chance of getting into hot water over an old, broken-down horse thief."[29] I decided that it would be better to make the poor devil walk back to Trinidad rather than risk having Horn or Owenby shoot him.

"I'm sorry about all this," Owenby apologized on the return trip to Walsenburg. He felt responsible for the entire fiasco and couldn't understand why he had been so gullible.

"I knew Black Bill and his crony were a couple of bums," Owenby said, "but for some reason or other I had a strong hunch they were tellin' the truth in this case. My hunches are usually more dependable."

Leaving Owenby at Walsenburg, Tom and I returned to Denver to report our findings. On the train I studied the big man sitting beside me. I was disappointed in his willingness to shoot down Black Bill in cold blood. His courage was unquestionable, but he was too quick on the trigger for a Pinkerton man. I was beginning to think that perhaps I had been wrong in recommending him to the renowned detective agency.

We arrived in Denver that night and obtained a room at the Brunswick Hotel. The next morning after breakfast we started up Seventeenth Street to Kramer's office. On the way I stopped to buy a newspaper. A glaring headline sprang up at me, stopping me dead in my tracks as I read the accompanying article. It confirmed Black Bill's story!

Two of the Cotopaxi train robbers had broken cover near Trinidad. The local sheriff, Brewer, had deputized several men, including Black Bill, and given chase. They had not traveled far when in the distance they saw two men preparing a meal over a camp fire. Their horses were staked out nearby.

"Those fellows might be the train robbers," Black Bill was reported to have said. "Maybe we'd better get out our rifles." The sheriff and his men were each carrying a Winchester rifle in his saddle scabbard.

"I don't think they are the robbers," the sheriff replied, "but even if they are, they won't dare resist us."[30]

The sheriff was wrong. As the posse drew near, both men unexpectedly jumped up from the fire and levelled their rifles at the approaching riders. One of them had a peg leg and the other was wearing a derby hat.

According to the article, they walked up to the possemen, and one of them asked, "Where are you bound for?"

"We are out hunting cattle," Sheriff Brewer had replied.

"Like hell you are," the man with the peg leg exclaimed. "You're huntin' us."

After taking all of their guns and tobacco, the perplexed manhunters were sent back to Trinidad empty-handed with the warning, "If we catch you following us again, we won't let you off so easy."[31]

"Let's get back to Trinidad quick, Tom," I said, handing him the paper. "It looks like Sheriff Brewer isn't the only fellow who got caught with his pants down." Neither one of us wanted to see Kramer now after this development. Maybe Black Bill and his hang-dog companion had been telling us the truth, after all. At the very least, it was a remarkable coincidence that Curtis and Peg Leg Watson should be found in the same vicinity where the two vagabonds said that they had stumbled on their camp. In any case, due to our skepticism Horn and I had certainly missed the boat.

We speedily gathered together the necessary equipment for a long chase, buying two new Winchester rifles, some blankets, and a mess kit. About nine o'clock that evening we emerged from the Brunswick Hotel with our guns and pack rolls, en route to the Union Depot.

"Let's go down to the corner of Larimer Street," I suggested, "and catch the next cable car."

"Oh, we can jump on right here," Horn said, walking out in the middle of the street. "Here comes one now."[32]

I followed him out into the traffic, each of us laden down with all our plunder. It was not a stopping zone, and the cable car rattled right on past us. Horn grabbed hold of the rear as it zipped by, intending to swing himself up to the door. However, he lost his grip and was thrown sprawling on the paved street, his pack roll, Winchester, and revolver scattering in all directions. He hit on his head and lay there unconscious as the traffic came to an abrupt stop and spectators began quickly gathering around us. I ran over to my fallen partner and lifted him to a sitting posture, but he was too stunned to stand up.

A newspaper reporter rushed up and started to question me. "What's the injured man's name?" he asked.

I gave the reporter a long, fictitious Irish name.

"Where does he live?"

I gave a phony address away down on Larimer Street.

Although dazed, Horn was soon able to get on his feet. I gathered up his guns and blankets. When I handed him his six-shooter, he tried to cock it. I snatched it away from him and put it in his holster. Then with the help of the conductor I managed to get him on the cable car, which was stalled with the rest of the traffic. A couple of cops came along and got the jam untangled. We got off on the viaduct and walked downstairs to the depot, where we bought a berth on the outgoing Santa Fe train. Horn was still groggy when we got on the Pullman; so I had the porter bring some ice, which I wrapped up in a towel and placed on his bruised head.

According to the newspaper report, the two fugitives were heading east from Trinidad; so in order to prevent them from getting too much of a head start on us, we got off the train at Rocky Ford, where we rented a team and a light wagon. We also bought two saddles and bridles, which we loaded in the back of the buckboard beside our pack rolls.

"Is there anything else we need?" I asked, since this was probably our last outfitting station for many weeks.

"Yeah," Horn grunted, "I reckon we'd better be takin' our coffins." He had been in a bad mood ever since his ignominious fall on Larimer Street.

We drove due south from Rocky Ford, hoping to either intercept the fleeing fugitives or pick up their trail if they had already gone by. Two days later we ran across the comparatively fresh tracks of three horses traveling in a southeasterly direction toward the New Mexican border. At the next ranch house we stopped to inquire about the horsemen we were following. There we learned that we were on the right track. We were told that a couple of days previously two desperate looking men—one with a peg leg and the other wearing a derby hat—had come riding by leading a pack horse. Because of their unusual appearance, they had attracted a good deal of attention. They were heavily armed and each had a several weeks' growth of beard.

"Those sound like the men we're after," I said to the rancher, "but with the start they have we're gonna need a couple of saddle horses to overtake them. Do you know where we could buy some?"

"The only one I have for sale is a four-year-old gelding, but there's a bigger outfit down the road a few miles. They could probably help you out."

"Let me see your gelding," I said. We accompanied the rancher to the barn where he caught a small, cream-colored mustang with dark stripes. I put my saddle on the pony and rode him around a little to get the feel of him. He had a nice gait and handled himself well; so I made an offer which was quickly accepted—a little too quickly, I thought, for I was used to dealing with horse traders.

After I had paid for the animal, Horn asked if he could ride him on down to the next ranch and see if he could find another mount for himself. My horse jumped around a little as Horn got on him, but he was soon brought under control. After Horn had left, I made arrangements with the rancher to take the rented team and buckboard back to Rocky Ford.

An hour or so later my riderless pony came stampeding back to the corral gate with two swearing cowboys in hot pursuit. As the runaway gelding came pounding past, I noticed that he had lost his bridle. The bronco slowed down somewhat when he reached home territory, giving one of the following horsemen an opportunity to rope him.

When the runaway was caught, the rancher and I hurried over to see what had happened to Tom Horn. The cowboys informed us that while they were showing him their remuda, his horse had suddenly started to buck.

"While he was tryin' to hang on," one said with a laugh, "his bridle broke and he was throwed off into some plum brush. Maybe he needs a few lessons in bronc ridin'."

"Don't underestimate that fellow," I said to the smiling horsemen. "He can teach you all how to ride broncos."[33]

I put another bridle on my jittery horse and went back with the cowhands to the neighboring ranch where the accident had occurred. There Tom was bargaining with the foreman about the sale price of two sorrels which he had picked out. When we rode up, I noticed that his face was scratched up considerably, but he seemed completely unconcerned about the mishap.

"Hello, Doc," he greeted. "I've got a couple of broomtails here for us. What do you think of 'em?"

"You only need one horse, Tom. I've already got mine."

"Oh, you don't want that half-broke bronc you're ridin', Doc. I've seen enough of him to know that sooner or later he'll get away and leave you afoot while he takes off for home. These two mares here are better broke and more dependable. Also, they've been runnin' together, and if one should get loose, she won't go far without the other."

It did sound like a better deal; so I agreed to take one of the sorrels if I could get back my money for the horse I had just purchased. Fortunately, the man from whom I had bought the striped gelding proved to be understanding about the matter. I told him that we were on the trail of two desperate train robbers and couldn't afford to take any chances of having one of our horses act up unexpectedly and leave us stranded. I pointed out that the horse had thrown my partner who was a better rider than I and that considering our dangerous mission, I didn't want to take a chance on a half-broke bronco.

"In that case," the rancher said pleasantly, "I'll take him back." He reached in his pocket and returned the money that I had paid him. "He's a little snorty for your kind of work."

Horn took his choice of the sorrels, picking the best looking one

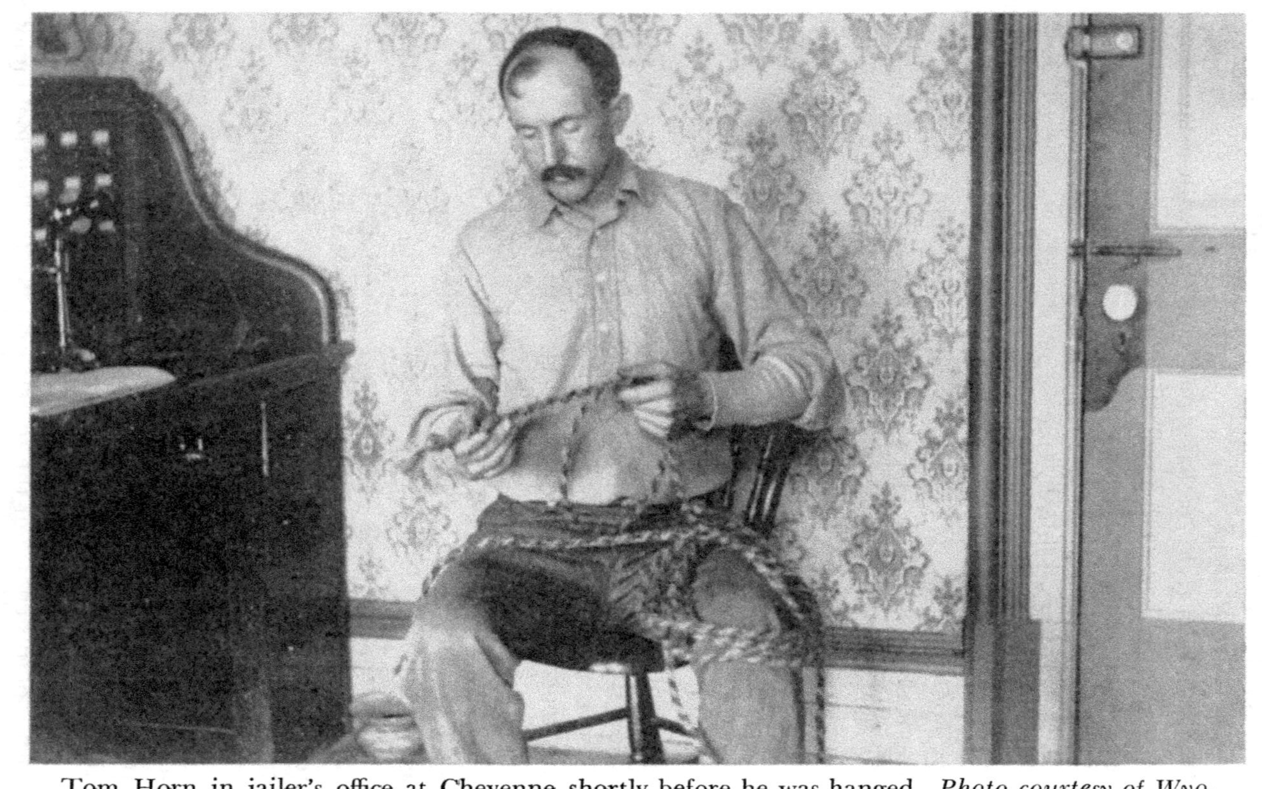

Tom Horn in jailer's office at Cheyenne shortly before he was hanged. *Photo courtesy of Wyoming State Historical Department, Wagner Collection.*

for himself. Having lost several hours of precious time, we tied on our pack rolls and resumed our way.

In spite of appearances my horse turned out to be the better of the two for traveling. Horn's nervous, high-spirited mare refused to settle down and pranced about so much that after the second day's ride she began to tire. My quiet, even-dispositioned mount moved along at a smooth, steady gait, which ate up the miles without tiring either horse or rider.

On the third day Tom broke one of his long sullen silences to say, "My horse is playing out. Since you're a lot lighter than I am, she would last longer with you riding her. What do yuh say we trade?"

To keep peace I complied. Tom was more and more showing a side to his character that I had never seen before. In my previous association with him on comparatively short trips he had been cooperative, full of stories, and a pleasant companion. Now, I was learning that on a long trail he was moody, insisted on his own way, and wanted the best of everything. This experience ended my close friendship with Tom, and I made it a point of never working with him again.

The fugitives were not hard to follow. They apparently did not realize that anyone was in close pursuit and made no effort to hide their trail. At each stop Peg Leg Watson left his peculiar imprint, and the pair did not avoid ranches or settlements along their way. They were even so sure of themselves that they often made a point of stopping to visit with local residents, admitting that they were wanted men and bragging about how they would kill anybody who was foolhardy enough to come after them.

Time after time we were told about these threats. Finally, I said to Horn, "These jaspers probably ain't kiddin'. When we run on to them, what do you think about bringing them back?"

"Let's leave 'em where we find 'em," he replied. "It don't look like they're gonna give us any other choice." I agreed.[34]

In spite of their seeming overconfidence, they rode surprisingly hard, and we had difficulty closing up the several days' gap between us.

Right from the start Horn and I had set up a man-killing schedule for ourselves. We would arise each morning while it was still dark and ride a strong, steady pace for fifteen or twenty miles. Then we would prepare a quick breakfast, allowing our horses to graze during the time. After eating we would continue on, jogging along for another three or four hours before taking another short break for lunch. Then, we would ride on until dark. This was the old Indian way of traveling after making a raid so as not to be overtaken by their victims.[35]

I hadn't put so many hours in the saddle for a long time, and after a few days I was as sore and stiff as a greenhorn. The strenuous pace finally even had its effect on Tom, and his discomfort was reflected in his cantankerous disposition. He would ride for hours without speaking, and when he did condescend to say anything, he was usually abrupt and surly.

The chase lasted forty-three days. We followed our quarry through southeastern Colorado into New Mexico. At Clayton, New Mexico, we discovered that they had caused quite a disturbance. While patronizing one of the sporting houses, they had got into a gun fight with several other customers who were members of a local gang of thugs. Peg Leg received a flesh wound in his chest during the fray. Being greatly outnumbered, the two outlaws had wisely got out of town as quickly as possible, going across the border into the panhandle of Texas. Here they struck the Washita River which they followed deep into the Indian Territory of Oklahoma.

Horn and I stayed one night with a Baptist minister and his family. They told us that the train robbers had passed by a day or so before. After making camp nearby, the two newcomers had come over to ask about the country. They frankly admitted that they were trying to get as far off the beaten trail as possible in order to escape the law.

"What will you do if someone should follow you?" the preacher's wife had asked.

"Well, ma'am," the man with the ever-present derby hat answered, "we'll just fall down and go to shootin'."[36]

After reporting this encounter with the desperados, the minister said, "I advise you to be very careful. They are pretty hard men."

"Don't worry," Horn grumbled. "We are hard men, too."

The trail led through Camp Supply, where twenty years before I had been a bullwhacker. Here I ran into an old friend of mine by the name of Amos Chapman. He was a former scout and Indian fighter, having lost a leg in a battle with the Cheyennes. It was pouring down rain; so we sought shelter, giving me an opportunity to reminisce with Chapman for a short time. He said that he had married an Indian squaw and was living with her and his half-breed kids on a little claim some miles out of town.

We followed the train robbers down the Washita through the entire Cheyenne-Arapaho Reservation. In this isolated area we ran out of grub. Game was scarce, and we had to postpone a few meals until we reached Beaver City, one of the few settlements in this Indian country. It was about as far away from civilization as one could get, and most of its white inhabitants were fugitives from justice. After eating and replenishing our stock of provisions, we went into the lone saloon to have a drink and try to find out when the men we were after had passed through.

There were a bunch of hard-looking characters standing at the bar, and a game of stud poker was going on at one of the tables. The group eyed us suspiciously, but after buying them several rounds of drinks, we broke through their reserve and engaged some of them in conversation. Tom was really dry after all the weeks he had been on the water wagon; so he bought a quart bottle and began to make up for lost time. It was obvious that anyone connected with the law was not welcome in this man's town, and I hoped that the whiskey would not loosen his tongue too much.

"Did any of you fellers happen to see a couple of saddle tramps come ridin' through here with a pack horse?" Horn asked, unexpectedly bringing up the all-important subject.

This question was followed by an ominous silence, and I held my breath wondering how my hard-drinking partner would handle the situation.

"What's it to you?" one of our drinking comrades asked finally. "Are you an officer?"

"Hell, no," Horn replied emphatically. "This is a personal matter. I'm a breeder of race horses, and a couple of bastards stole my my best stud."[37]

"Well, now, that's some different," another bystander commented. "A hombre has a right to steal a horse whenever he needs one, but he hadn't ought'ta take a prize stallion."

"That's right," Horn agreed. "My friend and I wouldn't be here if they had just took an ordinary horse."

In spite of the rapidly diminishing whiskey in Horn's bottle, he was doing so remarkably well that I didn't interfere. Before the quart was gone, he had obtained the necessary information. Curtis and Watson had gone through the day before. They stopped just long enough to have a few drinks and buy a quart of whiskey to take with them.

By this time it was late at night, and with some difficulty I persuaded Tom that we had better return to our room and get a few hours of sleep before leaving town. As I guided him up the board sidewalk toward the hotel, I said, "I'm glad I got you out of that place before you really got drunk."

"Oh, I was just hittin' my stride, Doc," he said, speaking more pleasantly than he had in days. "I handled those bums pretty well, didn't I?"

"Yes, you surprised me," I agreed, "and I'm glad to see that the liquor has improved your disposition."

However, his good humor was short lived, for the next morning he was nursing a bad hangover and was twice as cranky as before.

We continued down the Washita into the Comanche Indian country. Upon reaching their agency at Anadarko, we had covered several hundred miles and both our horses were sore-footed and tired out. The Indian agent was a Scottish Rite Mason, and in order to get his needed cooperation, I showed him my old Scottish Rite card, which I always carried. I told him that we would like to trade our horses for fresh ones, and he passed the word around to some of his Indians. They assembled a small bunch of their best ponies, and the horse trading was soon in progress. The exchange was made in short order, I paying ten dollars to boot and Horn fifty. Horn was more of a horseman than I and more particular in his choice.

There were no through roads or trails out of Anadarko going down the Washita. It was a cotton producing area, and what few roads there were led back and forth across the river to the various cotton gins. So, we hired a deputy marshal named Henderson to guide us southward through the brushy, unmarked country.

When we came in sight of Pauls' Valley, a town on the opposite side of the river from the route we were taking, we crossed the bridge into the settlement. We inquired around among the residents, but no one we talked with had seen the men we described. So, we assumed that the fugitives had continued on down the river without stopping off in town.

Several days later we spent the night in a ranch house near the Rock Island Railroad. A short distance away stood a box car equipped with a telegraph office, which was serving as an improvised depot. We learned from our host that the two outlaws had ridden past on the previous day; so in spite of all we could do, they were still maintaining their lead.

Tired and discouraged, I retired early while Horn and Henderson went out on the porch to have a smoke. A half-hour later I was awakened by a knock. Sleepily I lighted the kerosene lamp and opened the door. The rancher and a boy of about sixteen entered.

"I'm sorry to bother you," the older man apologized, "but my son here just came back from down the valley where he's been visiting some friends. He says that the two men who passed here yesterday are staying at the Woods' place just a couple of miles below here."

This news brought me to my senses like a dash of cold water. Wide awake now, I asked the boy to describe the men, and when he told me that one of them had a peg leg, I was sure we were nearing the end of the chase.

I thanked the youth for his information and asked him to tell my partners out on the porch that I wanted to see them. When Horn and Henderson came in, I said, "It looks like our luck is changing. I've just learned that Curtis and Watson are spending the night at a farm house two or three miles down the river."

"How come?" Horn asked skeptically. "The last I knowed they were a day's ride ahead of us."

"Apparently they've quit running," I said. "Maybe they're as tired as we are and want to rest up a little. Anyway, this is the break we've been waitin' for."

"Whose house are they stayin' at?" Henderson asked.

"The Woods' place," the boy answered.

"I know where it is," the deputy said. "Let's go down there right now and tackle them before they have a chance to pull out."[38]

"No," I disagreed, "it's early and they'll be on the alert now. Let's make the arrest just before daylight. That's when human vitality and watchfulness are at their lowest ebb."

"If yuh wanta wait till then," Henderson said, "why bother to arrest them? Let's just hide behind some jack oak trees and shoot 'em when they come out in the mornin'. That's the way they handle train robbers down in this country."[39]

"We'll do it my way," I said. While I usually went along with my associates on minor matters, I always took a firm stand when the occasion warranted it. "Now, let's get a little sleep. I'll wake you up at three o'clock."

At the designated time we got up and had a hurried breakfast. Then, taking the rancher along with us to divert suspicion, we set out on foot for the Woods' ranch house. It was very cold and still pitch dark. We reached our destination in about an hour, and, as pre-arranged, our host, who was well known in the locality, continued on up to the front door and knocked while Horn, Henderson, and I hid behind some trees.

At the sound of the knock a light appeared inside the dwelling and the door was opened. By listening carefully we could hear our host tell Woods that his wife was ailing and he wanted to borrow some brandy for her. The two men went inside the house, where our landlord presumably told his neighbor what the score was and asked where the outlaws were sleeping.

When they re-appeared, we were surprised to hear a deep, sleepy voice call out from the porch, "What the hell's going on here?" Apparently someone was sleeping on a couch beside the front door.

"Just a neighbor dropping by to get some medicine for his sick wife," Woods answered.

"This is one hell of a time to git sick," the sleeper commented, turning over on his squeaking bunk.

After the two friends had parted company, our accomplice started back up the path toward his ranch. As he passed by where we were hiding, he paused for a moment to whisper, "That was Curtis sleepin' out there on the porch. He's got a six-shooter. Peg Leg left early last evening for parts unkown but should return in a day or so. Good luck."[40]

I patted him on the back in token of our appreciation for helping us out, and he resumed his way. When he had left, I turned to my companions and said, "Let's give Curtis twenty minutes to go back to sleep and then rush him. I'll give the signal when the time is up."

This waiting period just before going into action is always the hardest part of a crisis. At this crucial time one is invariably under terrific pressure and expecting the worst. A man is much more likely to break at this stage than when he's in the thick of battle.

As the minutes crept slowly by, it began to grow light. In the distance we could hear roosters crowing from surrounding ranches. The early morning air was brisk, and whether from cold or tension, I noticed that I was trembling.

Finally it was time to give the long-awaited signal. It was now light enough to see each other in the breaking dawn; so grasping my Winchester firmly, I motioned to Horn and Henderson and we sprinted as quietly as possible toward the porch.

A hunted man, like a wild animal, develops a sixth sense of impending danger. Although we made hardly a sound, Curtis awakened before we reached him. Jerking himself up, he lunged for his six-shooter, which was hanging in its holster at the foot of the bed. He raised it to fire, but seeing the muzzles of three rifles staring him in the face, he hesitated.

"You might get one of us, Curtis," I warned, "but there will be two guns left to blow you to kingdom-come. Now, give me your six-shooter or we'll let you have it."

"Why didn't you come in the daytime instead of at this ungodly hour?" he snapped, handing me his gun. "Then, I'd have made it more interesting for you."

"That's what we figured," I commented. "We've heard all about your threats to shoot it out with anybody who followed you."

"So, you were too scared to face us in the daylight?" Curtis snarled sarcastically, apparently taking my mildness as a sign of softness.

After forty-three days on a difficult trail, Tom and I both were on edge and in no mood to take any abuse. So, when Curtis started to get insulting, Horn lost his temper.

He unexpectedly grabbed the outlaw by his long woolen underwear and jerked him out of bed. "I'm fed up with your cheap threats," Horn shouted. "When I first started hearing about them, I made up my mind then and there to leave you wherever I found you, and that's just what I'm gonna do."

"Don't kill him!" Mrs. Woods screamed, running out on the porch in her nightgown.[41]

This timely interference was all that saved Curtis's life, and he knew it. From then on we had no more trouble with him. After he was dressed, I put some light handcuffs on him and reinforced them with a piece of twine which Woods located for me.

"Did you fellows have any idea that somebody might be following you?" Horn asked.

"At the rate we were goin' we figgered only one man stood a chance of stayin' with us."

"Who is that?" Horn asked.

"An old sheriff by the name of Shores."

Henderson and Horn both glanced at me. "Would you know this old sheriff if you seen him?" Horn continued.

"I believe I would."

"If I told you that was Sheriff Shores over there," Horn said, pointing at me, "what would you say?"

Curtis looked me over with interest. "I'd say you were a liar," he finally exclaimed. "He don't look like Shores to me."

"I admit he's a pretty tough looker," Tom said, "but he's Shores all right."

I realized that after being on the trail for six weeks I wasn't much to look at. My face was weather-beaten to a dark tan and covered with a thick growth of beard. My hair hadn't been cut in more than two months, and my clothes were rumpled and dust-covered. I probably looked more like a train robber than the man we had just captured. My partner showed the ravages of the long chase also.

After breakfast I took our prisoner aside and had a confidential talk with him. "You look like a pretty decent sort of a fellow," I lied, "and I can't help but feel that Watson got you into this jam. If you'll tell me where I can find him, I'll see to it that you get off easy."

In spite of all my palaver, Curtis refused to reveal his accomplice's whereabouts. However, Watson's pack roll was still in his room, and Woods called our attention to one of his shirts hanging to a broken branch of a nearby tree. So, we assumed that he would be back soon. In examining the shirt we found a bullet hole in one side surrounded by a blood stain. This was undoubtedly the shirt he was wearing when he was shot in the brothel at Clayton, New Mexico.

"We heard about the gun fight," I remarked to Curtis. "How bad was Watson hurt?"

"Just a flesh wound. Although he bled quite a bit, it wasn't bad enough to slow up a tough hombre like him."

"So we noticed," Horn observed dryly.

There was no jail in the region to put our prisoner in, and we had no shackles. "What are we gonna do with him?" I asked Horn.

"He's a pretty slick customer," Horn commented, "and without irons it's gonna be a tough job to keep an eye on him. So, why don't you take him back to Denver on the next train and get him out of the way. Henderson and I can take care of Peg Leg when he comes back."

This sounded like good reasoning; so I made ready to leave with Curtis. Woods happened to have a discarded trace chain and padlock lying around in a shed; so I took them along to take the place of shackles. The key to the padlock had been lost, but I could open it with a nail.

Horn and Henderson accompanied us over to the box car to see us off. From here I sent a wire to the sheriff at Gainesville, Texas, asking him to meet me there on the train with a pair of shackles. I then thanked Henderson for his help and gave him my new Winchester rifle in part payment for his services. Horn also gave him a nice pair of spurs, and the deputy marshal seemed satisfied.

After getting on the train, I split open one of the prisoner's boots and padlocked the chain to his ankle. I tied the other end around a leg of our seat. Curtis objected to my cutting up his boot, but I told him that where he was going he wouldn't need it, anyway.

I treated my prisoner, as usual, with as much consideration as possible under the circumstanes. At one time during the journey, I talked with him a little about the train robbery.

"One of your accomplices," I said, "was described as a gangling willow of a kid who wore a slouchy hat and checkered shirt. I always sort of figured that he was one of Dick McCoy's boys—probably Joe, the escaped convict. Am I right?"

"No, Doc," Curtis laughed. "You're on the wrong track there. I will tell you this much. None of the McCoys had anything to do with this holdup."

"Well, that does surprise me some," I said. "They acted so damned guilty. But maybe they just didn't want to say anything to give their friends away. They did know, of course, who were involved?"

"Nothin' goes on in that country," Curtis admitted, "without the McCoys knowin' about it."

"If the McCoys didn't help you," I said "who the devil were those two other fellows with you and Watson?"

Curtis smiled but did not reply to my question.[42]

At Gainesville a big, fine-looking man wearing a sheriff's badge and a broad-brimmed hat got on the train. He entered our car and glanced around at the passengers as he strode down the aisle. He was carrying a square box in which I assumed were the shackles that I had ordered.

I looked up at him expectantly as he approached, but he kept right on going without paying any attention to me. I wasn't surprised because I wore no badge, and with my uncut hair, heavy beard, and worn clothes I didn't look much like an officer of the law.

"Sheriff," I called, getting to my feet, "I believe that you're looking for me."

He stopped and turned around, eyeing me curiously, "No, I don't believe so," he said. "I'm looking for Sheriff Shores. Do you know him?"

"That's me," I said, "even though I do look like one of Quantrell's raiders."

"Glad to know you, Shores," he said, shaking my hand. "Here are the irons you ordered."

"Much obliged. How much do I owe you?"

"Six dollars. They should be quite an improvement over that contraption you've got there." He pointed toward the old chain and padlock fastened to Curtis's ankle.

After the sheriff left, I got out my nail and went to work on the uncooperative padlock. When I finally worked it open, I took the trace chain off the prisoner and replaced it with the new shackles.

"Now I feel more respectable," Curtis remarked. "These ankle bracelets are more befittin' to a man of my station. After all, I'm no ordinary crook. I'm a train robber."

At Fort Worth we had to change trains. At such times I usually took off a prisoner's shackles, depending on the handcuffs to keep him from escaping. In this instance, however, since the cuffs were so light, I didn't dare take the risk. So, Curtis had to hobble between trains as best he could with his leg irons on.

While Curtis was a likeable person when he wanted to be, his cooperativeness didn't fool me any. I was familiar enough with criminals to know that his pleasant manner was primarily a front to throw me off-guard. If I relaxed and gave him the slightest opportunity to escape, he would try to do so, even if it meant shooting me in the back.

As Curtis mince-stepped toward the station in his shackles, a Negro called over to him, "Hey, mister, why didn't yuh learn to step short like yuh is now befo' yuh stole that hause?"[43]

Later on as we travelled through the Texas panhandle, some women began peddling delicious-looking fried chickens at many of the stations. They held the delicacies up to the car windows for us to see and smell, and I couldn't resist buying a couple for me and my prisoner.

It was well along into the night when we started pulling into Clayton, New Mexico. Curtis showed signs of uneasiness; so I said. "You seem a little jumpy. What's bothering you?"

He told me about the shooting scrape that he and Peg Leg had got into at Clayton. "If any of them fellers we tangled with happen to spot me, they'll be comin' aboard to lynch me just as sure as hell."

"Take it easy," I said. "I won't let them hurt you. If I can't handle them alone, I'll uncuff you and give you back your gun."

The train jolted to a stop at the depot, and a group of men carrying rifles got on and came walking through our car. When they appeared, the blood drained from Curtis's face and he whispered, "Better give me my gun."

I drew my revolver and held it in my hand as the newcomers strode up.

"Why, hello, Shores," one of them greeted unexpectedly. "What are you doin' here?"

The tension somewhat relieved, I reholstered my six-shooter and said, "I'm on my way to Denver with a prisoner. What are you gents up to?"

"Word has got around that this train might be held up," the man answered; "so we were deputized to guard it."[44]

Curtis and I breathed easier when we learned the reason for their intrusion.

"I've got a train robber here," I said, "but I don't think he intends to pull anything tonight. How about it, Curtis?"

"No, not tonight," Curtis replied with a smile. "You fellers can all go home."

Before reaching our destination the next evening, two men from the Pinkerton Detective Agency boarded the train to help me escort the prisoner on the last lap of our journey. They said that Tom Horn had notified them of my coming. When we pulled into the Denver Union Station, several police officers were on hand to relieve me of Curtis and take him to jail.

A day or so later Tom Horn arrived with Peg Leg Watson handcuffed to him. I learned that after my departure Horn and Henderson had kept a round-the-clock lookout for Watson's return. It was during Henderson's shift when the missing man finally came riding up the lane toward Woods' ranch house. The Woods' children were playing outside at the time, and Henderson told the oldest girl to run into the house and tell Horn to come out immediately. Horn sauntered out casual-like so as not to arouse any suspicion. When the unsuspecting Peg Leg dismounted in front of the house, both men covered him with their Winchesters and ordered him to put up his hands.

The only comment Watson made to them was that he should have known something was wrong when he noticed that his old torn shirt was no longer hanging up on the tree branch where he had left it. Horn and his prisoner left for Denver on the next train, taking the same route as Curtis and I. Watson with his game leg was an easy prisoner to travel with since he was not agile enough to make a run for it.

When their case came up for trial in the federal court at Denver, Watson and Curtis were both found guilty and given life sentences for robbing the United States mail. While they did not actually rob the mail car, District Judge Hallet ruled that forcing the mail agent out of the car amounted to the same thing. They were both taken to the House of Corrections at Detroit, Michigan, to serve their terms.

Peg Leg died there several years later.[45] I visited Curtis once as I was passing through Detroit. He seemed glad to see me and introduced me around to his fellow prisoners and the warden as "the man who run me down." He was looked up to as a sort of hero among the other convicts for having held up a train. He was an aristocrat in the criminal world.[46]

After serving about twenty years of his life sentence he was granted a commutation of sentence due partly to my efforts. His behavior while in prison had been exemplary, and I felt that after twenty years he had paid for his crime; so I took up his case with U. S. Senator Edward Wolcott of Colorado, and Curtis was pardoned. The Pinkertons and Mr. Kramer backed me up in the matter.

Curtis appreciated what I had done, and not long after his release I received a letter from him postmarked Portland, Oregon. He asked me to meet him on a certain date in the Wet Mountain Valley to dig up the money and gold retort which he said that he and Peg Leg had buried there right after the holdup.[47]

I wrote back thanking him for his unusual offer but said that the $1500 ($1000 from Mr. Kramer and a $500 reward from the U. S. government) I had received for helping arrest him and Watson was all that I could conscientiously accept.

I don't know whether he ever retrieved the stolen money or not, but that was the only time in all my many years as a peace officer and investigator that a train robber offered to share his loot with me.

FOOTNOTES

[1]C. W. Shores, "The Cotopaxi Train Robbery," original manuscript, Denver, Colo., Mar. 28, 1927. p. 1. In possession of Western History Dept. of Denver Public Library.

[2]*Ibid.*, p. 15.

[3]*Rocky Mountain News,* Sept. 1, 1891, p. 1.

[4]*Rocky Mountain News,* Sept. 2, 1891, p. 1.

[5]Shores, *op. cit.,*

[6]*Rocky Mountain News,* Sept. 1, 1891, p. 1.

[7]Shores, *op. cit.*, p. 2.

[8]*Ibid.,* pp. 7-8.

[9]*Ibid.*, p. 3.

[10]Jay Monaghan, *Last of the Bad Men,* The Bobbs-Merrill Co., New York, 1946, p. 120. Also, see Shores, *op. cit.,* pp. 3-4.

[11]Shores, *op cit.*, pp. 5-6.

[12]*Ibid.*, p. 4.

[13]*Ibid.*, pp. 4-5.

[14]*Ibid.*, pp. 4-5.

[15]Monaghan, *op. cit.,* p. 121.

[16]Doc Shores in his memoirs calls the man Burt McCarty, but since all other accounts refer to him as Curtis, Shores' memory, in this instance, was probably at fault.

[17]According to Shores, his proper name was J. S. Watson.

[18]Monaghan, *op. cit.*, p. 121.

[19]Shores, *op. cit.*, pp. 6-7.

[20]In his records Shores calls it the "Iron Springs Ranch," which is the same name he used for a ranch in southern Arizona where he captured a horse thief (see preceding chapter). In this instance he apparently was referring to "Mineral Hot Springs," located a few miles south of Villa Grove in the San Luis Valley.

[21]*Ibid.,* pp. 9-10.

[22]*Ibid.,* p. 10.

[23]*Ibid.,* p. 12.

[24]*Ibid.,* p. 11.

[25]*Ibid.,* pp. 24-25. For a further account of Ed Farr's death see Erna Fergusson, *Murder and Mystery in New Mexico,* Merle Armitage Editions, Albuquerque, New Mexico, 1948, pp. 99-100.

[26]C. W. Shores, "When First Appointed Special Agent of the Rio Grande Express Company," original manuscript, Denver, Colo., Mar.

4, 1927, p. 4. In possession of Western History Dept. of Denver Public Library.

[27]C. W. Shores, "The Cotopaxi Train Robbery," *op. cit.,* p. 13.

[28]Monaghan, *op. cit.,* p. 124.

[29]Shores, *op. cit.,* pp. 13-14. Several years later some Mexicans killed Black Bill Kelley near Trinidad for stealing their horses.

[30]*Ibid.,* pp. 14-15.

[31]*Ibid.,* p. 15.

[32]*Ibid.,* p. 16.

[33]*Ibid.,* p. 17.

[34]*Ibid.,* p. 21. Also, see p. 18.

[35]*Ibid.,* pp. 17-18.

[36]*Ibid.,* p. 18.

[37]*Ibid.,* p. 19.

[38]*Ibid.,* p. 20.

[39]*Ibid.,* p. 22.

[40]*Ibid.,* p. 21.

[41]*Ibid.,* p. 21.

[42]Shores says nothing about the capture of these two men; so if they were ever arrested, he apparently had no connection with it. He does identify them as two young men named Boyle and Grier. On page 14 of his account—*The Cotopaxi Train Robbery*—he writes, "Boyle's people lived over on the Hard Scrabble Creek about ten miles south of Canon City, and Grier was a Welsh boy . . ." He goes on to say that they met Watson and Curtis at the McCoy ranch where the train robbery was planned.

[43]Shores, *op. cit.,* p. 23.

[44]*Ibid.,* p. 24.

[45]*Ibid.,* p. 28.

[46]*Ibid.,* p. 27.

[47]*Ibid.,* pp. 27-28.

Chapter VII

Spring in the Gunnison country is associated with the promise of renewed warmth and life in a cold and barren land. It is a time of year when violent death and tragedy seem strangely out of place, but it was in this pleasant spring setting that I was called upon to solve a murder—one of the most uncalled-for in my entire experience as a peace officer.

One afternoon during the forepart of April, 1885, an unkempt middle-aged man walked into my office. He had a thick growth of jet black whiskers and the bleary eyes of a heavy drinker.

He introduced himself as Pat Cassidy and said that he owned a saloon at Sapinero, a small village thirty miles west of Gunnison.

"I just stopped in to tell yuh," he continued, "that I'm gonna have to kill some of the sons of bitches who are patronizin' my roadhouse."

I was somewhat taken aback at my visitor's frankness. "Is that the proper respect to show your customers?" I commented.

"They're a rough bunch," he explained, "and when they get liquored up, they try to take over the joint, servin' themselves drinks and pushin' me around like I had no rights. I've gotta kill a few of 'em to prove that I'm still runnin' the place."[1]

"There are other ways of handling the situation," I said. "If you have any more trouble, let me know and I'll come down and arrest them."

"I'll let juh know all right, Sheriff," he said meaningly. "Just remember what I told yuh." He got to his feet and without further comment walked unsteadily toward the door.

While I assumed that my eccentric visitor's remarks were inspired by a whiskey-inflamed mind, I somehow felt a twinge of apprehension about his threats.

"You'd better not try to kill anybody," I called out to him as he left, "or you'll have a lot more to worry about than someone taking over your saloon."

In the press of more urgent business I promptly forgot about Pat Cassidy and his strange behavior. However, it all came back with jarring impact a few days later when I received the following telegram. It was dated April 17th and read:

> Come down to my place right away. A man was killed here last night.
>
> Pat Cassidy[2]

This ominous message arrived about nine o'clock on a Friday morning, and the train had already left Gunnison for Sapinero and points west. So, I went over to a nearby livery stable and rented a team and buggy to make the trip in. I procured a rough box from the undertaker, W. A. Arey, to bring back the body for an autopsy. Then, accompanied by a justice of the peace named Col. S. M. Tucker,[3] I set out for Sapinero.

It was about a six-hour drive, and we finally arrived at four o'clock that afternoon. The streets of the village were deserted; so we drove up in front of the hotel and asked its proprietor, George Root, where Pat Cassidy's saloon was located.

"It's that place over yonder with the fence of beer bottles stacked around it," he said, pointing it out to us. "There was a drunken brawl over there last night and a man was shot and killed. He's still lying across that beer-bottle fence, right where he fell."

"Has anyone disturbed the body?" I asked.

"No, Cassidy said that you were comin' down today; so I told everyone to keep his distance."

"Has the dead man been identified?" Tucker asked.

"About all I know is what Cassidy told me when he came over

here this morning to wire you. He said the dead man's name was Mike Keating and that he came over from Leadville yesterday to see Bob Opeman, a young fellow who's workin' here with the section gang."

"What was the trouble all about?" I inquired.

"I don't know how the fight got started, but when Cassidy was here this morning, his face was all bloody and he said that he had killed one man and would like to kill another."[4]

"Thanks for your cooperation," I said. "This evening Col. Tucker here will hold a coroner's inquest; so we will get in touch with you then."

"I'll be glad to help out in any way I can, Sheriff. That joint of Cassidy's has long been a den of iniquity, and it's about time some action was taken."

Tucker and I got into our buggy and drove over to the designated saloon, surrounded by its unique fence of discarded beer bottles, piled like cord wood about four feet high.[5] Judging by the accumulation of bottles, the place did a roaring business.

The murdered man had fallen up against the inner side of this enclosure and then slid forward to the ground, taking part of the unusual fence down with him. He lay there on his back amid a pile of fallen beer bottles. He was a young man of about thirty and wore a dark pair of trousers and a woolen coat. There was no weapon on him except an ordinary pocket knife which I found in his pocket.

At first glance there was no mark of violence or evidence as to the cause of his death. Upon closer examination, however, we found a small blood-stained bullet hole in the left shoulder of his coat. An autopsy performed the next day in Gunnison by my friends, Doctors Rockefeller and Jennings, revealed that a .44-caliber Winchester bullet had pierced the deceased's left shoulder, and passed sideways through his chest, lodging in the right shoulder.[6]

Mike Keating had obviously been standing at a right angle to his killer when he was shot, as if he might have been turning to make a run for it at the last minute.

After our quick scrutiny of the dead man, Tucker and I carried him over to the buggy and placed him in the coffin-like box which we had brought with us. It was not an easy task since Keating was a big man. Then, we walked up to the front door of Cassidy's saloon and tried to enter. The door was locked, and no one responded to our knocks. So we procured a plank and rammed the door a few times, breaking the lock.

We stepped inside and peered around the dimly lighted room. A sickening aroma of stale liquor pervaded the place, and the bar and tables were covered with dirty glasses and empty bottles. Some of the glasses still contained whiskey as if a number of the patrons had departed suddenly without finishing their drinks.

The saloon's most distinctive feature was a large assortment of loaded guns hanging on the walls. These included two Winchester rifles, three shot guns, an old-fashioned musket, two revolvers, and a four-barrel pepper box.[7] A third six-shooter was lying on the bar. I broke it open and found three loaded and three empty cartridges in the cylinder. Since the powder in the barrel was dry and no longer had any odor, I assumed that the gun had not been fired in at least several days.[8]

"This place looks like an arsenal," Tucker observed. "Cassidy seems to have a liking for guns."

"A saloon is no place to keep loaded guns," I said. "It's no wonder somebody got shot."

There was a closed door at one end of the barroom, which evidently led into an apartment or bedroom. We knocked and then tried to open the door, but it was locked. When there was no answer to our pounding, we kicked it open.

There, lying fully clothed on a large double-bed, were Pat Cassidy and a woman of about fifty. At first I thought that they were dead, since Cassidy's face was a nightmare to behold. His nose and face were badly bruised, and his thick black whiskers were caked with blood. However, we soon discovered that the prostrate forms were not dead but merely sleeping off the previous night's drunken revelry.

On a stand by the bed was a glass and a big teapot half-full of whiskey. I shook Cassidy out of his stupor. He blinked his eyes in bewilderment when he finally became aware of me standing over him.

"Why, hello, Sheriff," he muttered, sitting up on the side of the bed. "I didn't expect you here so early."

"It's not early, Cassidy. It's past four o'clock."

"By God, is it that late!" he exclaimed. "We lay down around noon for a short nap, but we must've overslept."

He painfully got to his feet, and picking up the teapot poured a stiff shot of whiskey into the empty glass.

"Would you like a drink?" he asked, offering the glass to me.

"No, thanks," I said. "Drink it yourself. It'll probably be the last one you'll get for a long time."

He then offered the drink to Tucker who also refused. So, Cassidy drained the contents at a gulp and started to replenish it.

"That'll be enough," I objected. "Let's go in the other room where we won't disturb the lady. I want to ask you some questions."

When we were in the barroom, I came directly to the point. "Who shot that man lying outside there?" I asked.

"I did," he replied frankly, "just like I told you I would. The son of a bitch got to arguin' with me about payin' for his drinks, and before I knowed what was happening, he grabbed a poker and hit me across the face. Then, he got hold of that six-gun lying there on the counter and started shooting at me. He must've shot two or three times before I got down my .44 Winchester and shot back. He dropped the revolver and ran outside. I didn't know that I had hit him until I saw him lying out there this morning. But it was either him or me, Sheriff. A clear-cut case of self-defense."

Cassidy was quite persuasive, but I had examined the revolver he referred to and knew that it hadn't been fired last night. Consequently, it was apparent to me that he was lying. However, before arresting him I wanted to break down his story of self-defense.

I walked over to the bar and again picked up the revolver which he said that Keating, the murdered man, had used to shoot at him. I pulled out the cylinder and looked into the muzzle. I did it merely for the effect that it might have on Cassidy because I already knew what I would find.

"The powder in this barrel is as dry as a bone," I said. "This gun couldn't possibly have been shot last night."

In those early days when a bullet was fired, it emitted a large amount of burned black powder and left a strong, acrid aroma. For a day or so this powder had a tendency to collect moisture from the air, and then it would gradually dry out. Therefore, if the powder in a barrel was dry and no longer left any odor, it was sure proof that the gun hadn't been discharged for several days.

In spite of all this evidence to the contrary, Cassidy stuck to his story. "You're wrong as hell, Sheriff," he retorted. "That gun was fired last night by that feller lyin' out there on the beer bottles."[9]

I realized that I was wasting my time talking to Cassidy. He had made up his mind what he was going to say about the killing, and he was going to stay with it, come hell or high water. It occurred to me then that my best chance of finding out the truth was through the woman in the adjoining room. That is, if I could talk with her before she had time to compare notes with Cassidy.

"Is the lady in the next room your wife?" I asked.

"No, she's a widow who helps me run the saloon."

"What's her name?"

"Mrs. McIsaac."

"Colonel," I said, turning to the justice of the peace, "you keep an eye on Cassidy here while I go in and talk with Mrs. McIsaac."

"She'll tell you the same thing as me, Sheriff," Cassidy protested. "You're just wastin' your time."

I opened the bedroom door and walked inside, closing it behind me so that Cassidy couldn't overhear our conversation. Mrs. Mc Isaac had awakened and was sitting before a mirror combing her gray hair.

"I'm Sheriff Shores from Gunnison," I said, "and I'd like to ask you a few questions about the man who was killed here last night."

"There ain't much to tell," she snapped. "He just got drunk and refused to pay for his drinks. In the argument that followed he hit Pat with a poker and then started shooting at him. So, Pat had to kill him in self-defense."

This was the same story that Cassidy had told me; so he apparently had already briefed her how to testify. But she should be easier to break down than her paramour.

"Do you know who the dead man is?" I continued.

"He's a stranger around here, but from what he said I gathered that he was a miner from Leadville."

"Did you hear him say what his name was?"

"The man who was with him called him Mike."

"Was there anybody around besides yourself at the time of the argument?"

"There were two or three fellows from the section gang in here when the rumpus started, but they all had left before the shooting started."

"Who were they?"

She laid down her comb and turned toward me for the first time. I could tell that my bombardment of questions was beginning to bother her.

"You sure do ask a lot of questions," she remarked evasively.

"Mrs. McIsaac," I said, "you and your friend Cassidy are in serious trouble. A man has been murdered, and it looks to me as if you two were responsible. Your story that Cassidy shot him in self-defense won't hold up in court since I've seen the gun that Cassidy claimed the dead man used, and it hasn't been fired in at least a week. I will so testify, which will leave neither of you with an alibi to stand on."

She was listening to me intently; so I knew that I was getting through to her.

"Now, Cassidy could easily hang for this," I went on in a quiet, confidential tone of voice, "and you could get a long prison sentence for being an accessory. But if you'll cooperate and tell me the truth, I'll help you both all I can. I believe that I can keep you out of the penitentiary and prevent Cassidy from being hanged. How about it?" I smiled at her.

This little speech had the desired effect. Her attitude toward me mellowed.

"I didn't think we could get away with Pat's story," she said wearily. "What would you like to know?"

"Now you're taking the right attitude," I commented, "and it will be best for all of us. Now, let's start over. Did Mike, the murdered man, ever shoot at Cassidy?"

"No," came the faint answer.

"I noticed that someone gave Cassidy's face a good working over," I continued. "Did Mike hit him with a poker?"

If this were true, Cassidy still might have a good case of self-defense, even though he wasn't shot at. However, my natural assumption was that since he was lying about the shooting, he was also lying about the dead man's assault with the poker.

"No," Mrs. McIsaac admitted, "it was me who hit Pat with the poker."

This startling admission opened the way for a quick wind-up of the case. With her cooperation I was not long in gathering the necessary facts.

I kept the saloon closed and summoned a coroner's jury of six men with Col. Tucker acting as coroner. The three bystanders who had witnessed the dispute testified. These included Robert Opeman, who had been the murdered man's companion, and two other residents of Sapinero by the names of Cleary and Fleshingburger, who were shooting dice during the altercation. George Root, owner of the hotel at Sapinero, also testified, as did the defendants, Pat Cassidy and his mistress.

The inquest lasted until about ten o'clock that night when a verdict was reached that Mike Keating came to his death by a gunshot wound inflicted feloniously by Pat Cassidy. Mrs. McIsaac was found to be an accessory to the crime. From all of this testimony I pieced together the fateful events of the previous night.[10]

On Thursday evening April 16, 1885, Mike Keating and Robert Opeman went into Cassidy's saloon for some drinks. Keating was living in Leadville, but he had come down that day to visit Opeman, who was working on the section gang at Sapinero. While waiting for his friend to get off work, Keating had stopped in Cassidy's saloon off and on during the afternoon for a few drinks. However, he was still sober when he and Opeman came in later on during the evening.

The two men sat up at the bar, and Cassidy and Mrs. McIsaac served them from time to time. There were several other patrons present, some standing at the bar and others sitting at various tables. The latter included Fleshinburger and Cleary who were shooting

Early-day saloon similar to the one in which Mike Keating was shot. *Photo courtesy of Denver Public Library Western Collection.*

dice. These two men were among the last to leave and witnessed most of the disturbance.

Everything progressed smoothly until late in the evening when Cassidy asked Keating and Opeman to pay for their drinks.

Keating laid a piece of change on the bar and Cassidy pushed it back toward him. "That ain't enough," Cassidy objected. "That just takes care of the last round."

"We've already paid yuh for the other drinks," Keating said.

"That's right, Pat," Opeman agreed. "We paid each time that they were delivered. Don't yuh remember?"

"Are yuh tryin' to imply that I'm too drunk to remember?" Cassidy asked, becoming belligerent.

"Not any more so than we are, Pat," Keating replied agreeably. "We've all had too much, but don't yuh recollect that Irish coin —my lucky piece, I pretty near gave yuh when I paid for the drinks last time? You noticed it just in time or you'd have been short-changed and I'd have run out on my luck."

Cassidy scratched his balding head. "Yeah, I do seem to remember somethin' about a lucky piece, now that you mention it. Are yuh sure that all the other drinks are paid for? You two have been drinkin' up a storm."

"You bet, old fellow," Keating said, "I had a full weeks pay with me, and this is all I got left." He pulled a small handful of coins from his pocket. "I barely have enough to get home."

"We've paid for every drink," Opeman said. "You can take my word for it, and you and I have knowed each other for quite a spell, Pat."

"If you don't believe us, why don't yuh ask Mrs. McIsaac?" Keating suggested.

"I did and she said that yuh hadn't paid for anything as yet. But I do remember the Irish penny; so she must be wrong. Will yuh have a round on the house to square things?"

"You bet," Keating said. "Let's forget it."

After serving the drinks, Cassidy told Mrs. McIsaac what had transpired, but she still insisted that the young men had not paid. She and Cassidy had been drinking drink for drink with the rest of the house, and they were even further gone than their customers.

"You're too drunk to remember anything," Cassidy said to her. "Yuh shouldn't drink so much during workin' hours."

"You're a fine one to talk," the woman shrieked. "Just look at yourself. You're so drunk that yuh let those two young punks talk yuh out of a month's profit."

Her high, shrill voice attracted everyone's attention. Cassidy murmured some obsenity under his breath and told her to leave the room. She answered by grabbing an iron poker and giving him a a good wallop across the face. As the blood spurted from his nose, she raised the weapon to strike again, but Keating seized her arm and wrenched the poker away from her.

Bleeding like a stuck hog, Cassidy lunged at his mistress and grasped her by the throat. She screamed and fought back, but Cassidy bent her over backward and would have strangled her had not Keating once more intervened.

As soon as Keating had seperated them, Mrs. McIsaac dashed out the front door and ran over to the hotel, where she told George Root, the manager, that she was having trouble at the saloon and wanted him to return with her and help restore order. Seeing that she was drunk, he refused.

When she rushed out of the saloon, Mike Keating stepped back of the bar and said to Cassidy, "I'll tend bar for a while until you and the lady sober up a little."

Cassidy protested, but Keating, who was the stronger and the soberer of the two, took over. Gently but firmly he shoved the staggering proprietor aside and served drinks to the dice players, his friend, Opeman, and himself. One of the dice players paid for the round. Cassidy, seeing that his protests were futile, plumped down on a bar stool and let Keating assume control.

While Keating and Opeman stood facing each other on opposite sides of the bar, drinking and visiting, Mrs. McIsaac reappeared in the doorway. As she entered, she grabbed a revolver hanging near the entrance.

"What are you doin' back of that bar?" she said to Keating. "Now get out of this saloon or I'll kill you." She cocked the trigger.

Keating ignored her and went on talking to Opeman. A tense

moment followed in which everyone, except Keating, waited for the shot that didn't come.

Disconcerted by the Leadville man's complete indifference to her threat, she didn't fire but suddenly turned the gun on the others and ordered everyone out of the saloon, including Cassidy.

"Let's all of us git the hell out o' here," Cassidy said, starting toward the door.[11]

"Let's go, Mike," Opeman said, "I've had a bellyfull of this joint."

Opeman and the other customers departed, but Keating did not follow immediately. Cassidy walked as far as the front door with the others and then, shutting it, returned to the bar where Keating was standing.

While the others went their respective ways, Opeman stood outside the door awaiting his companion. He heard no disturbance inside, but suddenly the door was thrown open and Keating came running outside. There was a shot, and Opeman whirled around to see Cassidy in the doorway with a rifle in his hand. The saloon proprietor peered into the darkness for a moment and then went back inside.

"Is he shooting at us, Mike?" Opeman called over to his friend who had stopped a short distance away.

There was a long pause before Keating replied, "I guess so." His voice was unexpectedly hollow and weak.

"Did he shoot you, Mike? You sound sort of funny."

"I feel light-headed," Keating replied. "The drinks seemed to have hit me all at once."

He walked over to a nearby coal dump and sat down on it. Opeman followed suit, and the two friends talked for a short time. Keating was in such a stupor that Opeman again asked with concern, "Are you sure that you didn't get shot?"

"I guess not," Keating said vaguely. "This cool air should clear my head pretty soon."

"I feel a little groggy myself," Opeman said. "I think I'll go over to the section house and turn in. Why don't you come along with me?"

"No, not till I sober up a little. I might disturb the boys. I'll walk around for a while and join you later."

But death overtook Mike Keating before he had time to rejoin his friend at the section house. An autopsy showed that he died from a slow internal hemorrhage and that he may have lived for six to eight hours after being shot. In his drunken condition he probably never realized that he was dying.

After the inquest I arrested Cassidy and his mistress, intending to hold them there at Cassidy's saloon until morning when we could catch the eastbound train for Gunnison. Col. Tucker, the acting coroner, returned home that night in the buggy. Not long after he had left Sapinero a mob began gathering in front of the saloon. Many of them had attended the inquest, and their sympathies were all with the dead man. Whiskey had been procured and was making the rounds. The more the mob drank, the more determined they became to forcibly enter the saloon and lynch Cassidy.[12]

As the clamor grew, I decided to move my prisoners over to the hotel. Mrs. McIsaac realized the danger of remaining, but Cassidy was too drunk to know what was going on. Where he had obtained the additional whiskey was a mystery to me, but apparently he had it cached all over the place.

"They'll be chargin' the door soon," I said to Mrs. McIsaac. "Help me get Cassidy out of here and over to the hotel, or he'll be a dead duck for sure."

I took one of Cassidy's arms and she took the other, and we dragged him out the back door into the night. Under cover of darkness we managed to get him nearly to the hotel before we were observed.

"There's Cassidy!" someone yelled, pointing at us.

I pulled out my big six-shooter and, still pulling Cassidy along, shot a couple of times over the heads of the approaching mob. These warning shots delayed our pursuers long enough for Mrs. McIsaac and me to get Cassidy into the hotel lobby. Leaving him there with his mistress and the hotel proprietor, I went outside and advanced toward the rabble.

As I walked toward them, they quieted down somewhat so that I could make myself heard. "Take it easy for a minute and hear me through," I yelled. "I don't like Cassidy and what he has done any better than you do, but he's my prisoner and it's my job to take him to Gunnison tomorrow to stand trial, and I intend to do it even if it means bloodshed. So, unless you think that Cassidy is a man worth dying for, I advise you to break up and head for home."

"He sure ain't worth dyin' for," someone cried out.

"I agree with you," I said, "so let me handle him in my way, and I promise you that he'll get what's comin' to him."

"We want Cassidy!" somebody yelled, but the group gradually dispersed, and I returned to the hotel and took charge of my prisoners. During our long night's vigil I tried to get Cassidy to wash the blood off his face and whiskers, but he refused.

"I'm gonna leave it for the judge to look at," he said. "It might help my case."

The train pulled in shortly after breakfast. The box containing the body of Mike Keating was loaded on to the baggage car, and I boarded the coach with my prisoners. Upon arriving in Gunnison that Saturday afternoon, I placed them both in the county jail.

Their preliminary hearing was held on the following Monday, and Cassidy hired the law firm of Sapp and Brown—the two best lawyers in Gunnison—to defend him. On Sunday, the day before the hearing, they advised Cassidy to marry Mrs. McIsaac so that she wouldn't have to testify against him. So, I let them out of jail long enough to be married in my office before a justice of the peace.

In spite of this maneuver, however, the other witnesses and I who did testify against Cassidy persuaded the court to commit him to jail without bail pending his trial before the district court. There he was convicted of second degree murder and sentenced to sixteen years in the state penitentiary at Canon City.

Shortly after I escorted Cassidy to Canon City, his wife, who was discharged at the preliminary hearing, came there to live until he was released. But only a few years were left to them after Cassidy had paid his debt to society.

It all started on a promising spring day at a fair time of the year, but for Pat Cassidy, Mike Keating, and Mrs. McIsaac it marked not the beginning of life but the ending.

FOOTNOTES

[1]C. W. Shores, "Story of Old Patsy Cassidy, the Killer," original manuscript, Denver, Colo., Mar. 12, 1927, p. 1. In possession of Western History Dept. of Denver Public Library.

[2]*Ibid.*

[3]*Gunnison Review-Press,* April 18, 1885, p. 1.

[4]*Gunnison Review-Press,* April 21, 1885, p. 1.

[5]Shores, *op. cit.*

[6]*Gunnison Rievew-Press,* April 18, 1885, p. 1. Also, see Shores, *op. cit.,* p. 2.

[7]*Gunnison Review-Press,* April 21, 1885, p. 1.

[8]Shores, *op. cit.,* p. 1.

[9]*Ibid.,* p. 2.

[10]The following story of how Mike Keating met his death was assembled from eyewitness accounts written up in the *Gunnison Review-Press,* April 17, 18, 20, 21, 1885, p. 1.

[11]*Gunnison Review-Press,* April 20, 1885, p. 1.

[12]Shores, *op. cit.,* pp. 2-3.

Chapter VIII

During the eight years that I was sheriff of Gunnison County, my family and I lived in an apartment above the jail, where I also had my office. Although I had a jailer to help me, I was responsible for the care and safekeeping of the prisoners. There were some unique characters among my charges, and no story of mine would be complete without mentioning a few of them.

The most widely known of the men I held in custory was Alfred Packer, the notorious Colorado cannibal. During the winter of 1874 he murdered his five companions near the present site of Lake City and subsisted on their frozen flesh for nearly two months. At the time he was acting as their guide to the frontier town of Saguache, from which point the group intended to prospect the San Juan country of southwestern Colorado where gold had recently been discovered.

In March when the weather was more favorable for travel, Packer pocketed the money and personal belongings of his dead comrades and made his way through the snow to the Los Pinos Indian Agency, headquarters of the Southern Ute tribe. To sustain himself on the journey he carried strips of human flesh which he had cut from the bodies of his victims. He also carried with him a rifle and a coffee pot, in which he kept a fire burning since he was out of matches. Just before reaching the Agency he discarded the coffee pot and the incriminating supply of meat.

Packer spent a few days at the Los Pinos Agency and then went over the Continental Divide to Saguache. While in Saguache he met members of the original party of twenty-one prospectors who had started out with him from Salt Lake City to explore the San Juan. Due to the severity of the winter, the group had split up at the camp of Chief Ouray, head of the Uncompahgre Utes, near the present town of Montrose. Some of the more restless had braved the deep snows and cold weather to continue on their way, while the others remained at Ouray's camp until early spring to follow.

Upon gathering in Saguache, Packer was questioned about the whereabouts of his missing companions. He said that he had hurt his leg on the trip and was unable to keep up with the others; so they finally went on ahead without him.

This story about his being deserted was not generally believed, and when the Utah prospectors noticed that Packer had a lot more money than the twenty dollars he left Salt Lake City with,[1] they strongly suspected that he had killed and robbed his five comrades. These suspicions were told to General Charles Adams, the Los Pinos Indian Agent, when he came through Saguache.

In order to investigate the matter, Adams induced Packer to go back to the agency with him for the stated purpose of gathering a search party to look for the missing men.

During the search Packer claimed that he was lost and couldn't find the camp where he had last seen the vanished prospectors. In answer to various questions, he told so many contradictory stories that Adams became convinced of his guilt. In the meantime, some Ute Indians found the supply of meat that Packer had discarded near the agency. This was shown to the agency doctor who identified it as human flesh.

Upon this evidence Adams had Packer arrested on suspicion of murder. He was taken to Saguache and turned over to the sheriff there to await trial. He escaped soon afterward and was not heard from again for nine years.

With the coming of June, the deep snow disappeared in the mountains, and the decomposed, mutilated bodies of Packer's five victims were discovered two and one-half miles southeast of present Lake City on the eastern shore of Lake San Cristobal. Four of them lay in a row within arm's length of each other, while the fifth, who was identified as Shanon Bell, lay some distance away. The skulls of all the dead men had been split open with a hatchet, and Shanon Bell had also ben shot in the back.

Packer had apparently killed them while they slept with the exception of Bell, who must have awakened and started to run. Packer shot him in the back and then hit him over the head with the hatchet. It was a diabolical crime, but after becoming closely acquainted with the killer, I came to realize that it was entirely in keeping with his character.

After identification the bodies were buried where they were found. The burial ground is now surrounded by an iron enclosure, and a bronze tablet on a nearby rock reads:

> This tablet is erected in memory of Israel Swan, George Noon, Frank Miller James Humphries, and Shanon Bell who were murdered on this spot early in the year 1874 while pioneering the mineral resources of the San Juan country.

In March, 1883, nine years after Packer made his escape from jail, he was recognized at Fort Fetterman, Wyoming Territory, by Jean Cazauhon, one of the Utah men who had started out with Packer from Salt Lake City on the ill-fated expedition. The maneater was going under the assumed name of John Swartze.

Cazauhon went immediately to Cheyenne and notified the local sheriff, who arrested Packer and wired Sheriff Clair Smith of Hinsdale County, Colorado, where the murders had taken place. Sheriff Smith came to Cheyenne and escorted Packer back to Lake City where he was tried for murder. There on April 14, 1883, Melville B. Gerry, the district judge, sentenced Packer to be hanged a month later on May 19th at a place to be prepared in Lake City for that purpose.

Accordingly, a gallows was erected near the spot where the murdered prospectors were buried. Packer had hired two able lawyers to represent him—namely, T. C. Brown and Aaron Heims. Before the execution took place, they appealed the case to the state supreme court, which ruled that a person could not be hanged for commit-

Alfred Packer, the Colorado cannibal, as he looked in the Gunnison County jail while in custody of Doc Shores. *Photo courtesy of Library, State Historical Society of Colorado.*

ting a crime in Colorado before it became a state. Colorado did not become a state until 1876, while Packer's crime occurred two years previous to that time.

On this technicality the sentence was overruled and a new trial was ordered at Gunnison. Here Packer was found guilty of voluntary manslaughter and sentencd on August 5, 1886, to forty years in the penitentiary at Canon City. I was elected sheriff three years prior to this in the fall of 1883 and took over the office on January 1, 1884. Among the prisoners that I inherited from my predecessor was Alfred Packer whose case dragged on for several years during which time he was in my charge. After he was sentenced, I took him to Canon City chained to a cattle thief named Fred Meyers.

For the three years that I was associated with Packer, I learned a lot about him and none of it was good. Of all the prisoners that I held in custody during my eight years as sheriff Packer was the only one in whom I failed to find at least a few good qualities. He was slow-witted, cowardly, vicious, and a natural bully.

From his crudely written letters and my conversations with him, I learned that he had committed other serious crimes for which he was never arrested or prosecuted. Shortly after his escape from the Saguache County jail, for example, he murdered two young men east of Colorado Springs and stole their team and wagon. Later on near Tombstone in Arizona Territory he killed a prospector and took possession of his horse and pack mule. So, if one can believe him, and in this case he had no motive for lying, this is a part of Packer's story which has never been told.[2]

Packer had a persecution complex and took it out on everybody that he could, including his own relatives. It was part of my job to check the incoming and outgoing mail of the prisoners, and Packer wrote some of the most depraved letters that I have ever read to his sister in Pennsylvania. Among other things he accused her of neglecting him, and threatened to kill her when he was released from prison.

I kept these letters and showed them to Governor Charles Thomas when the *Denver Post* was putting so much pressure on him to pardon Packer.[3] The governor, in turn, showed them to the Board of Pardons which refused to pardon Packer. However, Governor Thomas did parole Packer finally in January, 1901, after he had served fifteen of his forty-year sentence. Terms of the parole provided that he could never leave the State of Colorado nor correspond further with his sister and other relatives whom he had threatened.

Many years after Packer's death, former Governor Thomas wrote the following letter to William C. Blair, editor of the newspaper at Lake City:

". . . Regarding Packer himself, the Denver Post bedeviled the life out of me during my whole term as Governor to pardon him, and its proprietors were bitterly vindictive because I would not do so. It so happened that I was in possession through former Sheriff Shores of Gunnison County, of a somewhat extended one-sided correspondence consisting of letters from Packer to his relatives. They were the foulest compositions that I ever read and were filled with all sorts of threats against them in the event he regained his liberty. I was under pledge not to make them public, but they were sufficient to justify a refusal of pardon even if he had any claim for consideration. I saw him several times during this period and talked to him at considerable length but saw nothing in his attitude to change my opinion. Finally, however, in view of reports concerning his health and also in view of the outstanding fact that his cannibalism was due to the pressure of starvation, I consented to parole him, conditioned in the most positive way, however, against his leaving the State or attempting to further correspond with his relations. Although the first of these conditions was presumed in the absence of express permission to leave the Commonwealth, I deemed it advisable to emphasize the fact very strongly.

I don't know what became of him nor when he died, but I am very sure that he was of no use to the community and probably a hinder to himself . . .

Sincerely yours,
Charles S. Thomas"[4]

After Packer was paroled, he lived in a little cabin near the town of Littleton. He became somewhat of a celebrity, and when he died there ten years after he was let out of the penitentiary, he had the

Alfred Packer's grave at Littleton, Colorado. From the markings on the tombstone, it would appear that Packer had served in the U. S. Army. *Photo courtesy of L. B. Dean of Denver.*

distinction of being buried in the Civil War Veterans' Cemetery at Littleton even though he never fought in the war on either side.

Packer tried to dominate his fellow prisoners in the Gunnison County jail, but there were two of them that he soon learned to leave alone. One was Virgil Wilson, a rancher of Montrose County, whom I was holding for safe-keeping until his trial. The authorities there wanted to give the populace a little time to cool off before taking him into custody to stand trial.

Wilson had shot his brother with a Winchester rifle and beat his skull in with a hammer. Then he threw the body into a well and emptied a straw tick over the corpse to better conceal it. As a further precaution, he piled a lot of barbed wire around the well on the pretense of keeping his cattle from falling into it but actually to prevent passers-by from stumbling on the remains. Nevertheless, the body was discovered and Wilson arrested.[5]

After Wilson was taken back to Montrose for trial, Packer wrote a number of iniquitous letters to him, calling him a lot of obscene names and threating to kill him if their paths ever crossed again. They reminded me of the vindictive messages that Packer had written to his sister, and I, of course, did not allow them to go through the mail. I still have them in my possession.[6]

Like most bullies, Packer was a coward at heart. Resentful of Wilson whom he feared and could not dominate, he took this safe and underhanded means of giving expression to his hatred and frustration.

The other prisoner whom Packer could not buffalo was a big, powerfully built coal miner by the name of Hugh McCabe, who was as dexterous with a knife as he was with his fists. For several years prior to his arrest he worked at the Baldwin coal mine, and I knew him well. I noticed that he usually carried a long clasp dirk knife which he used to cut his plug tobacco. Although it was a deadly-looking instrument, I never suspected him of using it as a murder weapon until a well-liked coal miner named Luke Curran was knifed to death in Baldwin in 1886.[7]

The killing occured in the evening shortly after a professional prize fight which from fifty to a hundred miners had been watching. As the crowd was dispersing, several men got into a fight, and during the struggle one of the combatants slashed Luke Curran across the abdomen. The blade was evidently long and sharp because it slit through Curran's vest and lay open his stomach. The wound was so deep that he died within a few minutes.

Two of my deputies—Lewis and Nolan—were at the camp, and learning of the murder they arrested three suspects—namely, Gaffeny, Kinney, and Hugh McCabe. They were taken to the mine superintendent's office and searched, but no knife or other weapon was found on any of them. A teamster was hired to drive the officers and their prisoners down to the Gunnison County jail in an old lumber wagon. As they left Baldwin, one of the spectators slipped McCabe a big .45 caliber six-shooter. In the darkness no one observed the act.

When about five miles out of Baldwin, McCabe unexpectedly jerked the gun from his coat pocket and shot it off directly over the head of Deputy Sheriff Lewis. Startled at the loud report, the team bolted. While the driver struggled to bring them back under control, both deputies jumped on the gunman and took the revolver away from him.

McCabe offered no resistance and laughed heartily at his little joke, "Don't think I was tryin' to kill you," he commented to Lewis. "I was merely testin' your nerve."

"I can't say that I like your sense of humor, Hugh," Lewis said, "but thanks for not killing me, anyway."

When the prisoners were brought to my apartment late that night, I registered their names in the logbook and put them in jail pending a preliminary hearing. I asked the officers if McCabe was carrying his long-bladed knife when they picked him up. They said that he wasn't, and I told them to go back to Baldwin and try to find it.

They returned to the coal mining camp and searched McCabe's living quarters without success. They then examined the vicinity where the knifing had occurred. This took a good deal of time since there was a thick layer of grass in the area. However, no trace of the missing knife was found.

They finally located it back of the wainscoating in the superintendent's office where the three suspects had been frisked prior to their being taken to Gunnison. In certain places the top of the wainscoating stuck out from the wall an inch or more, and while waiting his turn to be searched, McCabe apparently had slipped the closed knife down into one of these cracks. The handle and dagger-like blade were covered with dried blood, which was conclusive proof that it was the murder weapon.

The preliminary trial of McCabe and the other two suspects in the knife slaying was held in the city hall on the same day that the Alfred Packer jury was deliberating his case in the court house.

Late that afternoon I took Packer to the court room so that he would be present when the jury returned to render its verdict. While we were waiting for the jury to make its appearance, my undersheriff, Sam Harper, sent a messenger to the court house to inform me that the grand jury had cleared Kinney and Gaffeny of the knife slaying but issued a bill of indictment against McCabe charging him with the murder of the popular Luke Curran. The messenger went on to say that a huge crowd was rapidly gathering in front of the city hall and Harper was afraid to run the gauntlet and escort McCabe over to the jail without my help.

I immediately rushed Packer back to jail, which was only about a hundred feet from the court house. In my haste I locked him up temporarily in the steel cage instead of the iron cell, where I had kept him during his long confinement. Then I hurried over to the city hall. I made my way through the excited, angry mob and went inside the building where Harper and a couple of his friends were locked in the jury room with the prisoner.

"We can hold them off here," Harper said to me, "but they'll lynch McCabe sure as hell if we take him outside."

"We can't let them bluff us," I said. "A mob like that isn't hard to control if you don't panic. Follow me."

With an assurance I was far from feeling, I took McCabe by the arm and led him out the front door toward the throng of people. Harper and his friends followed close behind.

As we proceeded into the rabble, several of the ringleaders rushed up to grab our prisoner. I pulled out my revolver and said, "I'll shoot the first man who lays a hand on McCabe."

Harper and his associates also drew their six-shooters. This show of force put a damper on the enthusiasm of the would-be lynchers.

"You wouldn't shoot your law-abidin' friends to save that killer, would you, Doc?" one of them questioned.

"I sure will if you force me to," I replied. "Now, stand back and let us through."

Although there were the usual threats, the crowd got out of our way and no serious efforts were made to detain us. Upon reaching the jail I locked McCabe in the iron cell where I usually kept Packer.

Harper and I then hastened back to the court house with Packer. The jury had not yet appeared, but they were expected at any moment and the court room was filled to capacity with curious spectators.

While I was sitting there beside Packer, I heard a muffled roar, like the sound of a sudden wind. With all the commotion going on in the jury room, no one else seemed to notice the unusual noise. Fearing that a mob might be storming the jail, I left Packer in charge of Harper and hurried from the court room to investigate. As I was descending the steps, I almost collided with my jailer.

"McCabe has slit his throat," he cried out excitedly. "I was just comin' to get you."

We ran over to the jail, and there I found McCabe lying on his stomach in the front part of his cell. Blood was streaming across the iron floor in all directions. I grabbed the fallen man by the shoulder and turned him on his side. Although accustomed to sights of violence, I shuddered as I looked down at his grotesquely dangling head, which was nearly severed from his body. Blood was spurting from a deep gash which extended nearly from ear to ear. His jugular vein had been cut, and he had bled to death within only a few minutes. He certainly knew how to handle a knife even when it was directed against himself.[8]

Letting the body fall back face-downward, I went through the dead man's pockets in search of the suicide weapon. In one of them I found a jackknife with a small blade and a corkscrew. I recognized the knife as one which belonged to Packer, who had used it to cut his chewing tobacco with. However, there was no blood on the knife, and the blade was too small to have nearly cut off a man's head.

I continued my examination around the cell and finally discovered a bloody, straight-edged razor lying open on a narrow iron shelf in a front corner of the cage. Like the jackknife, the razor belonged to Packer, who had used it that morning to shave himself.[9]

In transferring McCabe to Packer's cell in my haste to get back to the court room, I had unwittingly made this suicide possible. I had intended to put McCabe back in the steel cell just as soon as the Packer jury had rendered its verdict, but McCabe beat me to the draw.

Prisoners in the jail who witnessed the suicide told me that after slashing his throat McCabe had laid the razor on the iron shelf and grabbed hold of the bars of his cell to brace himself. When the horrified onlookers saw the blood gushing from his throat, they began yelling for me and the jailer. This was the sudden noise, like distant surf, that I had heard in the court room.[10]

When the prisoners began shouting, the dying man turned loose of the bars with his right hand and shook his fist at them. At the same time he tried to speak, but only a gurgling cry escaped from his bleeding throat.

The yelling attracted a lot of people in the neighborhood, who assembled around the jail. When they learned what had happened, there was a good deal of criticism of me for leaving razors lying around where prisoners could get hold of them.

Overhearing one such remark as the coroner and I were leaving the jail with McCabe's body, I turned to the speaker and said, "If there is anyone else around here who would like to cut his own throat, let me know and I'll be glad to accommodate him with a good sharp razor at any time."[11]

I realize that I was talking a little out of turn, but the inconsistency of the mob sort of got my goat. Only a short time before, they were eager to lynch McCabe, but now after he killed himself in such a gruesome manner, their sympathy was suddenly aroused and they blamed me for the tragedy.

McCabe had no family in the area; so Hughie Frill, a fellow coal miner and his closest friend, claimed the body. Frill, I learned

Thomas Hurley, alias Hugh McCabe, grave and tombstone in Gunnison. Hurley, a prominent member of the "Molly Maguires" who terrorized the Pennsylvania coal mining camps in the 1870's, killed himself by cutting his own throat in the Gunnison jail Aug. 17, 1886. Words on tombstone read: "Born May 3, 1856; Died Aug. 17, 1886. May His Soul Rest in Peace."

later, was the man who had handed McCabe the six-shooter when he left Baldwin in the old lumber wagon.

The Gunnison telegraph operator showed me a copy of the telegram which Frill sent to the dead man's mother and brother. It read, "Tommy died last night. What shall we do with the body?"[12]

I was also shown the answer, which said, "Bury Tommy in Gunnison."

So, Hugh McCabe's real name was Tommy, I thought, and not Hugh. But Tommy what? The answer to this question was found in the name and address of his mother and brother in the return telegram, and it brought me up with a start. The wire was sent from Pottsville, Pennsylvania, and the senders signed their last name as Hurley. McCabe's real name then was *Thomas Hurley,* known throughout the nation as being one of the most prominent members of the notorious "Molly Maguires," who ten or eleven years before had terrorized the Pennsylvania coal mining camps.

The Molly Maguires were a secret society of coal miners formed about 1854 and named after an organization in Ireland. The members assisted the strikers in labor disputes by threats of violence and sometimes murder. Between 1862 and 1875 they attained considerable power in the coal regions of Pennsylvania, especially around Pottsville.

My friend James McParlan, who later became superintendent of the Pinkerton National Detective Agency in Denver, brought about their downfall. As a Pinkerton agent, he became an active member of the Mollies for more than two years. During this time he obtained damaging evidence against them and acted as the prosecution's key witness at a sensational trial in Pottsville which ended in June, 1877. In all, ten Molly Maguires were hanged and fourteen were sentenced to prison. These hangings, along with widespread public opposition, destroyed the Mollies as an organization.

Thomas Hurley was one of the worst assassins of the society, but he and a few accomplices made their escape when the others were arrested. In spite of a relentless search, the Pinkertons were never able to find him. I had a picture and a detailed description of the notorious killer, but time had changed his appearance so much that I failed to recognize McCabe as the Molly Maguire fugitive.

After being charged with the murder of Luke Curran, Hurley apparently felt that it was only a matter of time before his true identity would be discovered. So, he took the easiest way out for him by turning the long blade of his dangerous knife against its last victim—himself.

FOOTNOTES

[1]He stole around $1400 from his five victims.

[2]C. W. Shores, "The Story of Alfred Packer, the Colorado Cannibal," original manuscript, April 3, 1927, pp. 4-5.

[3]*Ibid.,* p. 6.

[4]*Silver World* and *The Lake City Times,* Dec. 4, 1930.

[5]*Ibid.,* p. 5. Wilson and his brother also went under the name of Prentiss. The murdered man was the first school teacher in the Paradox Valley. At one time the Wilson brothers were outlaws, which was why they changed their name to Prentiss upon coming to Paradox.

[6]After Shores' death most of his personal effects, including these letters of Packer, were destroyed in a fire.

[7]C. W. Shores, "The Story of Tom Hurley, Assassin, Murderer," original manuscript, Dec. 22, 1927, p. 1.

[8]*Ibid.,* p. 7.

[9]Apparently on the frontier, jail officials were not as particular as they are today in keeping razors and knives away from prisoners.

[10]*Ibid.,* pp. 8-9.

[11]*Ibid.,* p. 8.

[12]*Ibid.*

Chapter IX

One of my prisoners, curiously enough, was a hermit. I first heard of Reuben Dove in December, 1888, when a sub-contractor swore out a complaint against him for burning a big pile of railroad ties. According to the complaint, the sub-contractor had hired Dove to cut the ties, and then after they had been purchased, Dove set fire to them.

Before going out to arrest a man, I made a practice of trying to find out as much about him as possible. I learned that Dove was a recluse who could neither read nor write. He obtained his livelihood primarily from hunting and trapping, and only occasionally ventured out of the hills to sell his hides and purchase a few necessary staples, such as coffee, flour, and salt. He was described as a rosy-cheeked man with a Tarzan-like physique. No one seemed to know just how old he was, but if one were to believe the many accounts of his phenomenal feats of endurance and strength, he apparently was right at the peak of his physical prowess.

I was prepared to hunt down a half-civilized and dangerous adversary when my undersheriff, Sam Harper, and I packed our gear and caught the train for Crested Butte, where Reuben Dove had last been seen. He was reported to be staying temporarily with a rancher and his family several miles below the mining camp. While Dove did not have many friends, it was said that the few people who really knew him would do anything for him.

Harper and I got off the train two or three miles below the ranch where we expected to find Dove. We kept out of sight as much as possible in walking up to the house, since we knew that the hermit would take off if he saw us approaching.

Harper was acquainted with the family, and when we knocked on the door, we were asked inside and treated with courtesy. Only the rancher, his wife, and their mentally retarded daughter were present. There was no trace of Dove either in the house or about the premises.

When we inquired about his whereabouts, the rancher informed us that he had left afoot on the preceding night for Montrose to sell some hides. I might have fallen for this answer except that in an offhand remark he stated that Dove had taken a sack of flour with him. It struck me as unusual for a man to take flour on a trip to Montrose when he could easily obtain bread and other food at the many section houses along the way. If Dove took flour, his destination was more than likely in the opposite direction toward the high country.

During a lull in the conversation when the rancher and his wife went out into the kitchen to fix us a pot of coffee, I asked my undersheriff to try to get the truth out of the feeble-minded daughter. He had known the girl for a long time, and I could tell by her actions that she had a lot of confidence in him.

While we were drinking our coffee, Sam turned to the girl and said, "By the way, how is your colt coming along?"

This was the first time that anyone had directed any remark to her, and her face lit up in response as she replied, "He's sure growin', Mr. Harper. Would you like to go out and see him?"

This was the golden opportunity that we were waiting for. The two were gone only a few minutes, but in that time my undersheriff found out what he wanted. The girl informed Harper what I had suspected—namely, that Dove had not started out for Montrose as alleged, but had gone northward up a nearby canyon which led into the mountains, where he planned to hide out for a time. She also divulged that he departed early that morning, instead of last night as the rancher had said; so our fugitive didn't have much of a start on us. The girl cautioned Harper not to let her parents know what she had told him.[1]

After leaving the ranch house, Harper and I turned southward as if we were going to follow the railroad tracks back to Gunnison, which route Dove would most probably have taken if his destination had been Montrose. But as soon as we were out of the rancher's sight, we reversed our course and circled around to the designated canyon, which the girl claimed Dove would traverse enroute to his mountain hideout.

After we had progressed a mile or so we ran across the fresh footprints of a man, which we presumed to be Dove's, in isolated patches of snow. The trail was hard to follow since the tracks led for the most part over bare ground and rocks, leaving little, if any, imprint. Several times we lost them completely and split up on different sides of the canyon to re-locate them.

On one such occasion I was rounding a corner with my head down examining the ground when I unexpectedly came upon Dove sitting hunched over a campfire sound asleep. He carried a six-shooter in his belt holster, and a Winchester rifle was leaning up against a nearby boulder within his reach. He evidently had built a fire to warm himself and drowsed off for a moment. This was a lucky break, since it enabled me to get the drop on him without having to risk a gun fight with such a formidable opponent.

I tried to get the attention of my undersheriff, who was looking for tracks on the other side of the narrow canyon about fifty yards away, without awakening Dove. However, he was too far away to hear my whispers and too intent upon his search to notice my gestures; so I cocked my rifle, and pointing it at Dove, called out Harper's name. As I spoke, I rushed toward the sleeping fugitive, fully prepared to pull the trigger if he came to and grabbed for his gun.

Harper heard me this time and came running over. Dove opened his eyes and drew himself slowly up to an erect sitting position.

"Don't move," I threatened, "or I'll blow your head off."[2]

He made no move toward his guns, and I kept my rifle leveled at him while Harper took possession of his weapons. After he was disarmed, I clapped some handcuffs on him.

"I'm arresting you for burning railroad ties," I explained, quickly sizing him up.

After hearing so much about him, his appearance surprised me. Although his face was covered by a thick growth of beard, he looked quite human. In fact, he was what I would call a good looking man. His cheeks had a red glow of health about them, and his features were regular and pleasing.

"I've sort of been expectin' yuh," he said in a deep, quiet voice. "Can I move now?"

"Yes," I replied. "It's quite a long jaunt to Gunnison, and we'd better get started."

He got to his feet, standing several inches above Harper and me. He was magnificently proportioned, and I was suddenly glad that we had captured him without the necessity of a struggle. He looked strong enough to handle the two of us.

We took our prisoner to Crested Butte and caught the next train for Gunnison. Dove maintained an aloof silence during the entire trip. Before putting him in jail I searched him and found sixty-eight dollars in the small watch pocket of his trousers.

"I'll keep this for you until you get out," I said.

Dove refused to hire a lawyer and asked no one to go bail for for him; so I had to hold him for several months until the next term of the district court.

Dove accepted his imprisonment with philosophical resignation, but he kept to himself and wouldn't communicate with anybody. This reserve with most anyone else would have invited abuse and ridicule from the other prisoners, but because of his large size and foreboding manner, his fellow jail-mates respected Dove's privacy without argument or reservation.

I went out of my way to treat the hermit with consideration and win his confidence. From time to time when he seemed in the mood I engaged him in short conversations. He responded to my treatment and finally accepted me as a friend. One day I asked him why he had set fire to the railroad ties, and he confided in me the whole story.

He explained that the sub-contractor whom he had cut them for ruthlessly culled half of the ties by marking them with paint.

Dove was then paid for the rest, which the sub-contractor hauled away and turned over to the railroad company.

However, while Dove was away on a bear hunt, the sub-contractor gathered the cull ties and also turned them over to the railroad, piling them up with the ones he had paid for. When Dove returned from the hunt and discovered what had happened, he located the ties and burned up the whole bunch, culls and all.

I sympathized with Dove, feeling that he was a victim of circumstance. It was obvious that the sub-contractor had taken advantage of him. While Dove broke the law in his effort to even up the score by destroying several hundred dollars worth of private property, the course he took was a natural one for a hermit and backwoodsman. He was not the type of man to seek redress through a court of law.

After becoming acquainted with my anti-social prisoner, I learned to respect him highly. His word was as good as gold, and he was very dependable. Because of these traits, I often let him out of jail to perform various task for me, and I paid him out of my own pocket.

To illustrate, I at one time arrested two dentists at Crested Butte who were wanted in Denver for absconding with mortgaged property. I brought them to Gunnison, where I had to hold them overnight until the Denver authorities would arrive to get them.

On the train-ride down from Crested Butte one of them said to me, "I suppose you're going to lock us up?"[3]

"That's right," I replied.

"If you'll let us stay at the hotel, we'll pay five dollars in cash to anyone you choose to guard us."

"All right," I agreed after a moment's thought. "I know just the man to do it. Come on over to the jail and register, and then we'll go to the Tabor House and get you a room."

The man I chose to guard them was Reuben Dove. As I left the three of them in the hotel room, I said, "I hope that you gentlemen won't make the mistake of trying to get away."

"Not after seeing that guard of yours," one of them answered drily. "Where did you find that Hercules?"

When the district court finally convened, I went before the grand jury and told the jurors about Dove's excellent jail record. I enumerated the many odd jobs he had done so well for me and said that he was absolutely trustworthy.

"He admits that he burned the ties," I concluded, " and he will give you an accurate account of what happened and why he did so. While he has broken the law, in view of extenuating circumstances and his background, I feel that there was some justification for his action and recommend leniency."[4]

Following me, Dove appeared before the grand jury and gave his testimony. The jury refused to find a bill of indictment against him but recommended that he go before the district judge and tell his story, throwing himself on the mercy of the court.

Dove did so, and the judge gave him a light sentence of two months in the Gunnison County jail. After sentence was pronounced, I told Dove that I was appointing him a trusty and he would no longer be locked up in the jail. I assigned him a room next to the jail and had him serve out his term as a deputy sheriff and assistant jailer. He was very efficient, and I continued to pay him for his work. So, when he was released from my custody, he had a little stake to start life over with.

When he got out of jail, he went away back into the mountains, establishing his domicile under an overhanging cliff near Hubbard Creek, fifteen miles north of Paonia, Colorado. Here in this isolated country he spent the remaining thirty years of his life. He lived there alone the year around, trapping, hunting, fishing, and gathering wild honey. Each spring or early summer he ventured into the pale of civilization to sell his hides and pick up a few supplies.

His food consisted primarily of wild meat although he raised a garden near his hermitage in which he planted tobacco and a few vegetables. During the fall he collected potatoes and wild dandelions in flour sacks, which he hung on stumps and the branches of surrounding trees for winter use.

The hermit of Hubbard Creek became a western Colorado legend. It was said that while following a trail of some animal it was not unusual for him to walk sixty miles a day through the mountains. He made many of his own cartridges, filling discharged shells with powder and lead and using the heads of matches for priming.

Reuben Dove's hermitage on Hubbard Creek. Picture taken about 1920.

Dove was suspicious of strangers and greeted them with a gun in his hand. After his unfortunate experience with the railroad ties, he never did another day's work for any man.

One spring day in 1920 three acquaintances from the town of Paonia stopped at Dove's wilderness retreat to leave some salt and vegetables.[5] They discovered the old recluse lying on his bed, which was composed of a bear skin and a few blankets. Continous exposure, lack of a well-balanced diet, and old age had finally broken his powerful body. When found he had been hovering between life and death for nearly six weeks, scraping a meager existence from a few sacks of soft potatoes and dandelions hanging around in nearby sacks.

From his bed he was able to reach a pile of snow and the dripping sap of a box-elder tree, which had furnished him with his only supply of water during his illness.

Dove's three friends took him down to the haunts of man to receive medical care, but the hermit died soon afterward.

My association with Reuben Dove brought about a better appreciation of hermits and their mode of living. All that he wanted from life was to be left alone so that he could lead a completely independent and self-reliant existence. After seeing the gradual breakdown of these qualities in our society from soft living and dependence on government, it was a refreshing experience to know a man who chose the opposite extreme.

FOOTNOTES

[1]C. W. Shores, "An Honest Hermit and Bear Hunter—Reuben Dove," original manuscript, Denver, Colo., Dec. 22, 1927, p. 2. In possession of Western History Dept. of Denver Public Library.

[2]*Ibid.,* pp. 2-3.

[3]*Ibid.,* p. 4.

[4]*Ibid.,* pp. 4-5.

[5]Horace Curtis, a friend of Reuben Dove, personal interview, 1936. Also, see Wilson Rockwell, *New Frontier,* The World Press, Inc., Denver, Colo., 1945, pp. 173-175.

Chapter X

An entirely different type of prisoner than those I have mentioned was Charles Anderson, alias Charles Cole, a gentleman safe-blower. My first contact with this polished crook was during the Gunnison County Fair in October, 1886.[1]

There were a lot of strangers in town for the celebration, and my deputies and I were on the alert for trouble. So, when I saw John Steele, a prominent Gunnison hardware merchant, hurrying toward my office early one morning, I suspected that something was amiss. This assumption was confirmed when he reported that the safe in his store had been blown open and robbed during the night. The strong box, containing several hundred dollars in cash, and a drawer, filled with valuable documents, were missing.

I accompanied Steele back to his store and made a quick examination of the place. The thief had drilled a hole into the combination lock and put just enough giant powder in the hole to shatter the tumblers without damaging the safe or the contents within. This was unusual, since all other safe blowers in my experience showed no respect for the safe or any of the personal property inside it. Their standard way of operation was to pour powder into the cracks around the door and blast open the entire front of the safe, destroying it and much of the contents. Today instead of powder, nitroglycerin, or "soup," is used.[2]

The burglar had departed by way of a back window, which he

left propped open with a mallet. I crawled out the opening and located his footprints in the alley. Procuring my undersheriff, Sam Harper, we followed them to the railroad, where they turned northward between the rails in the direction of Crested Butte.

We had gone only a short distance when Harper, who was watching the ground on the left side of the railroad tracks, said, "Here he goes off to the left."[3]

The fresh imprints led us to the discarded strong box, which had been pried open and relieved of its cash. Beside it lay a chisel and a big broken rock, which had apparently been used as a hammer.

The robber's tracks returned to the railroad and continued up it for perhaps a hundred yards. Here they turned off to the right and proceeded to an old deserted house, which stood all by itself on the outskirts of Gunnison.

We looked through this neglected ruin, and in a conspicuous but sheltered spot under its crumbling foundation we found the missing safe drawer, crammed full of notes, checks, and other papers, which were valuable to the individual owners but not to the thief.

"It looks like this safe-blower went out of his way to put these papers in a dry, safe place where they would be found," I commented to Harper.

"That was a pretty decent thing to do," Harper said. "I never heard of a crook doing a thing like that."

From here we followed the tracks back toward Gunnison, losing them on a board sidewalk which led into town.

It was comparatively early in the morning when my undersheriff and I completed this part of our investigation. Most of the gamblers, carousers, and prowlers who had been up for the better part of the night were still asleep; so I decided to check through the various rooming houses and hotels for possible clues.

In examining one man's luggage I came across an opium pipe and all the paraphernalia used with it. The owner was known as Beef Steak Mike, and he was an extremelly tall fellow with the pasty complexion of a professional gambler. He often visited Gunnison and had the reputation of being an honest, high-class poker player.

I was after bigger game than an opium smoker who minded his own business; so I closed the grip without mentioning my find. As

I went out the door, Beef Steak Mike called out, "Sheriff, I'm much obliged to yuh."[4]

My search through the hostelries revealed nothing which would connect anyone with the safe robbery, but it did serve to narrow the field considerably by eliminating many of the newcomers whom I might otherwise have suspected.

That evening after the rodeo the gambling houses and saloons began to fill up. I went around to them all, casually observing the customers. While I was sitting on a bench in one of the saloons watching chances being sold on the next day's races, a blond, young man entered. He attracted my attention because he was one of the few visitors in town whom I had not seen before. He had the unhealthy palor of one who spends his life indoors, and he was sporting a drooping, colorless mustache.

He walked slowly up to the bar and ordered a shot of whiskey. As he gulped it down, I observed that one of his front teeth was missing. After finishing his drink, he glanced slowly around the room, and then left the saloon as quietly and deliberately as he had entered.[5]

A natural man-hunter has an instinctive feel for his work, just as in any other profession, and as soon as I saw this washed-out newcomer, I had a hunch he was the man I was after.

The fact that he was one of the few visitors in town whom I had not investigated made him, of course, an obvious suspect, but there was more to my suspicions that just that. I realized that I was after an unusual criminal. No ordinary thief would have blown open a safe with such finesse and respect for other people's property. His pattern of work set him apart, in my judgment, as a man of above-average intelligence and sensibilities. The way a thief operates reflects to some degree his character, and there was something about the over-all appearance of the stranger which fitted my estimate of the safe-blower. While first impressions are often deceiving, I decided to play my hunch to the hilt.

Sam Harper was tending gate next day at the fair; so I described the suspect and told him to let me know immediately if he entered the grounds. It was not until late afternoon that he finally showed up, and I was notified right away.

I changed into a different colored suit than the one I had worn on the previous night and, removing my badge, went out to the fair-grounds. It took me quite a while to locate my man in the big crowd, but I finally spotted him near the race track talking with some tough-looking women. I then contacted a former deputy of mine and hired him to shadow the suspect and find out where he was staying. Unfortunately, I chose the wrong man to do the job, and he lost his quarry somewhere in West Gunnison.

Since this was the final day of the fair, the elusive stranger would probably soon be leaving town. Therefore, that evening at eight o'clock I was on hand to meet the incoming train from Denver. It had not yet arrived; so I sat down on a bench just inside the depot's entrance where I could get a good view of people coming in and going out. In order not to be too obvious in my scrutiny, I bought a newspaper and pretended to be reading it.

I was just about to give up my vigil when at the last moment the young man appeared and took his place in the dwindling line at the ticket window. I folded my newspaper and stepped up behind him.

I had anticipated that if and when he showed up he would be carrying a bag of some kind, and I had planned to arrest him on the spot and go through his luggage in hopes of finding his drill or some other evidence which would link him with the burglary.

However, he was carrying no baggage of any kind when he entered the depot, which put me at a distinct disadvantage. It would be useless to arrest him without some sort of evidence, and, in all probability, he wouldn't be carrying any on his person. While he had no reason to suspect that anyone was on his trail, he apparently wasn't taking any chances of getting caught with the goods on him. He was a smooth operator and a deliberate one.

When his turn came at the window, I heard him ask for a ticket to Montrose, fifty miles west of Gunnison. The Montrose County Fair was starting there on the next day; so apparently he was going to work that town also during the festivities.

I watched him get on the train, and before the train pulled out, I had a friend of mine go through his car to make certain that there was no luggage in his seat. It puzzled me why he would leave town without any baggage, and I wanted to make sure that some accomplice had not slipped a grip in to him. My emissary reported that there was no bag of any kind in the suspect's compartment; so I was left in somewhat of a quandary. When I next saw my suspect in Montrose several days later, he had a valise, but how he got it there I will never know. At any rate, I decided that it would be futile to arrest him until I had a better case against him; so I let him leave on the train.

Although I wasn't making much progress, I was by no means through with the case. Next morning I again visited the hotels and rooming houses of Gunnison to locate where my blond friend had resided while in town. I described the suspect at each place, and finally the landlady of a West Gunnison rooming house said that a young man who answered the description had stayed there during the fair. She showed me the register where he had registered as Charlie Cole, St. Louis.[6] I looked closely at the unusual handwriting so that I would recognize it if I saw it again.

Armed with this additional information, I caught the train that night for Montrose to continue the chase. Upon arriving I procured a room, and as I was registering, the name Charlie Cole caught my eye. He had again given St. Louis as his residence, and the handwriting was identical to the registration that I had seen in Gunnison.

I asked the clerk if he remembered the man. He replied in the affirmative and said that he had stayed there only one night.

"Did he have any luggage?" I asked.

"Yes, he was carrying a black leather grip. I remember it particularly because it was awful heavy. Are you acquainted with the gentleman?"

"In a manner of speaking," I said.

It was possible that Charlie Cole had left town when he checked out of the hotel, but I doubted it. With so much activity going on, the fair would provide a good setting in which to practice his devious profession.

I walked out to the fairgrounds, figuring that if Cole were still in town he would eventually turn up there. After a long search, I espied him near the grandstand visiting with some girls, who, judging by their highly painted faces and fancy dresses, were from the red-light district. I had seen him fraternizing with the same type of women in Gunnison; so appartntly he had a weakness for them.

This time instead of getting someone else to shadow Cole I did it myself. After leaving the fairgrounds, he went directly into the center of town. There were enough people on the streets to make it easy to follow him without arousing his suspicions.

Upon reaching Main Street he led me a merry chase going into one store after another as if he were shopping around. Occasionally, to keep up appearances, he purchased an inexpensive item. In each store that he entered he would gradually work his way back to where its safe was located, all the time examining the merchandise with profound interest. However, each time he passed by a safe, he gave it a moment of scrutiny. I knew enough about professional safe-blowers to know what he was looking for. He could tell by the make of a safe and its locks whether it had a burglar-proof cash box in it or not. If it had, he would mentally cross it off his list for a possible future visit.[7] Most of the safes he looked at were simply fire-proof receptacles and easy for a skilled safe-cracker to break into. Consequently, he had a lot to choose from.

After visiting the various stores in order to spot the location and make of their safes, Cole proceeded to the outskirts of town where he went into a small rooming house. I could have gone in and arrested him then and there, but I first wanted to find out if his black valise was in the room and not cached away some place. I was depending on it to furnish the needed evidence, and I didn't want to show my hand until I got possession of it.

In order to ascertain whether or not the grip was in Cole's room, I obtained the help of my hotel landlady. I told her who I was and explained the importance of my getting hold of the valise in question. So, she agreed to help me out. She had just recently moved to Montrose and was not well known in the town.

In compliance with my instructions, she went out to the rooming house where Cole was staying and told the elderly woman who owned the place that she was looking for a room. The proprietor said she had no vacancy at the time but that one of the rooms would probably soon be available since the young man who stayed there was only renting it by the day. My landlady asked to see it, assuming

Picture taken from west side of corner Cascade Avenue and Main Street looking east up Main Street in Montrose. Lots Hotel on northeast corner, Robinson grocery on northwest corner, Buddecke and Diehl general store and freighting outfit next to grocery store. This is the way Montrose Main Street looked in 1886 when Doc Shores arrested Charlie Cole, alias Charlie Anderson, the expert safe blower. *Photo courtesy of Tom J. Reeves.*

that the young man referred to was Charlie Cole. The occupant happened to be out; so the old lady showed it to her. My emissary then returned to the hotel and informed me that the black grip I was seeking was there.[8]

Until then I had kept away from the Montrose peace officers, but now that it was time to act, I needed their cooperation. I looked up the town marshal and asked him to accompany me on my mission.

He agreed to do so, and we walked over to the rooming house. It had two front doors facing the board sidewalk. I knocked on the first one we came to, and when no one answered, we proceeded over to the other door, which my landlady said led into Cole's room. I again knocked, and this time when no one responded, I rammed my shoulder against it and broke the lock. The impact made quite a crash, and as we entered, the startled proprietor made a sudden appearance.

"Madam," I said, flashing my badge, "we are officers and want to see what is in that leather grip over there in the corner. I'd like to have you stick around while we open it."[9]

"No, I don't want to have no part of it," she exclaimed, turning around and making a hasty exit.

As she left, I said, "I'll reimburse you for any damage that I've done."

The grip was locked; so the marshal and I pulled it apart at one end so that I could slip my hand into the crack. While I didn't have much freedom of movement inside the valise, I pulled out a number of items, including a double action Colt six-shooter and a half-dozen new ladies' kid gloves with some of their fingers missing. These gloves were unusual articles for a man to be carrying around and puzzled me.

The marshal was getting jumpy and kept peering out the window.

"Let's get the hell out of here," he said finally. "Your man is liable to show up at any moment, and we don't have a search warrant."

"Don't worry," I said. "I'll take care of him. Here, help me pull this thing apart again."

As soon as I had forced my hand into the small opening to dig around for more evidence, the marshal suddenly gasped, "Here he comes up the street. I can't afford to be caught in a compromising position like this."

He let go of the valise and ran out into the street. The locked grip closed like a vise over my hand. I glanced through the window and saw Cole approaching about two blocks away. The marshal had crossed to the opposite side of the street and was heading for town as fast as he could walk.

I put the bag between my feet and pulled out my imprisoned hand, scraping off a good deal of skin as I did so. Then I hastened outside. Cole was still far enough away that the chances were he hadn't noticed which house I had emerged from.

Even though the grip had so far produced nothing of great importance, I still believed that once I really got into it I would discover the necessary evidence. At any rate I decided that the time had come to arrest Cole and take my chances on getting him convicted. Otherwise, now that I had shown my hand by breaking into his room, he would likely skip town and disappear.

Grasping the six-shooter in my overcoat pocket, I turned down the sidewalk and walked toward the thief. As we neared each other, I watched him closely out of the corner of my eye, ready to draw my revolver in case he made a sudden move. While I didn't think that he had observed me or the marshal coming out of his room, he was nobody's fool and might have had his suspicions aroused.

He showed no sign of being alarmed, and when we finally came face to face, I jerked out the revolver from my overcoat pocket and ordered the surprised victim to put up his hands.

"What's this all about?" he asked as he slowly complied with my request.

"I'm arresting you on suspicion of robbery," I replied. "Turn around with your back toward me."

He did so, and I quickly frisked him for a gun but found none.

"Now, let's go back to town," I said. "You lead the way and I'll follow along right behind you."

When we got to Main Street, I noticed a sign on a small building which read "Justice of the Peace." I escorted Cole inside and introduced myself to the J. P. I explained that my prisoner was wanted in Gunnison County for committing a crime and asked permission to keep him in the Montrose County jail for a day or two until I could take him to Gunnison for a preliminary hearing.

While in the judge's office I searched the prisoner and found a peculiar-looking watch key which I had seen before in John Steele's hardware store. This was my first piece of tangible evidence connecting Cole with the burglary. I also found the key to his leather grip. He wasn't carrying as much cash as I would have supposed after his recent haul. Either he was quite a spender or had the stolen money hidden away some place.

While searching him I asked, "What is your name?"

"Charlie Cole," he answered pleasantly. I, of course, suspected that this was an alias and discovered later that his real name was Charlie Anderson.[10]

"Where are you from?" I continued.

"St. Louis."

"What is your business?"

"I'm a stone cutter."[11]

I had noticed that his hands were very soft, like those of a person who had not performed any physical work for a long time.

"Have you cut any stones lately?" I asked.

"No," he said, observing my glance at his hands. "I've been sick for a long time."

I smiled at his anwser. He looked like a pretty healthy specimen to me. His smooth, white hands were not the result of poor health but reflected his indoor profession, which certainly wasn't cutting stones.

After interrogating and searching the prisoner, I took him over to the county jail and had him locked up. The next day I returned to the rooming house, where I retrieved the grip and made a settlement with the old lady, both for the prisoner's bill and the damaged door.

As I had hoped, the grip disclosed some pertinent evidence. It contained more ladies' kid gloves, some with their fingers removed. This phenomenon continued to amaze me until I discovered in the grip two cartridges made from the fingers of one of the gloves. Each cartridge had been cut down to the diameter of a lead pencil, and a small amount of powder, a cap, and a fuse had been inserted.

In blowing a safe Cole would drill a hole into the combination lock and then place one of his home-made cartridges in the opening. The resultant explosion was just strong enough to shatter the tumblers, permitting the safe to be opened by merely turning the knob.[12]

The drilling machine was all that I needed now to have an air-tight case. Since it was not in the valise, I assumed that Cole had hidden it in the vicinity of the Montrose rooming house. Consequently, I hired some boys to search the area. They hunted for the machine all afternoon, but were unsuccessful. Nevertheless, I paid them for their efforts, and before leaving Montrose offered a ten-dollar reward to anyone who discovered it.

When I arrived in Gunnison with my prisoner, I took him before a justice of the peace for a preliminary hearing. On the basis of my testimony and the evidence which I had found in the grip, the court found a bill of indictment against him and held him under a good-sized bond until the next term of the district court. Since the court did not convene in Gunnison for six months, Cole was in my custody for quite a spell.

The residents of Gunnison soon learned that I had a professional safe opener in jail, and whenever any of the businessmen mislaid their combinations or had trouble opening their safes, they made a practice of asking for Charlie's assistance. I would oblige by escorting him to wherever his unique talents were needed.

It was interesting to watch him open a safe. Before starting, he would sandpaper the tips of his fingers until they were so sensitized that they could feel the least jar of a tumbler when it fell. He told me that he kept his fingers soft and sensitive at all times by wearing gloves and doing as little physical labor as possible.[13]

When twirling a dial, he not only made use of his highly developed sense of touch, but he also utilized his acute sense of hearing. He would press his ear up against the combination to listen to the delicate workings of its mechanism. He could work most combinations if given sufficient time. He confided in me that the only reason he ever blew a safe was because it was quicker, and time was of the essence in his trade.

About two weeks after Cole's arrest, I received word that his drilling machine had been found near the Montrose depot. Some railroad men ran across it while tearing down a platform by the railroad tracks. The machine had been hidden in the timbers underneath the platform along with some drills, caps, powder, and more ladies' kid gloves.

These items corresponded with those I had already found in his valise; so he could not very well disclaim them. This additional evidence gave me such a strong case against Cole that when the district court met, his lawyers advised him to plead guilty. He did so, and the district judge sentenced him to five years in the state penitentiary.[14]

When I was taking him to Canon City to serve his sentence, I said, "By the way, Charlie, I've often wondered how come you took the trouble to put those papers under that old deserted house near Gunnison."

"To preserve them for the owners," he replied earnestly. "They were no good to me, and it seemed like the only honest thing to do."

Charlie Anderson, alias Charlie Cole, was the only honest thief that I ever escorted to the state penitentiary at Canon City.

FOOTNOTES

[1]C. W. Shores, "The Capture of an Expert Safe-Blower," original manuscript, Denver, Colo., Mar. 15, 1927, p. 1. In possession of Western History Dept. of Denver Public Library.

[2]*Ibid.*, pp. 6-7.

[3]*Ibid.*, p. 1.

[4]*Ibid.*, p. 2.

[5]*Ibid.*, p. 3.

[6]*Ibid.*, p. 4.

[7]*Ibid.*, pp. 10-11.

[8]*Ibid.*, p. 4.

[9]*Ibid.*, p. 5.

[10]*Ibid.*, p. 10.

[11]*Ibid.*, p. 7.

[12]*Ibid.*, p. 11.

[13]*Ibid.*, p. 8.

[14]*Ibid.*, p. 9.

Epilogue

Doc Shores' career as a lawman did not end with the expiration of his second term as sheriff of Gunnison County. For the next twenty-four years he served in the order named as special investigator for the Denver and Rio Grande Express Company, the Denver and Rio Grande Railroad, the Globe Express Company, and chief of police of Salt Lake City.

After leaving Gunnison in 1892, he moved to Grand Junction and later went to Denver, where he spent the remaining years of his life. He owned property in Gunnison until his death and visited his old home town frequently. He died there October 18, 1934, at the age of 89. He was buried in the Gunnison Cemetery beside his first wife, Agnes, and his younger son, Cyrus Wells, Jr., who preceded him in death.

Typical of the many obituaries written about him in newspapers thruout the state was the following article in the *Gunnison News-Champion*:[1]

"Last Friday morning death wrote Finis to one of the most interesting and colorful lives that has ever been identified with the West when Cyrus Wells Shores, known all over the state as Doc Shores, passed quietly away at the local hospital. He had been sick only a few days, his death being attributed mostly to advanced years. Had Doc Shores lived until November 11, he would have been 90 years old. Yet, despite his years, one seeing him on the streets would

Doc Shores as an older man. *Photo courtesy of Mrs. Lucille B. Hartman.*

never guess that age. His straight carriage and brisk walk would do credit to a much younger man.

"With him at the time of his death were his wife and son, Frank, who had been summoned when his condition became serious. Mr. Shores had made his home in Denver of late years, but each summer came back to his first love—Gunnison County—the scene of his early-day joys, sorrows, and exciting experiences.

"Few men have had so interesting a life as Doc Shores. When he was sheriff of Gunnison County, often men lived by the gun as well as the pick and shovel, and bad men were rampant in every section of the then untried West.

"This pioneer's life reads like a story book tale. Born in Michigan, Nov. 11, 1844, one of ten children, he started early in life to make his own way. Answering the call of the West, at that time the genuine article—wild, untamed and alluring, Mr. Shores came to Hays, Kansas . . . That was in 1867.[2] Part of that trip was made by steamboat from St. Louis to Fort Bend,[3] the fuel necessary to produce steam being wood. In later years Shores used to recount with amusement how the crew of that boat would stop it every so often while on the trip in order to chop more wood. That journey took 60 days, and Shores, who was among the best marksmen on board, kept the boat well supplied with fresh meat.

"From 1867 to 1871, Shores was a bullwhacker across the plains of Wyoming, Montana, New Mexico, Kansas, and Colorado . . . Many times on these perlious trips the party had hair-breadth escapes from roving bands of Indians that at that time terrorized the country.

"Colorado was then experiencing all the excitement of gold discoveries, and in the late seventies Mr. Shores' attention was turned toward Gunnison, then a booming metropolis of 50,000 people. He arrived with his wife in 1880 and from the beginning was closely identified with the history of Gunnison County, whose boundaries at that time included what are now Delta, Montrose, Gunnison and Mesa Counties.[4] Along with the gold seekers, investors, promotors and other pioneers seeking a new field, there came the lawless element to prey upon a new country. Here it was that Doc stepped into the limelight as a peace officer. In 1883 he was elected sheriff of the county, holding that office for eight years. He was strictly of the old-school type of peace officer. A typical westerner, not of the blood and thunder, nor the movie idea of what western sheriffs were, but a man who served his fellow men honestly, fearlessly, and justly. He was deadly in action and was a number one shot, and once he started out after a lawless character he got his man. Among the bad men that felt the heavy hand of the law as represented by Doc Shores was Alfred Packer of maneating fame whose capture in Wyoming was finally accomplished, and he was brought to Gunnison and placed in Doc Shores stout jail, where he remained until taken to the penitentiary. He knew such famous pioneer characters as Wild Bill Hickock, Tom Horn, and others . . .

"To recount, even in part, the many exploits in which this fearless man participated in the trailing and capture of train robbers, cold-blooded murders, and other desperadoes would fill a good sized volume . . .

"After leaving Gunnison Mr. Shores was for a time special criminal investigator for the Denver and Rio Grande and later held the same job for the Wells Fargo Express Company.[5] In 1915 he was appointed chief of police of Salt Lake City,[6] serving in that capacity so well that some of the lawless element brot influence to bear on some higher-up to the extent that a long-forgotten city statute was dug up setting forth the claim that a non-resident could not hold office in the Mormon city.[7] Shores returned to his home in Denver, where he spent his declining years. Each summer he would come to Gunnison, enjoying renewing acquaintances with early-day friends. . . .

"Mr. Shores was married twice. His first wife was Agnes Hoel to whom he was married in Michigan before coming to Gunnison in 1880. Two sons were born to this union, one of whom C. W. Shores, Jr., died some years ago.[8] Mrs. Shores passed away in September, 1908. She was noted for her poems and was an artist of considerable ability.

"Some years ago Mr. Shores married Miss Hattie Stevenson, sister of Archie Stevenson, one of his early-day friends in Gunnison, and teacher in the public schools here when he was sheriff. She and his son, Frank, survive him.[9] A sister, Mrs. Alice Burch, lives in Grand Junction."[10]

A letter about Doc Shores in the April, 1961, issue of *True* (The Man's Magazine) is in keeping with his character and contains a concluding anecdote to further remember him by:

"My wife's uncle, Doc Shores, was mentioned in your story as an employer of Horn at one time. Doc was a really ripe character. My father-in-law liked to tell about the time Doc took him into a saloon in Fort Hays. Standing at the bar with a couple of beers before them, Doc was talking to Dad when a shooting broke out behind their backs. Doc turned cooly, glanced briefly at the dying man on the floor, and picked up the conversation without a hitch. When they left the saloon he remarked to Dad: 'Let that be a lesson to you. Always mind your own business.'

—French Rowlen
Chicago, Ill."[11]

FOOTNOTES

[1]Agnes M. Winters, "Doc Shores Dies Suddenly Last Friday," *Gunnison News-Champion,* October 25, 1934, p. 1.

[2]This is an error. Shores did not go to Hays, Kansas, until 1870.

[3]His trip from St. Louis to Fort Bend was made in 1867, but it had no connection with his going to Fort Hays, which occurred several years later.

[4]The present boundaries of these four counties were established in February, 1883.

[5]This is another slight error. Shores was special criminal investigator for the Denver and Rio Grande Express Co., and the Globe Express Co., but never for the Wells Fargo Express Co.

[6]A letter dated May 26, 1960, from L. C. Crowther, present police chief of Salt Lake City, states, "Please be advised Cyrus Wells Shores was Salt Lake City's 18th Police Chief. He served from January 17, 1916, to May 8, 1916." Letter in possession of Western History Dept. of Denver Public Library.

[7]Shores' legal residence at the time was Denver.

[8]Cyrus, Jr., died during the flu epidemic in 1918.

[9]Frank and Hattie followed Shores in death on Dec. 18, 1948, and May 7, 1950, respectively.

[10]Mrs. Burch was the last survivor of Doc Shores' nine brothers and sisters.

[11]French Rowlen, *True,* April, 1961, p. 10.

www.ingramcontent.com/pod-product-compliance
Lightning Source LLC
LaVergne TN
LVHW010051110826
845155LV00028B/285